BENEATH
THE SURFACE

BENEATH THE SURFACE

KILLER WHALES, SEAWORLD, AND THE TRUTH BEYOND *BLACKFISH*

JOHN HARGROVE

WITH

HOWARD CHUA-EOAN

palgrave
macmillan

First published in 2015 by PALGRAVE MACMILLAN® TRADE in the
United States—a division of St. Martin's Press LLC, 175 Fifth Avenue, New
York, NY 10010.

Palgrave® and Macmillan® are registered trademarks in the United States,
the United Kingdom, Europe and other countries.

ISBN: 978-1-137-28010-7

Library of Congress Cataloging-in-Publication Data

Hargrove, John (Animal trainer)
   Beneath the surface : killer whales, SeaWorld, and the truth beyond
Blackfish / John Hargrove with Howard Chua-Eoan.
 pages   cm
   Includes index.
   ISBN 978-1-137-28010-7 (alk. paper)
   1. Killer whale. 2. Killer whale—Habitat. 3. Captive marine mammals.
4. Aquatic animal welfare. 5. SeaWorld. I. Chua-Eoan, Howard. II. Title.
QL737.C432H3675   2015
599.53'6—dc23

                                                        2014039895

Design by Letra Libre, Inc.

First edition: March 2015

10 9 8 7 6 5 4 3

Printed in the United States of America.

To all the killer whales that I had the privilege
of building relationships with and swimming
with for so many years—you gave me everything.
But most especially to Takara, who taught
me so much and whom I loved the most.

CONTENTS

PROLOGUE

Freya was refusing to follow any of the signals I had taught her. It wasn't as if she didn't know what I wanted. She just wouldn't cooperate—nor did she want any of the fish I had in my hand. She pushed at my torso with her head, propelling me with her mouth, which remained obstinately shut. Her nearly 7,000 pounds of orca muscle directed me farther into the middle of the pool, farther from the safety of the perimeter.

I dropped the fish, letting the food that would have been her reward sink to the bottom of the pool; I then used my freed hands and my body to try to deflect myself away from Freya, to get out of her way. But that didn't work. She countered every move I made like a skilled soccer player—and I became the ball she was so nimbly positioning in her game. With her shut mouth and the beak-like tip of her rostrum—the anterior tip of her head—she pushed me right to where she wanted me, the center of the pool, as far as possible from solid ground and from the help of the other trainers who were watching in horror from the sidelines. With a sudden slide, she looped beneath the surface, vanishing from my sight.

But only for a moment. She came back at me from beneath, slowly and deliberately, turning sideways to make contact with the left side of my body, first with her chest, then her stomach, her genitals, and her flukes, the huge fins that make up her tail. She stopped. Her right fluke was submerged; but her left fluke stuck out into the air, just a foot or two away from my head. Was she going to strike me in the face? If she did, the force and weight could easily break my neck and kill me. But she decided to tease me some more, swirling around to face me, her blue eyes bulging, wide and strained.

Outwardly, I appeared calm but I knew that Freya, with her hyperacute sense of hearing, could detect that my heart was beating faster with anxiety. The rush of blood through my veins only increased as she continued to refuse to respond to every signal, including an attempt to draw her to the other side of the pool by way of a five-syllable emergency underwater tone set off by trainers on land. She was in charge now—and my fate was of her choosing. I was desperate for some inkling that she might still be willing to cooperate with me and the other trainers. But Freya wasn't playing. I could see it in her wide-open, upset eyes, the red veins showing around the blue irises. The muscles of her back were tight. I recognized the sounds she was emitting. They were signs of an oncoming episode of aggression.

She submerged in front of me to about three feet. The water was murky but it was midday so I could still make her out from where I floated in the pool. I kept eye contact with her even as she was underwater. She was still upset.

I knew what was coming. As calmly as possible, I told the trainer positioned closest to me on land to get ready to call the paramedics.

Just then, I felt a suction beneath me. Freya had rolled sideways and finally opened her mouth. The underwater vacuum pulled me down even as she moved toward me. I felt her teeth pressing on my hip bones, just over the wetsuit; the entire width of the middle of my body was in her jaws, like a twig in a dog's mouth, one that could snap with just the wrong amount of pressure. To give some perspective: the largest great white shark ever caught weighed 5,085 pounds; Freya was more than 1,000 pounds bigger.

She pulled me underwater but chose not to puncture me before releasing the grip of her jaw. I floated back to the surface, facing her. I had both hands on her but she went under and rolled again. She came at me once more, grasping me in her jaws, pulling me under a second time before releasing me, allowing me to float upward. I knew that this could well become a pattern—I'd seen it happen before when orcas would toy with birds that had strayed into their pools—or when they turned on their trainers. She might come back to drag me under again and again until I became unconscious in the water from the repeated dunking. But I was determined not to die.

At the surface, I kept my cool and asked one of the trainers on land to once again produce the emergency recall tone. Originally devised for emergencies, it was a signal for the whale to stop everything, leave behind the trainer in the water, head toward and focus on a trainer on land, and put their chin up on the pool's rim to await the next set of instructions. Freya had ignored the tone when we first tried it. But this time, she chose to follow it. I instructed the trainer to be ready to use her whistle—which Freya would recognize as a positive sign that she was doing the right thing—and to put a hand into the water, a behavioral stimulus and powerful message to Freya to stay at the perimeter so she wouldn't head back for me. I told the trainer to have a bucket of fish beside her so that she could immediately reward Freya when she heeded those signals. Whales are zealously aware of the rituals of reward—and we had trained them to recognize a whistle as a precursor to a reward and the human hand as a symbol that had to be heeded. This time, Freya accepted the food. She had finally deigned to be rewarded.

I kept looking at her eyes. They were still bulging, clearly a precursor to incidents of aggression. Even though she was facing the perimeter, she kept looking at me as she headed toward the trainer on dry land. The eye muscles of orcas allow them to look backward—or anywhere they want—no matter in which direction they are swimming.

The incident was not over yet. Freya was taking the prize but was not yet prepared to give me up. I knew that the moment I made a move to swim to safety, she'd turn around and, with the stunning speeds orcas can achieve instantaneously, catch up with me in no time and grab me once again. She would be furious that I was trying to escape. In that case, she might no longer toy with me.

I chose to gamble. I asked the trainer on land to use her hand to point Freya back toward me, a basic signal the whales are taught early on. "*What?*" she asked in disbelief. I shouted back, repeating that she should send Freya to me right away. Timing was of the essence. If the trainer didn't point the whale back fast enough, while Freya was still feeling rewarded for behaving well, still feeling that this episode was turning out positively for her, then Freya was going to become aggressive again. If she did choose to return to that state, her behavior would most likely escalate into something I couldn't get out of. I knew all too well what she was capable of doing to me. I swam to position myself exactly in the middle of the pool to make it clear to her that I wasn't trying to get away.

Freya followed the trainer's direction and swam back to me. She was calm. I asked her to complete three simple behaviors we had taught her and she performed them perfectly. Then, at my request—and as she had learned in earlier sessions—she propelled me through the water, my torso beneath her head, my arms wrapping up around her lower jaw up onto her rostrum, my feet resting on her pectoral flippers. She pushed me forward to the edge of the pool where another trainer waited with a bucket. Once I was by the rim, I stepped up and out, quickly took all the fish available—about 15 pounds' worth—and fed Freya all of it to reward her for cooperating, for letting me go, for performing the pec-push that had brought me back to land. The encounter had taken less than 15 minutes. I looked back at the water, at what could have been the end of my life at the age of 27. My knees were shaking.

Dread and wonderment both are at the heart of my relationship with killer whales. More than a dozen years have passed since that encounter with Freya. Before and since, I have had other experiences—both fearsome and wonderful—with many orcas. These experiences were what I had hoped for in my life. The whales were my passion.

By the time I ended my orca training career in 2012, I was one of the most experienced orca trainers on the planet. I had started as an apprentice at SeaWorld San Antonio in 1993 at the age of 20, becoming a trainer in the corporation's premier facility in San Diego two years later. From 2001 to 2003, in the south of France, I took up the challenge of training orcas that had never worked with humans in the water before. After spending the next five years trying to transfer my passion to other careers, I returned in March 2008 to the one I loved the most, heading back to SeaWorld San Antonio, where I worked until I resigned in August 2012.

I worked with 20 different whales, swimming with 17 of them across two decades. Most are still alive. I loved those charismatic and complex beings. I can't quite call them animals; the whales are beings just as we are beings. And these orcas have been a more intimate part of my life than most humans. Dr. Ingrid Visser, who has spent many years studying the killer whales of New Zealand, told me, "If you have a question about orcas, frame it as if you were asking about people." The answer, she said, would often be surprisingly similar.

I had worked hard to get in peak physical form to be able to qualify to work and swim with killer whales, and the years I spent with the whales were a privilege. I will treasure them forever. It is a sentiment that I share with almost every person who has ever reached the highest ranks of SeaWorld's orca trainers. We were dedicated to working and performing with the whales; and we steadfastly believed we were doing what was best for the orcas. Our lives were so intertwined that we felt as if we could channel what the whales were feeling. We had a special kind of language, having developed a rigorous though imperfect form of communication based on the scientific notions of behavioral psychology to condition the whales to perform for the thousands who showed up for each show at SeaWorld's Shamu Stadium. No one else on earth could even pretend to read a whale's mind. We did. And we all knew what a great privilege it was—because it was extended to us by the whales themselves. Each day, each captive whale had the choice to allow us in—or to shut us out.

We were a small band of brothers and sisters: there have been perhaps no more than 20 top-ranked trainers at any one given time across the three SeaWorld parks during the company's half-century of existence. We spent as much time with each other as we did with the whales—competing with each other as we tried to push our careers ahead but also collaborating for the good of the orcas in our charge. I am not a scientist and, while this book will delve into the natural history of killer whales—into how they live in the wild—my story involves the lives of orcas seen through the eyes of the men and women who trained them to perform at SeaWorld. We swam with them. We kept them healthy. We saw them give birth. We watched them suffer. We suffered with them. We looked them in the eye and caught a glimpse into their souls. Sometimes, we saw joy. Sometimes, we saw things that were terrifying.

No SeaWorld trainer has been allowed into a pool to perform with a killer whale since February 24, 2010, when Dawn Brancheau, one of the most skillful and experienced of our small club, was killed by the 12,000-pound male orca Tilikum in Orlando. This horrific and tragic incident was the focus of the 2013 documentary *Blackfish*. Immediately after Dawn's death, SeaWorld pulled its trainers out of the water in all three of its facilities—not just in Florida where the death occurred but also in San Antonio, Texas, and in its premier park in San Diego, California. Soon after, the Occupational Safety and Health Administration (OSHA), the federal agency in charge of safeguarding Americans in the workplace, cited the corporation for violating safety codes and said that, in order to avoid a penalty, trainers and killer whales should never be as close to each other as Dawn and Tilikum were—and Dawn wasn't even swimming with Tilikum when she was attacked. OSHA's August 2010 citation cited SeaWorld Florida for a "willful" violation of safety codes and said that a remedy would be to "prohibit animal trainers from working with killer whales . . . unless the trainers are protected through the use of physical barriers or through the use of decking systems, oxygen supply systems or other engineering or administrative controls . . ."

Being in the water had always been an integral part of the trainer's relationship with the whale—and a central part of the public spectacles in Shamu Stadium. But in 2014, after four years of fighting the OSHA citation in court and voluntarily pulling its trainers out of the orca pools, SeaWorld was forced to accept that trainers would never do "waterwork" again. All interaction with whales would be from the perimeters of the pools—known as dry-work—or from very shallow water on ledges built into the pools. The trainers were effectively grounded.

Along with my former colleagues at SeaWorld who have been landlocked since, I may be one of the last of a generation of human beings who can say that they performed with orcas in the water. To be part of such a historic and exclusive club fills me with conflicting emotions. I enjoyed those moments and so did the whales. It gave them something to do in captivity. But in the broader perspective, it was unsettling because our experiences were just a part of a rapacious corporate scheme that exploited both the orcas and their human trainers.

SeaWorld's corporate marketing strategy turned the orcas into the pandas of the sea, commercial and cuddly, with little hint of the complexities of killer whales and the effects of confinement on them. The terrifying monsters were domesticated and tamed through public relations and entertainment, transformed into performers appropriate for family-friendly theatrical settings. Backstage, the corporate ideology was paradoxically the reverse: unemotional, matter-of-fact and driven by dollars and cents. In the eyes of management, the animals perform as they do because they are trained to respond to behavioral cues imposed after repetitive psychological reinforcement. The company's official dogma for the trainers: Don't anthropomorphize those animals; don't give them human emotions. It's okay to love the whales, but don't let sentiment get in the way of your job. The whales are a company asset on the ledgers—difficult to replace, of course, but ultimately a matter for spreadsheets.

I believe in something greater and deeper about orcas. Every time a killer whale looked me in the eye, I saw intelligence shine through and felt his or her emotions. I sensed a presence in the orcas that is closer to the power of the myths surrounding their species, a consciousness that is both approachable and beyond human probing. They are both compelling and unfathomable.

The orcas are only memory to me now. All I have are photos and video footage of my life with the killer whales. I left SeaWorld in August 2012. My body was a painful wreck after years pursuing my hazardous occupation. It was no longer physically possible for me to go on. But I had also had an intellectual conversion. I had been a SeaWorld loyalist since I was a child—a true believer in the company's vision of cross-species interaction as a way to teach the virtues of nature conservation. But though I was thrilled to be part of the orcas' lives for so long, I finally came to the realization that if I had to live their lives, it would be hell. Captivity is always captivity, no matter how gentle the jailer.

My human colleagues are part of a more complicated legacy for me. After I ended my career and began to speak out against SeaWorld, I lost most of my trainer friends who remained working at SeaWorld. I understand their predicament and why they have abandoned me. It took me years to make my decision to speak out. It wasn't easy. Sea-World is a gigantic entity, with a corporation's access to many levers of power: lawyers, politicians, the media. Against that behemoth, you can feel utterly alone and powerless. When you are trapped by a whale that has gone over to the dark side, you still can hope that you can look the orca in the eye and redirect him or her. But in SeaWorld the corporation, there is no soul to peer into.

I can never walk back into a marine park where any of the whales I worked with live—not into the three SeaWorld facilities in the United States, not into the one in Spain that the corporation helps to manage, nor into the one in France where I worked for two years and which does business with the multibillion-dollar American theme park empire. It's not just because of my conviction that SeaWorld's treatment of its orcas is wrong—though that is what I now believe. What prevents me from returning is my awareness of the emotional distance—the knowledge that even if I did enter the park, I would never truly be near the whales. I was so close to them, physically and spiritually. Of the 30 living whales that SeaWorld currently owns, I've worked with

12 of them. Of the 12, I did waterwork with 10. To return as a visitor to a theme park, to see them presented in a show as if I had never been part of their lives, would be too painful to endure.

I had a boyhood dream that came true, almost magically, like something out of a children's storybook. In time, I discovered that the gorgeous dream was only part of the story, that the bigger story was more of a nightmare, for myself and for the whales. I have lost the whales; they are no longer in my life, and that breaks my heart. But I have gained something else: a new path that is becoming clearer as time passes. I want to remember the whales and share them with you. I want you to know what I have learned so we can save them together.

1

MONSTERS AND OTHER PEOPLE

What happens when a six-year-old boy sees his first orca?

It was my first trip to SeaWorld Orlando with my parents and I was immediately captivated by the killer whale's compelling combination of beauty and danger. The orcas were enormous and they were killers, swift and sleek and toothed. And yet they were gentle and friendly to the trainers in the water with them. Those men and women were not ordinary people. Even though they were puny in size compared to the orcas, the trainers were contoured like gods. There was something almost supernatural in the way they performed in harmony with the killer whales. I wanted that power too. I not only wanted to have a killer whale. I wanted to be one of the people who trained them.

I could not have been the only one so inspired that summer day in 1980. There were at least 5,000 other people in the audience in SeaWorld cheering and applauding as the orcas performed with the trainers. The spectacle at Shamu Stadium was a magical combination of water and muscle—both human and cetacean—as the whales and their trainers sped through the pools and leapt into the air with acrobatic poise. I had never seen anything like it before.

I was a few weeks shy of seven but I knew from the moment I saw trainers and whales appear together that I wanted to be part of that world, to become a member of that small troupe of wonderworkers who could talk to the whales, who could understand the orcas' responses, who were not afraid of the enormous jaws, fins, flippers and flukes that came crashing down, splashing water out of the show pools. I wanted to be one of the select few who were an intimate part of the whales' lives.

I began to dream that day. There must have been others in the audience who fantasized about it as well. But I was certain that I was going to make my dream come true.

Summer vacation for me always meant a road trip with my parents. And in 1980, my mother and my stepfather decided we'd all go to Orlando. We couldn't afford to fly so we drove the nearly 900 miles from our home among the bayous of east Texas to the theme park capital of America. The contrast was dramatic: Orange, Texas was a monotonous, flat swampland while Orlando was punctuated with architectural extravagance, from Cinderella's castle in Walt Disney World to the adamantine giant golf ball of EPCOT Center. And then there was SeaWorld.

At first, it was the dolphins that had my attention. My parents couldn't drag me away from their petting pool. It had taken long enough to wait my turn to touch the animals and I can still remember how profound the experience was. But I would soon shift my fascination from the dolphins to much bigger things.

We joined the crowds headed into Shamu Stadium. The coliseum for killer whales was already the largest animal performance space in the marine park, far bigger than the theaters built for the dolphins or the sea lions and otters. Seated in the middle of an audience that was a third the size of the entire population of Orange, Texas, I was visually and emotionally overwhelmed as we watched the spectacle unfold. I was mesmerized by how the whales followed signals as ephemeral as a magician's hocus-pocus gestures. The creatures would come and go to the slapping of water by their human co-performers—a miracle that was almost biblical to me.

I began my campaign to join SeaWorld soon after that first show, when my parents took me to meet the trainers and ask them questions. Each year from then on, I would insist that we return to SeaWorld—if not in Orlando, then in San Antonio, after a branch opened there in 1988. At every visit, after each show, I would hound the trainers, asking them what they did to get their jobs and what I had to do to become one of them.

After SeaWorld opened in San Antonio, I was at the marine park ever more often. I always brought detailed technical questions for the trainers about animal behavior. But I also knew then (and know now) how awkward some of the questions from well-meaning visitors can be. I've been asked things like, "How'd you get those sharks to do that?" or "How do they get their vegetables in the water?" My questions may not have been that unknowing but I must have annoyed the trainers with the sheer volume of my queries.

When I was 12, I started a two-year letter-writing campaign, sending off missive after missive to ask for counsel and guidance from the trainers and from SeaWorld executives and managers. I wanted nothing else. I just had to make this dream come true.

I guess that even as a child I was looking for a way out of Orange, Texas. And what greater fantasy could there be than to escape to a life swimming with the world's most magnificent marine predator?

There was nothing awful about Orange itself. You'd go to church on Sunday, taking your pick from a bunch of Southern Baptist congregations. For fun, you'd take a three-wheeler or four-wheeler into the woods. You'd go mudding. Whatever your choice, it usually involved the woods.

The one real thing that always got people excited was the football rivalry between the two local high schools: Little Cypress Mauriceville versus West Orange Stark. My cousin Tracy remembers my trailing along to all her pep rallies. The underlying ugliness was that Little Cypress was the white school and West Orange was the predominantly black one. In my town, in the 1980s, the races still lived apart, coming together only to clash via football—with all the combined awfulness of sports fanaticism and bigotry. Orange, however, had nothing on the notoriety of the city of Vidor, just about 20 miles away. The Ku Klux Klan marched there well into the 1980s; and when black families moved into public housing in Vidor during that decade, they were greeted with burning crosses.

The whales—as dangerous as they might be—were much more attractive than some humans.

The moment we returned from that first trip to SeaWorld in Orlando, I got my hands on everything I could read about killer whales. We had a set of the *Encyclopaedia Britannica* at home, and I studied every article it had about orcas, whales and dolphins. There really wasn't much. It only contained two pages about dolphins. Technically, killer whales are the largest members of the dolphin family (which is part of the cetacean group to which whales belong) but trainers and even most scientists refer to orcas as whales. In any case, the encyclopedia simply wasn't enough to satisfy me. Nevertheless, I read those articles again and again; eventually the pages were so worn out they practically fell out of the volume.

A few years before, in 1977, the movie *Orca* had come out in the theaters. It's the story of a male killer whale who goes on a rampage after humans kill his mate and her calf. I found it on VHS after one of our family's summer trips to SeaWorld and watched it repeatedly. I always rooted for the whale. But *Orca* seemed strangely unappealing to me—and I am certain it was because the humans and the whale were set against each other.

I loved movies. My mother's sister, Aunt Darlene Tindel, recalls how excited I was when she got her first VCR—the first member of my extended clan to get one of the new machines. I couldn't wait to stay over for a weekend, and when I finally did, we went out and rented ten movies.

The film that spoke to me most eloquently was *The Big Blue,* Luc Besson's 1988 film about the relationship between dolphins and a free diver—a specialized swimmer who can descend to immense depths in the ocean on a single breath without scuba gear. I wanted to be the star, Jean-Marc Barr, whose character, Jacques Mayol, assumed many qualities of dolphins because of his love for those marine mammals and the sea. At the end, after a series of diving competitions, he realizes he is dying as a consequence of a contest with his best friend and closest rival—a tragic incident that ended in his friend's death. A distraught Mayol chooses to return to the waters to perish in the depths as well, giving up the human love of his life, played by the actress Rosanna Arquette. As he drifts toward oblivion deep down in the sea, a dolphin appears to take his spirit to its proper home. I watched the film so often the tape of my VHS copy of the movie snapped.

Both movies were prophetic about my life in specific but small ways. One of the "stunt" whales that appeared in *Orca* was Corky, who would become the first killer whale I would ever swim with when my career as a trainer in SeaWorld took off. As for *The Big Blue,* a lot of the movie takes place in Marineland in Antibes, France where I moved in 2001 when I accepted a supervisor position of its killer whale training program.

I slowly absorbed what was out there about killer whales—fact and fiction and legend. The scientific name of the species, *Orcinus orca,* echoes with allusions to classical and modern monsters—from Orcus, a Roman spirit of the underworld, to the Orcs, the huge goblins from the fiction of J.R.R. Tolkien. Ancient writers saw the voraciousness of killer whales—epitomized in the relentless waves with which they attacked larger cetaceans—as a metaphor for the insatiability of death. In North America, the orca was seen as a kind of werewolf, the whale being the wolf spirit transformed in winter to guide the indigenous peoples toward the seals that would sustain them in cold weather—just as the wolf guided them to deer in warmer months. On both hemispheres, the myths of the killer whale satisfied the meaning of the word "monster" at its origin—from the Italian *mostrare,* to show or to demonstrate, that is, in effect, to teach. Because of its power and its intelligence, the orca was expected to teach cosmic lessons of life and death to a human race that, by the twentieth century, had become estranged from nature.

Books and popular culture provided fun facts about orcas. But I believed that the real answers to my questions could come only from one place: SeaWorld. I continued to write letters to several people in the company, asking for the requirements I had to meet to become a trainer. All that pestering was in addition to the annual trips to Sea-World in Orlando and years later San Antonio, where I'd line up to see the trainers after their performances and then pepper them with the same questions.

One day in 1985, I got the detailed answers I had been asking for. It was both bracing and terrifying. Dan Blasko, the director of animal training at SeaWorld in Orlando, was kind enough to reply. I was floored that someone so high up in the organization would take the time to write back to me. But I was also devastated by the response. He was very polite but not particularly encouraging. He said that since there were few positions available and so many applicants for them it would be best for me to have back-up plans for careers in other fields. He was courteous but quite firm when he said that there was an extremely high likelihood that I was never going to get my dream job. He was being realistic—and kind—but it punctured my fantasy that simply wanting something hard enough would make it happen.

Blasko, however, also mapped out everything that he believed a good applicant for the job of SeaWorld trainer had to have on his or her resume. I needed a degree in either psychology or marine biology, scuba certification, public speaking experience and volunteer work with animal welfare organizations. Most importantly, I needed to pass a grueling swim test that seemed to require lungs as powerful as a cinematic free diver. My hopes could well have been dashed by Blasko's frankness, but I was determined to learn the basic requirements he outlined—or surpass them—so that when the time came and a position opened up at SeaWorld, I would get the job.

Ever since I was child, water has always been a part of my world—and it provides a powerful dichotomy in my life. Even at a young age, I knew that water can give, and water can also take away.

Water almost killed my mother. I was just four when the accident that nearly took her life occurred. But the impression it left on me was so powerful that even before I became obsessed with whales, I was determined that I would become a good swimmer, so strong and comfortable in the water that it would feel like home.

My stepdad liked to go out in boats and would convince my mother, who was never comfortable in them, to accompany him. On one weekend trip on the Sabine River, not far from Orange and right on the Louisiana border, they tooled around in one of those small aluminum boats with a motor. Suddenly, a bigger and more powerful boat sped by and the wake capsized my parents' craft, tossing my mother and stepfather into the water. There was no kill switch for the motor, so the now-unmanned boat began to circle in the water. My mother, who was wearing an orange life jacket, was about to surface when the propellers of the boat's motor slammed into her chest. The life jacket was both a blessing and a curse. If not for the preserver, her chest and breast area would have been ripped to shreds. The thickness of the jacket prevented that. However, it had now become massively entangled in the propellers themselves. Unable to remove herself from the jacket, she was now caught underwater and was beginning to drown.

In the meantime, the boat whose wake had knocked my parents into the water returned to the scene and its crew was helping my stepfather in his frantic search for my mother. She told me years later that she could hear them screaming her name. She was submerged for what eyewitnesses said was easily close to two minutes or more. In the end, she managed to free herself. Fortunately, the vest and its straps had so clogged up the motor that the blades had stopped spinning. She went to the hospital with bruising and tissue trauma at chest level. When I finally saw her, I was not allowed to hug her.

I was very young but I was still aware of the severity of the event. Even before the accident, I was obsessed with water and would even practice holding my breath in a full bathtub. I was already taking swimming lessons and now had even better reason to work hard at them.

Years later, when I was already well under way in my SeaWorld trainer career and a success in the water, the other side of the dichotomy would strike at my family again. I used to admire my cousin John Carroll, who was ten years older than I, seeing him often at reunions at my maternal grandparents' home in Big Thicket, Texas. The family always called him John Carroll; it's a Southern thing.

He and a friend were on a fishing trip in the Gulf of Mexico when they got lost in the middle of a storm, thrown into the water by the tempest. The two men, wearing life vests, tied two coolers together so that they could hold on to them as they floated in the sea. After hours adrift overnight, hypothermia quickly set in and both men struggled to remain conscious. When they floated to within sight of an oil rig, John Carroll's friend said he would try to swim there for help, telling my cousin to hold on. But the man realized that he was too weak to make it to the oil rig and swam back to the coolers. When he returned, however, John Carroll was no longer there. The authorities presume he lost consciousness and slipped out of his life vest into the deep. His friend was rescued by the Coast Guard, which had been searching for the men.

I continued my annual trips to SeaWorld with my family. I knew who all the trainers were, and by the time I was 14, I had two definite idols among them—people whose talents and temperaments I wanted to emulate.

Anita Lenihan always gave me a lot of time. She came out of the SeaWorld San Diego facility, the premier park in the empire. She was honest about herself and what a career at SeaWorld would demand. She'd always talk to me while I waited to speak to the orca trainers after the performances—and I'd listen even though she worked with sea lions and not with the whales. After all, as a senior SeaWorld trainer, she was a valuable source of information. She never sugarcoated anything. She'd tell me how she'd never be able to pass the swim test if she had to try out for SeaWorld anew. She was happy to work with the sea lions, despite knowing that all the prestige came from being in Shamu Stadium. She had a great touch with the animals both up close and on stage during the shows. Years after I first began harassing her as a child, I would work with Anita as an apprentice trainer in San Antonio. My opinion of her has never changed, only grown stronger.

My other SeaWorld idol was her complete opposite: Mark McHugh. He was the star of Shamu Stadium. No one questioned his athleticism and showmanship, which was seemingly superheroic. I would learn when I worked with him in San Antonio that, like some stars, he was difficult and temperamental and chose to lead by inducing fear in the staff. He was never mean to the wide-eyed kid begging to speak to him after the show. But he never gave me time. As much as Anita was self-deprecating, Mark was self-aggrandizing. He called the shots, and his opinions spoke even louder than those of SeaWorld executives who ranked much higher in the organization. Yet seeing him on stage, swaggering with authority, I could not deny his power and charisma, and I wanted to emulate some of the qualities he possessed.

As a teenager, I had to try to figure out who I was while living in a conservative part of already conservative Texas. When I realized I was gay, I knew it was time to disentangle myself from Orange. I ran away from home, taking a bus to Houston.

I was determined to make life work out for me even though I got to the city knowing no one. I had no money and no idea where I was going to live. This was the early 1990s, when AIDS was still killing gay men at an alarming rate and advanced medications were not yet available. But I was lucky. I found gay friends in Houston who gave me direction and guided me. If it weren't for them, I would not have been able to pursue my dream. I've returned that favor to a few who were close to falling victim to the wrong people at the wrong time. When you're young and naïve and trying to come to terms with your sexuality, there are sometimes more mature men with money who take advantage of that vulnerability. These are monsters too. You grow up quickly in that environment. I became street smart.

In Houston, I proceeded to check off all the things I needed to do to get a job at SeaWorld. I got my scuba certification. I enrolled at the University of Texas in Houston to study psychology, just as Dan Blasko had recommended. I took classes full-time at night school and worked full-time during the day. I picked up extra money as a lifeguard.

I also drove down to Galveston to volunteer with the Marine Mammal Stranding Network, where I helped with beached animal recovery on the weekends. That was heartbreaking labor, particularly one animal necropsy that I got to assist in. A mother dolphin and her calf had been caught in a gillnet—the kind that hangs vertically, its bottom edge anchored by weights. Suddenly, the element that was their home and refuge became the very substance that threatened them. The mother dolphin realized that she and her calf were running out of oxygen and that they had to make it to the surface immediately or drown. In desperation, she plunged deeper into the water, driving herself against the sea floor to try to get under the net and scoop her offspring to safety. It was all in vain. Mother and calf died. She had been nursing the baby till the end. We found fresh milk in the calf's stomach. The mud in the mother's mouth was evidence of how hard she was ramming herself against the bottom to get out from the net.

I kept up my swim training. I knew that one element of the swim test was diving to the bottom of the pool on a single breath. It wasn't quite the epic immersions depicted in *The Big Blue* but the pool was more than 25 feet deep at Dolphin Stadium and 40 feet deep at Shamu Stadium. You don't learn to go deep—and stay deep—just by being a good swimmer and leaping off a diving board.

I prepared for the dive portion of the test by every so often taking a wave runner out into the Gulf of Mexico, jumping into the water and going down as far as I could—about 30 feet. The objective of each dive was to grab mud, bringing up proof that you had touched bottom. The deeper you go down into the water, the greater the pressure and the compression on your lungs, resulting in a smaller capacity to retain oxygen.

Later in my career and after years of swimming with killer whales at Shamu Stadium, I would learn the benefits of having gone repeatedly down to such depths: your eardrums become more flexible the more often you are in deep water. Most other trainers had to pinch their noses to equalize their eardrums during a deep dive. Fortunately for me, that was something I never had to do. I would feel my eardrums readjusting on their own. Equalizing was easy and effortless.

Even as I did all the prep work to qualify for a potential job opening at SeaWorld, I planned to plow through college for the next four years. The degree was a requirement—or so Blasko had said. Then, something unexpected happened. The pestering I had been doing for years paid off.

In 1993, management at SeaWorld San Antonio had an apprentice trainer position to fill and asked the experienced senior trainers if they knew anyone who might qualify. Several said, "That kid who keeps coming to ask us questions," explaining that I met all the criteria. One of them got word to me. My chance had come—earlier than I expected. I was not going to let it pass, even if I was nowhere close to college graduation.

I would not be the only one trying out for the job at the Animal Training Department of SeaWorld. Twenty-seven of us, all with scuba certifications, showed up for the swim test that September.

It took place at Dolphin Stadium. The temperature of the water there is warmer than at Shamu—though it is still chilled to about 60 degrees and much colder than a backyard swimming pool. First, we had to swim 125 feet underwater in a single breath and then dive 25 feet down to retrieve a weight from the pool floor. The challenge was not to surface prematurely during the dive to the bottom or the underwater swim. There was also a timed freestyle swim element in the test.

On the day of the swim test, I woke up with a sinus infection—a result, I think, of too much practicing in the Gulf of Mexico. That kind of blockage can be dangerous when diving deep, with the possibility of more infection and the perforation of the eardrums because of your inability to equalize pressure. It had the potential to end my career before it started. That did little to improve my stress levels. But I would rather have died during the swim test than pass up the opportunity.

Only three of us made it to the final round. We would go through a battery of interviews with the top trainers (including the star of the show, Mark McHugh); we would all go on stage to prove we had the presence and confidence to speak on a microphone in front of a crowd; also our diving form would be carefully scrutinized by the judges.

Then they sent us home to wait. It would take a month before a decision was made. It was agonizing. After the first week without news, I was convinced I didn't get the job and that they wouldn't even bother to tell me. But finally Human Resources called me. They had picked one apprentice out of the three finalists: and it was me! My dream was coming true. I was going to be a SeaWorld trainer.

2

THE FANTASY KINGDOM
OF SEAWORLD

I have absolutely no doubt that SeaWorld will go down in history as a legendary enterprise. Since its founding in 1965, the theme park has provided Americans and the rest of the world with a compelling model of a particular kind of modern mythology: that of apparent harmony between animals and human beings. In the SeaWorld cosmos, the paradise that has been the dream of many cultures throughout history is finally at hand.

To people hoping for a world in tune with nature, SeaWorld could well have been the peaceable kingdom predicted by the prophet Isaiah, except instead of the wolf living in friendship with the lamb, the earth's two most dangerous apex predators—*Orcinus orca* and *Homo sapiens*—swam and played together as God meant it to be at creation. If you had any doubt, all you had to do was buy a ticket for a show at Shamu Stadium in San Diego or San Antonio or Orlando and you could see the miracle for yourself. After being hired as an apprentice trainer at SeaWorld, it was now my job to help maintain and enhance that myth of perfect interspecies co-existence.

I joined as a true believer. And, even when there were inconsistencies in the SeaWorld doctrine, I chose to believe—most of the time, happily—in the watery cosmic vision I was becoming part of. Like all successful organizations—be they businesses or religions— SeaWorld had its holy writ, a kind of theology at the heart of its existence.

And, thus, in the beginning there was Shamu.

Shamu was the first superstar of SeaWorld, the primordial orca goddess of the marine park, making her appearance in the second half of 1965 to capture the imaginations of park goers. She was the first killer whale in SeaWorld's collection and her name would live on and on, as if Shamu herself was immortal. Every show was about Shamu; every whale at the center of the spectacle was called Shamu; any companion to the principal whale in the show was somehow explained away as Baby Shamu or Grandbaby Shamu or Great-Grandbaby Shamu. Shamu would never die. At least, not in name.

The original Shamu died in 1971. But every whale that starred in the shows staged in the central stadium named in her honor would be called Shamu. It was so important to SeaWorld that her memory live on like that of a legend beyond compare that, for a long time, the actual names we gave the whales were secret. The public never really knew that Takara was called Takara, or that her nickname was Tiki; or that her mother's name was Kasatka. Or that the whale we called Corky was the same animal with a cameo in the movie *Orca*. Few members of the public knew who Keet was; or Ulises; or Katina. That's because SeaWorld felt the need to keep the fantasy of Shamu going. She was to be adored forever.

SeaWorld may have set itself up as a kind of paradise—all theme parks do—but even the Garden of Eden was part of a morality tale.

The original Shamu was the first killer whale to be intentionally captured from the wild and made part of a show. Three other orcas had previously been put on display elsewhere, but they had been caught while tangled in fishing nets or had survived harpoon attacks or had been ill when they fell into human hands. Those orcas were exhibited in aquariums or in the low-budget marine parks that dotted the Pacific coast of North America in the mid-1960s.

The most popular of the initial trio was a male who had swum into a salmon net off the town of Namu on the coast of British Columbia in June 1965. The fishermen who found the orca sold him for $8,000 to Ted Griffin, an aquarium owner from Seattle who had dreamed for years of capturing and swimming with orcas. Griffin would become the key figure in the creation of the half-century-old industry of performing orcas. He named the orca Namu for the town near the waters where the whale was found.

Until then, orcas had been considered extremely dangerous. But the brief life and death in captivity of an orca named Moby Doll had changed all that. Moby Doll was male but when he was harpooned during capture, people at first thought he was female. He wasn't supposed to have survived in the first place. The Vancouver aquarium wanted to create a life-size replica of a killer whale and sent hunters out to kill one on July 16, 1964 and bring its corpse back to use as a model. The sculptor Sam Burich recounted to local newspapers the moment of the harpooning: "It looked me right in the eye, and I looked right back. I just let him have it." The wounded whale struggled for over two hours, with members of his pod repeatedly pushing Moby Doll up to the surface to breathe. Burich attempted to finish him off from a small boat but after several rifle shots, the whale would not die, the paper stated. Since they couldn't kill the whale, they took him into captivity. After partially recovering from the shock of the harpooning, Moby Doll proved that orcas, despite their popular murderous name, could be friendly, even docile. Moby Doll, however, would not survive long; after less than three months, he developed a skin disease and, more fatally, a fungal infection to his lungs. He lived just 87 days in captivity.

It was Griffin's thunderbolt of enterprise to turn the discovery that orcas could be gentle with human beings into a business model. Within a month of transporting Namu from Canada, he was swimming with the orca at the Seattle aquarium he owned. He made a movie with Namu as well, further transforming the image of the "killer" into that of a giant black-and-white dolphin, reminding Americans that orcas are classified as the largest of delphinids and related to a bottlenose celebrity then on television. This was the time of the hit NBC show *Flipper,* about the heroic and lovable dolphin friend of a human family in Florida. With Griffin's help, the once-feared orcas slowly became lovable too. It was a welcome change from a reputation that, at one point, was so malevolent that the US military slaughtered killer whales as potential security risks to American bases in the northern Atlantic.

Namu's demeanor and popularity drew crowds to Griffin's aquarium. And so Griffin went into the orca-capturing business. His next prize was a young female orca from Puget Sound captured on October 31, 1965. Envisioned as a companion to Namu, she was named Shamu. Almost immediately Griffin leased and eventually sold Shamu to a year-old theme park that had opened on Mission Bay down the Pacific coast in San Diego, California. That park was SeaWorld.

Marine parks had existed in the United States since the late 1930s; and some began to feature performing dolphins by the 1950s. In the early 1960s, the founders of SeaWorld took the concept of marine mammals performing for audiences to the scale of Disneyland (which had opened in Anaheim in 1955). Milton Shedd, an investment banker, and three partners proposed a phantasmagorical park to the San Diego officials in charge of vetting projects for a large property on Mission Bay. The journalist Conor Friedersdorf has described the original pitch, which included an underground amphitheater that would allow the audience to peer into an enormous, illuminated aquarium, where a man in scuba gear would reveal the wonders of the sea—and the exotic, sometimes frightening examples of marine life—captured behind the glass. There would also be a lagoon around which visitors could dine while enjoying shows stocked with elephant seals, walruses, Sniffles the pilot whale and penguins trained to march like soldiers.

Much of the proposal—at least architecturally—became reality when SeaWorld opened on March 21, 1964. The park also included hydrofoil rides and other kinds of entertainment. The partners wanted to make money even as Shedd pursued higher aspirations. As Friedersdorf relates, the SeaWorld founder would tell potential financial backers, "Your investment in SeaWorld is a means by which you can participate in the public's ever-growing fascination and curiosity about the marine environment." In other words, the success of Shedd's business model required the park to cultivate the visitors' curiosity about and concern for the animal life of the oceans—a perfect balance of environmentalism and capitalism. SeaWorld also had one of the foremost whale experts among its founding fathers. Says Howard Garrett of the Orca Network, a nonprofit opposed to killer whales in captivity, "Dr. Ken Norris gave SeaWorld immunity from criticism and an aura of ultimate scientific authority among those who questioned the effects of captivity on marine mammals or the ethics of holding them for attendance revenues. The company has continued to promote his rationale of education and conservation as a cornerstone of its operating principles long after his departure in 1976, even as SeaWorld went in a completely different direction."

The park attracted about 400,000 visitors in its first year of operation—though its transformative star would not arrive till almost a year later. Shamu was dramatically flown in on December 20, 1965. The prospect of a performing killer whale proved not only irresistible but a stroke of inspiration. With the legendary sea beast in its midst, SeaWorld became an even greater success story. As the company closes in on its half-century, each of its parks is attracting more than four million visitors a year.

To this day, the centerpiece of any visit to SeaWorld is the show in Shamu Stadium that was developed to showcase its original star cetacean. There has been one significant change: since the death of Dawn Brancheau in February 2010, trainers no longer swim with the orcas during performances. Otherwise, though the sets have become glitzier through the decades, the basic elements and story line remain the same. There is an initial segment of wonderment in which a human being—represented by a star trainer—discovers the existence of whales and is awed by their strength and size, and more importantly by the mammal's seeming willingness and eagerness to be friends with people. That is impressed upon the audience by a bang-up opening number with multiple aerial leaps and splashes to show off the skills and athleticism of the whale as it responds to signals from trainers. The emotions deepen in the middle of the 25- to 30-minute show as the trainer puts the whale through several acts, offering proof of how whale and trainer can cooperate—and how gentle and loving that relationship is. The trainer appears to be in an affectionate relationship with the whale; the whale appears to be enjoying playing with its human colleague. The third segment and grand finale showcases the most spectacular waterworks behaviors, including breaches, bows and breathtaking gyrations through the air by the whale at the behest of human trainers. The members of the audience are splashed with water so they can feel that they have become part of the relationship. Trainers who have swum with the whales feel that the show has become less exciting because of the restricted contact and the ban on waterwork. But even as the company tries to promote other zoological wonders and forms of entertainment in its facilities the show and the killer whales remain the focal point of the park.

I still remember the first show in which I participated. I had just been hired as an apprentice trainer and I knew my parents were coming up from Orange, proud to see me finally part of the show to which they had taken me summer after summer. At barely 20 years old, I wasn't as muscular then as I would become. I recall being uncomfortable in my wetsuit, which I felt was too big and had too much slack in it. But I felt a sense of accomplishment: it was a Shamu Stadium wetsuit, after all.

I didn't really do much that was show-worthy. I had a couple of simple scripted lines on a microphone like "Ladies and Gentlemen, welcome to Shamu Stadium." Otherwise, my principal job was to set up buckets full of fish around the pool for the trainers to reward the whales with or to open and close the gates when the experienced trainers working the whales asked for that to happen. I contentedly absorbed the glamor. Or what I thought at the time was glamor. After all, the people in the audience probably thought I was a trainer working with the whales.

My key responsibility that day was spotting. I was positioned on the porch, a shallow shelf that projected on to the main show pool where I could watch what was happening in the water. Whenever a trainer was in the water during the show, spotters kneeling on the two porches on each of the long sides of the main pool looked out for him or her, providing visual or verbal communication in case of an emergency, passing along alerts between a trainer in the water with the whale and an experienced trainer at another location in the stadium.

As an apprentice trainer, it wasn't my job or in fact within my abilities to interpret what was going on around the whale or how it would affect the orca's behavior. Apprentices acted strictly as a means of communication between two trainers working the whales. Still, it was important for apprentices to convey the information to trainers so that they could figure out whether small things—maybe a member of the audience throwing an object into the water—might lead to big bad events. It was important to know whether the orcas were annoyed with all the possible repercussions of multiton animals showing 5,000 people how unhappy they were.

The orcas were watched carefully and closely at all times. That should have been an early clue to me that the ideal of perfect harmony between man and beast could unravel.

For all of SeaWorld's lovely mythology about orcas and humans getting along, the relationship is, well, complicated. The historical realities behind the fantasies are harsh.

When Namu was trapped in the nets off the coast of Canada, members of his family pod gathered around him, trying to figure out how to free him. As Griffin transported him to Seattle by way of an ocean-pen towed by a boat, a number of orcas surrounded him, but were unable to solve the problem of setting Namu free. Namu himself emitted what one person recalled as painful shrieks and cries. Eventually, most of the bigger orcas—probably male—slipped away, leaving Namu alone with only the company of three whales: an older female and two younger ones, most probably his mother and his siblings.

They stayed with him as long as they could. They too finally slipped away, unable to rescue him.

Namu did not live beyond the year in which he was captured. Suffering from a bacterial infection, he rammed his head against the side of the pool in Griffin's Seattle aquarium. He drowned. Some accounts say he was trying to escape. Others said he was confused and addled by the illness.

Griffin was heartbroken—and, over the decades, he would tell reporters again and again that he missed Namu intensely. But he continued to hunt down whales, using explosives to herd them into areas where they could be netted. Several whales died at various stages of the capture process—including mothers killed in order to make it easier to take away their calves. And while SeaWorld officially says it now regrets the way it got hold of its first whales—that they were the victims of cruel methods—there is no doubt that Griffin supplied the marine park with the first several animals that made the company's fortune, including the whale whose name is chanted and cheered at the park with every show.

Shamu herself did not have a happy ending. Griffin had sent her on to SeaWorld because he said she and Namu turned out to dislike each other. Shamu was also recovering from trauma. Griffin had harpooned and killed her mother during the capture; Shamu had seen it happen.

On April 19, 1971, SeaWorld decided to use Shamu in a promotional photo session with a model dressed in a bikini. The model, a secretary at SeaWorld, was to take three rides on Shamu. But by the second ride, the whale was showing signs of annoyance. On the third ride, Shamu refused to follow a command and, in the ensuing confusion, the model fell into the water. The whale bit her on the lower torso and limbs and, for several minutes, refused to let her go. The model survived the attack but spent several days in the hospital, where she received more than 100 stitches. She was scarred for life. In the ensuing lawsuit, SeaWorld provided documents that revealed that Shamu had bitten two people before, including a trainer, but no one had warned the model.

Shamu was pulled from working the shows and she died four months after the incident. The cause of death was pyometra, a hormonal imbalance that causes blood poisoning by allowing bacteria to enter the whale's uterine lining. It is an illness that almost never infects orcas in the wild.

These were the open secrets of SeaWorld, the history everyone who worked there knew but very few cared to discuss out loud. They were inconvenient truths, the skeletons in the family closet. Nevertheless, Shamu's name lives on in the signature spectacle of the theme park. More than just a captive whale, Shamu—nine years old, just a child really, when she died—had become a brand.

Being hired as an apprentice trainer meant that I was going to be closer to the orcas. It did not automatically mean I was going to train them. Still, I considered myself lucky. There was no guarantee about which stadium a trainer would work in. An apprentice might end up spending his or her entire animal training career never working with orcas. SeaWorld management decided where trainers would be assigned based on their skills and how they might best benefit the company. I know countless trainers who spent their entire careers at Dolphin or Sea Lion Stadium even though they wanted nothing more than to be at Shamu Stadium.

I had made sure I fit the Shamu bill. I was in the gym every day, lifting weights. You could see the effects in a wet suit, even though there was still more slack in it than I wanted there to be. It didn't hurt to be young. I was eating right. I was working out. You can't be shy or timid about wanting to work at Shamu. You can't be passive. You've got to let people know what you want. You've got to show people that you have the skills—both animal training expertise and athleticism— to be the choice they are looking for.

It must have worked. In 1993, less than two months after I turned 20, I not only got the apprentice job in San Antonio, I was immediately assigned to Shamu Stadium. I was ecstatic. My dreams were coming true faster than I expected. I quit college—after all, I had enrolled only to earn the degree I had thought necessary to apply for the job. I was ready to throw myself at work.

As a young wannabe, every time I spoke to the trainers, I was intensely focused on how to get into Shamu Stadium, not just on how to be hired by SeaWorld. I was always curious about the age at which the other trainers knew they wanted to join SeaWorld and what their path to the job was, often comparing myself to them. Occasionally, I'd meet trainers who, despite years of experience at SeaWorld, weren't at Shamu. I'd be surprised. Why would anyone not want to be working with the killer whales? Some said they didn't want to take, or think they could pass, the much more difficult swim test at Shamu Stadium; others felt that Shamu Stadium was a stressful environment and no fun. Or they were afraid of the whales. I didn't understand that. I was attracted to the pressure, knowing every move you made was under scrutiny, that your life might be on the line.

To officially qualify for Shamu Stadium, even as an apprentice trainer, I had to pass another swim test. This time, it would take place in the stadium itself, where the water was even colder—48 to 52 degrees Fahrenheit—in order to limit the bacterial growth that might harm the whales. It was 12 to 15 degrees colder than the water for the dolphins—and that was already about 15 to 20 degrees cooler than a regular pool. Such low temperatures can sometimes cause what is called shallow water blackout, a loss of consciousness from lack of oxygen, exacerbated by the low temperatures, which can kill you. To make it more difficult, instead of a 25-foot dive, I would have to swim to the bottom of the Shamu Stadium front show pool, which is about 40 feet deep, to retrieve a five-pound weight. Meanwhile, the single-breath, beneath-the-surface swim was 140 feet long, 20 feet longer than the one required at the Dolphin Stadium pool. Immediately after, I had to do a timed 250-foot freestyle swim. I also had to be able to exhibit upper-body strength by grabbing a ledge high above the surface of the pool and pulling myself up from the water and onto land. All of this had to take place within ten minutes. But I was confident. The test itself was the least of my worries. A very personal challenge had emerged a couple of weeks before.

On my first day of work, I showed up at SeaWorld San Antonio and, after I was done at Human Resources, a white Chevrolet truck pulled up to drive me to the main stadium. I was stunned when I saw who the driver was: Mark McHugh, my former childhood idol and now boss at Shamu Stadium. He was very encouraging and said I had shown great skill and athletic ability during my first swim test. That was a huge boost to my ego and my confidence. Things were going well, I thought, and this was just day one on the job.

As we spoke, however, McHugh casually said, "I almost voted not to hire you because I thought you might be gay."

I said nothing but I felt as if I had been kicked in the stomach by someone who was not just one of my bosses but also a person I had idolized as a hero for years. It hurt. I was suddenly afraid of losing the job I had spent all my life trying to win. I knew I would have no problem passing the swim test at Shamu Stadium. I was prepared for it. McHugh's remark, however, triggered my first career crisis. I quickly decided what I had to do: an important part of me had to go back beneath the surface, back into the closet. It wasn't what I had expected. But I was willing to do anything to work with the whales.

Even after being assigned to Shamu Stadium, I was not yet allowed to touch the animals or interact with them in any way. I certainly could not be in the water with them. A senior trainer had to be nearby whenever the apprentices were close to the edge of the pool. The whales can easily come out past the pool's perimeter and grab you. Even setting up buckets of fish in certain spots required you to be spotted by a senior trainer. But I was still nearer than I had ever been to the whales. It thrilled me to be in such close proximity to them, to discover things that I had never noticed before and to learn the way SeaWorld worked to keep its great marine stars alive and seemingly healthy.

The first whale I saw after I got my job was Kotar, the largest of the five whales in San Antonio at the time. You couldn't miss him. He weighed approximately 8,000 pounds. In the SeaWorld universe, only Tilikum in Florida—at 12,000 pounds—and, as he grew, Ulises in San Diego—approximately 10,000 pounds now—were more massive. Corky, a female in the San Diego facility, was about the same size: 8,200 pounds.

Yet even with an amazing specimen like Kotar, many things were amiss. For one, his dorsal fin was collapsed. It was a physical characteristic he shared with all of the adult male orcas at SeaWorld. I would soon learn that the cause is confinement: floating motionless at the surface of the pool without support for the height and weight of the dorsal fin leads to the collapse. This was even more pronounced at the Texas and Florida parks, where heat is a factor. Captive whales bake in the sun and suffer from sunburn and dehydration. Orcas in the wild spend much of their time fully submerged. SeaWorld's pools may be large in human scale but they do not in any way approach the breadth and depth the orcas have available to them in the ocean. In captivity, the broad sail-like dorsal fins so characteristic of male orcas remain exposed to the air and to the sun more often than those of killer whales in the wild.

Even as an apprentice trainer, I realized how fragile these creatures were. But the observations just made me redouble my efforts to care for them. I believed in SeaWorld's declared mission: that allowing humans to see these magnificent creatures at the marine park would help preserve the species in the wild because people would appreciate them and contribute to conservation efforts.

Like a nurse at a hospital, I was taught to observe and record each whale's behavior patterns and note them down in the meticulous documents kept by SeaWorld. I literally watched every breath a whale took at certain points, multiple times per day. Orcas will breathe once a minute; if they are performing a particularly strenuous part, they might breathe two to three times a minute depending on how much effort they have to expend. What is normal depends on the scenario. If their respiration is abnormally elevated, this can indicate something else is going on that involves their health. If I suspected an abnormality, I would immediately inform a supervisor. We would then monitor the whale's respirations again during a five-minute period and also evaluate what was happening socially between the specific whale and the others in the park. If the rate was still above normal limits, we would call the veterinarians, while continuing to record respirations and observing the whale.

Counting the number of times each whale breathes during a five-minute interval multiple times a day was an important chore. As was food preparation. It was my chief introduction to the immense efforts required to keep the animals alive in captivity. Food preparation sounds too professional. What I was doing was filling buckets with fish.

An individual whale can eat from 150 to 300 pounds of fish a day. Huge amounts are delivered constantly, arriving at the park frozen solid. The apprentices and the trainers thaw the fish overnight, running water over the herring, mackerel, smelt, salmon and, in California, squid. Each whale had a specific diet that required making certain the buckets contained the proper proportions and percentages of each fish. Then the buckets would have to be weighed, heavily iced and refrigerated to keep the food from spoiling. When it was time for the training sessions or shows to begin, the apprentices would lug 30-pound buckets of fish in each hand, running to and from poolside toward the trainers they were assigned to shadow. The fish had to be constantly available so that the trainers could reward the whales when they chose to.

The bucket brigade continued to toil once the show and sessions were over. (During certain times of year, there would be fewer shows a day so we'd make sure the whales were parceled out their daily quota of fish through learning sessions.) We'd have to scrub the stainless steel buckets clean because of the accumulation of fish scales and what we called "gack"—the crud left over from mashed-up fish and squid bits that solidified into bacteria-attracting gunk. Insufficiently cleaned buckets would attract the bugs that can kill whales. Every single scale had to be scrubbed and picked off. The supervisors would check the buckets, which were then bleached and hung out to dry.

Soon enough, the excitement of arriving at SeaWorld San Antonio was over and work settled into a predictable routine. One night, I sat down exhausted after scrubbing and thought, "This is what I passed the swim tests for? Icing and bucketing fish?" I had become part of the Shamu Stadium team but I didn't expect to be doing so much scut work and backbreaking manual labor. Apprentice trainers were also constantly in scuba gear helping clean the pools or looking for any foreign objects the whales might accidentally swallow.

But that backbreaking tedium was incredibly important. In the wild, the orcas find their food in the ocean. There are no schools of fish for the whales to chase and feed on at SeaWorld. Without that freedom, the captive orcas were completely at SeaWorld's mercy.

We easily went through a 1,000 pounds of fish a day to keep the five orcas in San Antonio at that time fed. Every week, we monitored their weight to make sure it was optimal. Each of the SeaWorld parks has a large stainless steel scale in a section of one of the shallower back pools that the whales are trained to slide up on. They have to position themselves perfectly on the scale, without a fluke or flipper hanging off. If part of the whale touched the water, it would affect the accuracy of the measurement on the digital display. Precision was critical.

If a whale had gained or lost too much weight, we'd adjust his or her diet by increasing or decreasing the percentages of certain fish in their base level of daily food. The herring, mackerel, smelt and salmon all have different caloric values and we'd vary the mix according to what the whale needed to get to his or her target weight. The basis for how much food a whale got was constantly in flux—among the factors that we calculated into their diet were age, the time of year, activity level and pregnancy. In California, we included squid to help with hydration because of the mollusk's high water content. Even when the whales were at a healthy weight, almost all of them hated squid. It was something you had to train them to accept and eat.

The trainers taught the whales what might be called "eating etiquette." They had to learn to keep their heads up with their chins on the pool wall and not to play with their food. Sometimes, when whales were too heavy, they would lower their heads just far enough so that their mouths filled with water, causing all the fish to sink to the bottom. That would be a reason for the whales to break from control with their trainer (what is called splitting) and submerge to play with the food. It's the equivalent of a child who isn't hungry being sat at a table for dinner, picking and playing with the food and not eating. Heavy or overweight whales don't have appetites or an interest in food.

As fascinating as learning about orcas was—even from my junior perch—the hard labor of apprenticeship frustrated me. A salary of $6 an hour and no health insurance did not help either. However, all of that motivated me to look for a way to move up the ranks.

San Antonio was the newest of the SeaWorld parks. It was also the biggest in terms of square footage. For its part, the park in Orlando was praised by management for the precision of its showmanship during the Shamu Stadium shows. But neither San Antonio nor Orlando had the prestige of San Diego, the oldest of the facilities.

The California whales had always had a significantly larger repertoire and higher criteria—that is, more exacting limits in terms of accuracy and difficulty—for the behaviors they were trained in. As a result, the whales were in better shape and more motivated to perform. For example, Takara held the record for bows: 60. She had the stamina and willingness to do it. Good luck getting a whale in Texas to do more than four or five bows in a row without terminating the session!

As an ambitious apprentice, I constantly inquired about how things were done—and was fascinated by what I heard about California's methods. The International Marine Animal Trainers' Association conference used to hand out awards every year for the best new behaviors learned by whales. The California park always took home prizes for categories such as Best New Novel Behavior or Best Criteria, the latter being awarded for achievements in ever-higher levels of difficulty, say, the fastest-swimming whale or the orca who performed the most bows or rose to a significant height out of the water. SeaWorld

San Diego was always on top when it came to getting the whales to do the most creative and novel acts, a testament to the facility's mastery of the behavioral sciences. Senior management in Texas and Florida conceded to me and others that the San Diego trainers were the best in applying the principles of behavioral science—that is, they were what was called the "strongest behaviorally"—and that the whales in that facility had the highest criteria and largest repertoires. I made up my mind that I wanted to end up in California.

Despite being the newest of the SeaWorlds, San Antonio did not have the resources that had been poured into San Diego and Orlando. The trainers had to do their work with less. Still, it had its advantages. Of all the parks I've worked in, San Antonio had the cleanest facilities. The Fish Room where we prepared the food for the whales was spotless. You certainly wouldn't find a scale in a cleaned bucket. Or under-iced fish. In that part of the care and feeding of whales, San Antonio was exceptional. But, in other aspects, it wasn't San Diego.

Once again, I caught a break. In my second year at San Antonio, a manager told me that an associate-level trainer position—the next step up from apprentice—had opened up in San Diego. I got on a conference call interview with several senior managers and got the job. All I really ever knew was Texas. Now I was headed for the original SeaWorld—and the bright lights of California. It was the beginning of a chapter in my life that would permanently shape me as a trainer and as a person.

3

THE EDUCATION OF
AN ORCA TRAINER

After I moved to San Diego, I bought a surfboard. Like everyone else who'd heard of the fabled California coast, I thought I had to learn to surf now that I lived there. But surfing would never become a habit with me—not after I began to get into the water to work with the killer whales of SeaWorld San Diego. Why would I want to get up at 6:00 a.m. to catch a wave when I could go to the office and actually ride on the back of a killer whale? There's no sport that lets you do that. Certainly no other job that I know of.

I arrived in San Diego in 1995 with a kind of smugness. I had finally accomplished what I had longed for since I was six years old. The facilities at the California park were of the same class and quality of a Disney theme park. SeaWorld San Diego is the Yankee Stadium of marine parks—that is, if you like the Yankees.

I drove there solo in my beat-up white Mazda truck with a U-Haul attached, carrying all my belongings. I drove 25 hours from San

43

Antonio because I didn't have enough money to stay at a motel on the way. I was deliriously happy. I was even getting a pay raise: to $10.50 an hour from my starting apprentice rate of $6.05 in 1993. I couldn't believe how brilliantly beautiful San Diego was when I finally got there: cloudless sky, no humidity, iconic lines of palm trees. I knew too that, unlike in San Antonio, I could live openly as a gay man in California.

I was even more ecstatic when I got to SeaWorld itself. From the employee parking lot, you can see the bridge over San Diego Bay, connecting to Pacific Beach. And finally, there was Shamu Stadium, the place I had dreamed of working.

After orientation on that first day, I took a lunch break to see the whales. Shamu Stadium in San Diego is bigger than its equivalents in San Antonio and Orlando. It seats 6,500 compared to the 4,500 in Texas. California also had more whales—six at that time compared to the five in San Antonio. The orcas in San Diego were bigger and more impressive. At the age of 22 and standing there in the cool air, free of the sticky heat of Texas, I was as entranced by the killer whales as when I was a child. When I got to the stadium, I caught the tail end of a training session. I got goose bumps at the sight of the trainers—Robbin Sheets, Lisa Hugueley, Ken "Petey" Peters and Curtis Lehman, the very people who would shape the way I pursued my career—calling the whales over to chin-up at the edge of the pool. They were the people I wanted to be.

That day marked the start of two years of learning on the job with sea lions, walruses and otters. After that I was moved to Shamu Stadium, promoted and began to wear the wetsuit of a SeaWorld orca trainer. And when the time finally came for me to get into the water with the orcas, Robbin, Lisa, Petey and Curtis would teach me how to go about doing that with the kind of personal style and professional wisdom that cannot be found in books. They would teach me the rides of my life.

One of the most exhilarating and dangerous of those rides was the hydro hop. Only the most experienced trainers at Shamu Stadium get the opportunity to learn and perform what is considered to be the most challenging and dangerous behavior with whales in the water. In essence, you steer the whale to the bottom of the pool, then turn back toward the surface, where you and the orca explode out of the water and the whale throws you up in the air. The goal is to achieve a perfect dive and not to land on or be hit by the whale. Depending on the size of the whale, you can easily reach almost 30 feet in the air—comparable to the height of a ten-meter diving platform. The consequences of performing this incorrectly are immense. Having done more than a thousand hydros and rocket hops throughout my career, I can say there's no feeling like it in the world. That is, when everything goes right.

I prepared for the hydro even before I was a high-enough ranked trainer to be eligible for it. In San Diego, I trained with the head diving coach at the University of Southern California (USC). I went off the five-meter and ten-meter platforms just to get used to the heights and to learn how to dive with the correct form. I told the USC coach, "You know, in maybe ten months I'll be doing this act with the whales and I'd like to start learning to be great at it now." I was so sure of myself—so sure that I was going to get what I wanted. I was young and still quite naïve.

Every whale is different but by the time you work with an orca on a hydro, both of you will have trained together for months or even years. Trainers have a dominant foot that they use not only for balance but to help send signals to the whale by applying pressure. The dominant foot has to be exactly located on the whale's rostrum so you don't slip off. There is no special footwear for this: just black dress socks that provide your feet with no good way to get a grip on the whale's smooth, glass-slick skin. (There was a period we tried something like a scuba booty but we reverted to socks.)

I happen to be left footed. Most trainers are right footed. You steer the whale by shifting the weight and the direction of your body. You use your feet to indicate the speed you want to go. Two feet firmly on the whale is a signal to swim at normal speed. If you drop one foot and gently tap with pressure three times, the whale knows it is time to swim fast. It's like power-steering—except that the car is a killer whale and the steering wheel is your body.

I float on my stomach, my feet on the whale's rostrum, the orca propelling me forward in what trainers call a "foot push." The whale is so sensitive to the way my body is positioned that the moment I arch my back skyward, expanding my chest in a forward motion with my arms spread, the orca knows that it is time to go underwater. I am foot-pushed down into the pool. I direct the whale as far as we can go—36 feet in San Diego, 40 feet in San Antonio. The whale descends at an angle so that I am upside down underwater, heading straight toward the drain at the bottom of the pool, propelled at huge speeds by tons of killer whale.

The force of the water as you descend is a tremendous gush. It is both physical and aural. The sound is almost overpowering. There is nothing gentle about it. You feel it press hard against your body. You feel the energy of the water in your ears. And every now and then, the thought flashes through your mind, "What if I don't pull this off? What if I get hurt?"

The force of the water against your body flushes those questions out of your brain because you are now descending head first into the depths. You have to remember to be precisely positioned in the pool for the moment when the two of you turn upward. If you are not, it could result in being too close to the glass or stage, which would turn the dive into a bone-shattering catastrophe. There is no margin for error. You think of other trainers who have ended up with broken necks or backs or have had their careers ended by injuries. The adrenalin goes thrilling through your body with fear and anticipation. This is happening whether you want it to or not. There's no bailing.

Your concentration goes back to your foot. The dominant foot has to stay in the perfect spot or your foot will slip off with potentially disabling consequences. If the water pressure going down was harsh, the journey up comes at you with the power of an onrushing train. You can't see a thing because there is so much salt water flowing against your face, at your eyes. That sound and the fury are like a massive action movie sound effect. Imagine being in an underground subway platform with a passing train directly overhead as the ceiling shakes and you can't hear anything else—that's the best way I can describe it.

You hit the air, rising faster than thought. It's now all in the timing. You push off the whale's rostrum at the same instant the whale throws you off it. You loop into space and hit the arc, flying through the air, as the whale dives in. You both return to the surface.

The hydro—along with the rocket hop (which is almost like the hydro except you are positioned before emerging from the pool on the orca's pectorals, not on the rostrum)—is the pinnacle of whale-and-trainer interaction at the shows staged at Shamu Stadium. They are the culmination of decades of hard work and fine-tuning by generations of trainers—as well as the scores of whales, many now dead, who have been the denizens of SeaWorld's empire. I was fortunate to be part of those amazing years, when human and cetacean could mingle in the water. I would discover as I grew in the job and as a person, however, that all this spectacle was built on shallow reasoning. Tragedy has since curtailed acts like the hydro. What I have just described—the exhilaration and the danger—are no longer part of the trainer's repertoire. I look back at what I was able to do with much nostalgia but also much wisdom.

What I do not want to be lost is the ingenuity that allowed humans and whales to perform together so magnificently. I do not want people to forget that we were once able to swim with killer whales—to forget the almost magical knowledge we accumulated in our quest to know them, to convince them to work with us.

So, how do you begin to train a killer whale?

First, a slap of the water.

Slapping the water is a call-over, and training an orca to respond to that signal is the foundation of the thousands of small steps and behaviors that, paired with reinforcement and the whale's recognition of the sound of a whistle as a sign of correct behavior, form the intricate choreography of SeaWorld's shows. Before you can work with an orca, the whale has to learn to come to you. The whales are so perceptive that they can tell trainer from trainer even if the humans aren't in the water; they can detect strangers on the perimeter of the pool; they know whom they have to please to get what they want; and they play favorites. It is always advisable to be on the good side of a whale. And if they are to work with you, they must know who you are and why you matter.

You and the whale—even an adult whale that already has a repertoire of behaviors—need to form a strong relationship, with a lot of give-and-take and reciprocity, knowing where both of your limits are. The whales know you as well as you know them: for example, they are aware of how long humans can stay underwater on a single breath and often adjust for that. Most importantly, the whales must realize that a specific trainer will be someone who is a positive part of their life, not just in terms of rewards of fish. Nothing about training orcas is easy. You have to be patient. You need the whale to buy into the relationship.

Slapping the water to call the whales over appears simple but it is a trained behavior. And it is only the first step. Through training, conditioning and the process of association, you and your hand—in the eyes of the whale—can be extended into a pole that you use to guide the animal as you shape behaviors. Again by extension, the whale can respond to a small cube of ice that you toss into the water, its ripples becoming the spot where you would have slapped the surface. You shape what you want the whale to do through positive reinforcement. The behavior you want is paired with food or something else the whale enjoys. You can pair the desired behavior with any signal you choose: visual, tactile or audible. Through careful, slow steps, whatever type of signal you choose will ultimately elicit the behavior you have trained the whale to perform.

This training—approximating behavior by way of a gradual approach—essentially takes the whale forward step by step toward a goal, with the trainer psychologically reinforcing all the correct moves along the way, with food mostly but not always. You can use a variety of reinforcers—what might in ordinary language be called "rewards"—that a particular whale enjoys. Each animal is unique and a good trainer discovers what it is that each orca finds rewarding.

By the time you are in sync with each other, the signs become not just a way of getting a whale to do what you want him or her to do—to spin through the air, to bow, to swim fast along the perimeter of the pool. They also become portals into their souls, a way to fathom their ancient intelligence.

Apprentices at Shamu Stadium aren't expected to fully absorb the principles of behavioral psychology until they have successfully completed two years of training. Even after two years as a trainer, it would still be some time before they would be allowed in the water with the whales and many more years after that before they could do everything with the whales.

There is so much technical information to learn that you sometimes feel you will never absorb it all. But with hard work and continuous observation of how trainers work, your knowledge grows and the theories become comprehensible. Until then, apprentices can have no interaction with the orcas—not even as they are dashing by the glass cutaway into the pools with buckets of fish and the whales are peering at them longingly. Peering at the fish, to be exact. Every human interaction with orcas can potentially reinforce an unwanted behavior. The trainers reminded the apprentices of this again and again. It was hard not to want to interact when the whales were right there but we couldn't afford to have the orcas feel rewarded for things they shouldn't be doing.

The whales are opportunistic and will take advantage of situations when people or trainers with whom they have no day-to-day relationship come into the picture. They can sense who the apprentices are—or at least have a good idea which humans have less authority—and can take advantage of those scenarios, often in malevolent ways. One night, after I swam with Takara for an entire show, ending with a surf ride on her, she and I headed to the back pools of the stadium, where an apprentice was waiting to help gate Takara in one of the pools. She appeared to be calm, chinning up at the perimeter in front of me as the gate closed behind her. The apprentice had to walk across the gate to the other side to chain and secure it. As soon as the young woman took her first large step across the top of the gate, Takara split from my control. The orca turned and slammed her 5,000-pound body into the unchained gate. The force completely knocked the apprentice trainer's feet and legs off the gate. Fortunately, the young woman had tremendous upper body strength and she was able to grab the railings to keep from falling into the pool. When Takara realized she had not gotten her way, she swam back to where I was and chinned up at the perimeter again, right in front of me, as if she did not have a care in the world. The apprentice, however, was in tears. The incident was a perfect example of the opportunistic nature of a predator—and how instantly an orca can choose to go to the dark side and back again. While she had a relationship with me that she wanted to preserve, she had none with the apprentice crossing the gate. I do not want to imagine what might have happened if she had succeeded in knocking the woman into the pool.

Moving to SeaWorld San Diego was the big career break in my quest to work directly with orcas. However, before I could qualify to handle killer whales, I had to learn the basics of behavioral psychology—in practice, not just theory—and to prove it to my bosses by working with sea lions and walruses. I had to show that I not only knew the principles of animal training and the basic tricks of the trade but that I could use them in an enterprising way to make animals impress a crowd with what they could do. I had to show my supervisors that I could accomplish what was expected of me but also prove to them that I had the talent to do much more. Every animal species has its quirks; and each one teaches you to be patient in different ways. I learned valuable lessons from the sea lions and walruses.

You can't just go from filling buckets of fish to surfing on the back of a killer whale, much less jumping into a pool with an 8,000-pound orca older and wiser than you are. Hands-on experience with other, smaller animals is essential to moving on to dealing with an enormous and dangerous predator like a killer whale. Even so, sea lions, weighing up to 500 pounds or more each, can be formidable. With their large canines and substantial weight, they are more imposing and much bigger than seals, which are rotund and slow. Sea lions are also temperamental when unhappy and can deliver nasty bites with those sharp canines.

Walruses are even bigger, reaching up to 1,000 pounds. When I got to San Diego, trainers had been banned from waterwork with walruses because of a near-fatal drowning a decade earlier after one animal, perhaps too playfully or aggressively (no one seems to have ascertained) grabbed on and held a trainer under water for a prolonged period. I believed we could—and should—go back into the water with the walruses and decided to petition to be allowed to do so. It was a daunting process. I had to argue my case before SeaWorld's all-powerful Behavioral Review Committee—which oversees training policies and micro-manages all trainer activity. I told them that walruses had to be desensitized to having trainers in the water with them so that, in case someone slipped and fell into the pool, there would be much less of a chance of another grab-and-hold incident. They were convinced. And so, just as I turned 23, I had made it into the SeaWorld books as a trainer who was able to revive a risky act. It was the kind of enterprise and forethought the corporation was looking for in trainers they would assign to Shamu Stadium.

The sea lions and walruses also taught me a more subtle skill, one I appreciated after much day-to-day, practical experience. Every sea lion or walrus was different; each one required a relationship specially tailored by the trainer. As I made progress with the sea lions and walruses, I could sense where each one was in his or her head. Within two years, I was at the point where my ability to judge how an animal would behave was instinctive.

I paid my dues for about two years at Sea Lion stadium, and more than just that, I enjoyed the experience. I loved the animals I worked with. As time passed, I noticed the effects of captivity on them—arthritis from having to live and perform on hard concrete instead of the sandy beaches that were their natural habitat; blindness from the chlorinated salt water they swam in because of outdated filtration systems. The facilities were practically unchanged since the 1960s. It would take many years for the significance of these observations to sink into my consciousness. At the time I just thought they were part of the inevitability of age and the passage of time. I was not yet at a point where I could question SeaWorld's mission.

At Sea Lion Stadium, I labored alongside some great trainers whom I admired—Greg Stryker, Tasha Bogden and Dawn Otjen—and I learned a great deal from them about their craft. I saw how much they loved the animals and developed good and strong training relationships with them. Even though it wasn't Shamu Stadium, I was happy. This is where I built my foundations in the theory and practice of behavioral psychology essential to a trainer's technique and success. Even at Sea Lion Stadium, it was clear that the California park was on much more solid theoretical and practical ground than the Texas park. The trainers in California had a detail-oriented focus on precise behavior and it showed in the way the animals performed. As a result, the repertoire of San Diego's orcas was much more extensive and the level of difficulty—the quality or criteria—of the behavior was of a much higher standard.

One of the coolest experiences I had was with Hercules, a surplus sea lion SeaWorld acquired from the US Navy. He had been trained to dive to hundreds of feet beneath the surface to tag warheads on the sea floor so they could be recovered. One day, however, Hercules decided he wasn't going to dive below a certain depth anymore. He just flat-out refused. The Navy having no further use for him, Hercules was offered to us. Before we could bring him over to SeaWorld, trainers needed to establish a relationship with Hercules. I and one of my colleagues were selected to go to the Navy and work with Hercules. When we arrived, Hercules jumped onto the back of one of the Navy's Zodiac boats as he had been taught to do and off we went into the open sea where we worked on several behaviors with him over a number of visits. He was finally brought to SeaWorld San Diego, where he was trained for shows. It was an opportunity and a challenge to teach an animal naive to shows.

Despite the engrossing work, it was no secret to anyone at Sea Lion Stadium that I wanted to be moved to Shamu once I was promoted to Trainer level. Only when you reached that rank could you finally begin to do high-quality, hands-on work with the whales. It was also the level you needed to reach to begin to do waterwork with the whales. I did everything I could to be promoted to Trainer level in the minimum time required. The path was narrowing to my goal, and there were others who wanted to reach it as well. On average, management at SeaWorld transferred trainers to Shamu once every year or two; there were many other trainers ahead of me on the list.

Some trainers at Sea Lion Stadium waited ten years but never got a chance to work with orcas. Still, I continued to be surprised that not all trainers wanted to go to Shamu. I worked with a couple of them who were excellent behaviorists but were very happy at Sea Lion stadium. Working with killer whales was the proof I needed to show that I had made it, that the promise I made to myself as a child and announced to my relatives and friends had been kept.

Luckily, a couple of orca trainers unexpectedly left SeaWorld at about the same time and positions suddenly opened at Shamu. I was one of only a few trainers in more than a decade to be moved directly from Sea Lion Stadium to work with the orcas, bypassing Dolphin

Stadium. Almost everyone else had to go through Dolphin first. Management had been impressed by my skills at Sea Lion.

I was moved to Shamu at the same time as my best friend and roommate, Wendy Ramirez, who had been at Dolphin. We were about the same age and had similar upbringings—mine in Texas, hers in Oklahoma. I was happy to be going to Shamu with a friend. It's very much like going to a new school. It's good to have a friend when you walk in. There was an intimidating amount of knowledge and practice to be learned at Shamu. But we were there for each other. There was also a lot of danger at Shamu. Despite our love for the whales, we knew we were putting ourselves in harm's way working with animals that weighed several tons each. As good friends, we became our own mutual support group. There were many days that were tough and if you didn't have a thick skin before, Shamu Stadium would give you one really fast.

In the wild, every whale knows its place in its family and in its pod— and who has precedence over the other. But in a marine park, that hierarchical structure is both repressed and supersized. From my experience, the captive killer whale is a massive collection of smarts and emotion—as well as sensitivities and suspicion. They can be divas, needy of attention and jealous of what you do with other whales. While sea lions can be temperamental, they aren't the apex predators of the sea. Nothing in the ocean hunts killer whales as prey. They know they are at the top of the pyramid.

The practical reason to begin with sea lions and walruses was that, despite their size, they were still closer to human scale. The work was much more forgiving because even if a sea lion became aggressive, even if it bit you, that wasn't going to kill you. But if a whale is aggressive and decides it wants to take out its frustrations on you, the potential for catastrophe goes up exponentially.

Whenever a trainer took a break, going on vacation for example, he or she could not just get back into the water with a whale immediately after returning to work. There would have to be a period of what I would describe as respectful distance, in which the trainer provided enough attention to the whale without getting back into the pool as if he or she had never been away. It is not as if the whale has forgotten the trainer. I don't think whales ever really forget.

There are no guarantees that what you have learned will always work. There were some in the Animal Training Department who knew every term in the books, every psychological theory and every behavioral principle. But when they were in front of an animal, they simply couldn't apply what they'd learned. The animal is constantly changing in front of you. The whale is making a series of sometimes contradictory decisions based on what is happening in the immediate environment, based on diverse stimuli that intrude on the simple scenarios set out in the textbooks. You are making behavioral decisions in a constantly shifting environment with a "free-thinking" animal. By necessity, you have to be able to change and adapt your behavioral decisions as you size up the situation you and the animal are in. A trainer has to watch for every factor the whale might be paying attention to.

Almost everything I had to know at SeaWorld I was taught by other trainers. It is lore that has been passed down from one generation to another. We like to think of it as behaviorist knowledge, just to give it a scientific patina; and what we do in planning out training is as meticulous and as complicated as any engineering flowchart or the diagram of a chemical reaction. But, when it works, it is sometimes like magic.

As trainers, we are adherents of behaviorist principles, believers in slowly teaching the animals one "trick" or behavior after another and stitching them together into an act they then perform when show time comes around. The principles have proven to work again and again— and thus have the sheen of science. Because behaviorism delivers both practical results and has a powerful philosophy behind it, I still find it nearly impossible to use the word "trick" instead of behavior. It goes against my core programming.

Each step in training an orca is mapped out in detail, long before we get to the pool and the whales. We establish the criteria that must be met for the training to be considered successful: how high must the whales leap up into the air; where should they look when we ask them to pop their head above the surface of the water? We also plot out how we do the training itself. Everything is taken into account: how we stand; where our hands are; eye contact; the way we point at the whales so they know which pool to head toward. The whales notice everything, so we have to make sure that our signals have nothing extraneous to them each time we ask the whales for a behavior. For example, the whales can figure out whether a bucket has fish in it or not—and whether or not you are worth listening to because you may not have food to reward them with. So don't shake out your only bucket in front of the whales, making it obvious that it's empty.

With patience and a detailed understanding of each whale, you can train an orca to do almost anything. When the orcas went after and killed seagulls that strayed into the park, we figured out how to train them so that the killer whales would, first, fish out the carcass from the pool for us; then learn not to tear the carcass apart after they killed the bird; finally, we managed to get them to give up a seagull— alive and intact—if we got to the whales in time, just as they were about to set upon the visitor.

As a trainer, I never liked being described as an entertainer and resented the policy at SeaWorld that required us to go through dance steps and do choreography as part of the Shamu show. I thought we should really be keeping our eyes on the whales. Nevertheless, I cannot deny that there is an artistry that comes with the work of the best trainers. Every act at SeaWorld—even the simplest ones—is composed of a number of behaviors. Putting them together is an art. Over and over again, I've studied videos of my favorite colleagues— men and women who have not only done the hard work but who are also able to combine those signals into one smooth, seamless performance.

Whales are assiduous about following instructions and the initial lessons are ingrained deeply—including whatever miscues might have occurred in training. If you lead them astray, the mistake will be difficult to undo; you will only frustrate them by trying to dial back the instructions. Every step in teaching a new behavior must be planned out and executed carefully. Kasatka—the mother of my favorite whale Takara, whom I worked with at both San Diego and San Antonio—was quite intolerant of human failure. If you caused her to fail, she'd let you know it. A few whales—like Kasatka, Takara and Orkid—were so unforgiving that only the most experienced trainers were entrusted with them, particularly in the water.

For waterwork, the most experienced trainers, who work in teams, are typically assigned to no more than three whales. That is already difficult because the animals have such complicated personalities and have idiosyncratic needs. But whoever was on Kasatka's team, for example, definitely had to focus more of their time and attention on her because, as a dominant female guarding her social position, she was considered the most dangerous whale at SeaWorld during waterwork. I had to make sure I spent a lot of quality time with her to ensure my relationship with her was sound and we trusted each other.

Fortunately, the very first whale I was assigned to in San Diego was Corky. She was a bit of a celebrity, having been the stunt whale in *Orca*. She was always in high gear, always wanting to go fast. I was the trainer but, essentially, Corky trained me. And I am eternally grateful for her patience. At 8,200 pounds and in her early 30s, she was the largest female in captivity in the world and every bit a legend.

Corky already knew every trick in the book. She had also worked with enough neophyte trainers that she had her own special way to treat them: gently. It was as if she could sense our confidence—or lack of it—from the way we touched her. If you were a new trainer performing a hydro on Corky, she would take you down only about 20 feet before stopping and pulling back up to complete the performance, throwing you more gently above the surface.

Only after your confidence registered with her, perhaps with the firmness of the touch of your hand or foot—or the position of your body—would she take you all the way to the bottom of the pool, 36 feet below the surface. Then she'd use her enormous flukes to kick into high gear, swimming at an incredible speed and exploding through the surface with a dramatic flourish, launching both you and her into the air. She made trainers look good.

Trainers are indoctrinated to believe that whales behave the way they do because of the mosaic of psychological reinforcements we have constructed for them, reinforcements that are ultimately based on one primary object: food. This unsentimental perspective stems from the tenets of behaviorism, which declares that what matters is the performance elicited from a stimulus, from what can be observed and quantified. This materialist perspective, of course, eliminates the interior life of a whale, which, being left to our imaginations, is not properly the subject of science. Without the step-by-step, pains-taking choreography we practice with them—and reinforce with food as well as other things—the spectacles of SeaWorld would be impossible.

However, a good trainer has to be able to look into the interior life of an orca to figure out how the animal will behave. Corky's caution with newbie trainers was completely untaught. What kind of tangible reward would she have had for modifying her behavior in a way that humans can only interpret as being "nice" to a newcomer? Is it just the mystery of her "personality"—even if she isn't a person?

I sense this quality about Corky because I have dealt with other whales that don't behave the same way. Take Keet, a much-traveled orca. Now in San Diego, he spent most of his life at the Texas park and lived for a while in SeaWorld's Ohio facility, which closed in December 2000. Like Corky, he was a "learner whale." But he was a badly conditioned one. New trainers would work with him, and because of their inexperience, often reinforced poor effort or criteria. As a result, he became lazy. He'd do things that were just a little less than right, enough to get by—and then was fed fish as a reward for that imperfection. Imprecision is not a virtue in a theme park where a wrong move or a swerve a few inches off could have disastrous results. That is what happened to me.

While completing the hydro, most orcas almost instinctively dive the other way to avoid hitting the trainer. But Keet didn't when I performed with him in San Antonio during a night show in 2009. All 7,500 pounds of him drilled me in the middle of my back directly on my spine upon reentry into the water. I heard my back crack—it was the kind of sound a chiropractor would make when he worked on your vertebrae. I was literally stunned.

Still underwater, I put both my hands on him, making sure that his jaw was closed. I grabbed his rostrum, which was the signal for him to haul me onto the stage. I wasn't even sure I was going to be able to move as I surfaced on his back. Fortunately, I had full range of motion. But I could feel my back was tight and getting tighter by the moment. After the show, I asked a trainer to unzip my suit and look at my back. There was already a perfectly round circle on my spine, the impression of the tip of his rostrum. It was as if someone had traced the rim of a large drinking glass on top of a couple of my vertebrae.

I went to the SeaWorld doctor the next day thinking my back could be fractured. It wasn't. But by then I was into my second decade as a trainer and my body, which had taken other batterings before Keet's, was being worn down. (On another occasion, Keet and I were almost in a catastrophic collision when another trainer sent him breaching into an area of the pool unaware that I was in the water. I managed to get out of the way. Barely.)

Being hit by a whale was a constant hazard for trainers doing waterwork. I knew Keet was not being aggressive. He was just a lazy whale and wasn't paying attention because he had been poorly reinforced through the years. If a whale wanted to be bad, there would be no question of intent to do harm.

Trainers talk about "the bridge" all the time. For us, it is a technical term. But the bridge also has poetic resonance. For those of us who worked the orcas day-to-day at SeaWorld, the bridge is the period of time between the correct response by a whale from a signal for a behavior and the orca getting his or her reward—be it fish or a rubdown or something else that the whale enjoys. There are many different ways you can "bridge" a whale. The most obvious is the sound of the whistle we hang around our necks. But you can also use a tactile bridge—touching them—or visually get their attention by pointing or putting your hand up. The underwater computer-generated "emergency" tone is also used as a bridge, a signal of approval and the advent of reward. Following the signal, the whale would then return to its trainer. Any type of tactility would be interpreted by the orca as a "bridge"—even something as subtle as kissing the whale. The whales would understand that they were correct and had been bridged and rewarded.

For a trainer, the bridge is symbolized by the whistle around his or her neck. It is not only a tool but a mark of status: it's a sign that you have reached a level of competence, proving yourself worthy of being part of the small coterie of people in the world who know how to handle and read the ways of the orcas. I earned mine when I first started in Texas as an apprentice, though that was really for surviving a hazing as I did not rank high enough at all to work directly with the whales yet. But the whistle I treasured most I received in San Diego, when I was deep into the principles and practice of behaviorist science—and seeing the results of it in my interactions with the orcas themselves. There was no ceremony, just someone handing me a box and saying, "This is your bridge."

During a career spanning three different killer whale parks, I had two different whistles. The whistle has helped me get out of life-or-death situations. That's because it is a manifestation of the bridge and encapsulates that moment when you tell the whale "job well done." Because there is always the potential for a killer whale to grab your whistle and drag you underwater by it (and it has happened), the whistle hangs around our necks on a lanyard connected to a rubber o-ring that will break if it is pulled with any force. It would certainly snap with the power of an orca grab—and not take you into the water.

Whistle, lanyard and o-ring form a kind of rosary, a subtle reminder of how suddenly the hour of death may come upon you when working with orcas.

Orcas need food, so fish will always be a primary form of reward. The trainers will always be figures of authority because the animals know human beings are their only source of fish. But the whales understand and appreciate more than mackerel and salmon.

California was the champion of a training philosophy of rewards that looked beyond food. The trainers there believed in challenging the whales—the orcas certainly had the intelligence to take up a challenge. We let them show it. SeaWorld San Antonio would sometimes use secondary reinforcers—like rubdowns and playtimes—but not to the extent or in the same context they were used in the California park. We were taught to believe it was not only possible but that it was a good thing to train whales without food to reinforce behavior. In San Diego, we regularly interacted with the whales during training sessions or shows, including waterwork—without using fish for reinforcement. That would be inconceivable in Texas.

In California, we removed the immediate focus from food. That increased the importance of the whale's relationship with the trainer and his or her ability to make the orca feel rewarded and positive about every training situation. It raised the relationship to a higher level. There was, of course, always a bucket of food readily available in case of an emergency.

When material rewards were not the sole method of reinforcing behavior, the whales were forced to think more, to associate the human trainer with complex linkages of stimuli. The process, I believe, enriched their existence in SeaWorld. We also reinforced them with playtime, which again broadened their concept of reward to include physical interactions with trainers and with each other. Using this variety of reinforcement, the whales were more motivated and more engaged with their trainers.

Experienced trainers at the other facilities knew of San Diego's philosophy—and many of them disagreed with it. Even though all three parks are part of a single corporate SeaWorld, each facility has its own management—with varying approaches and styles with regard to orca training. SeaWorld San Antonio did not believe in elevating risk levels by interacting with the whales without primary reinforcement—that is, fish. In California, on the other hand, the trainers were taught that by doing just that, you developed stronger relationships with the whales—and were therefore safer.

The play sessions and trainer interactions are rewards in and of themselves. In behavioral jargon, any reward other than food is categorized as secondary reinforcement. But secondary doesn't mean it is unimportant. Takara liked to solicit for her favorite secondary rewards. She enjoyed having her tongue rubbed and patted, and me to grab it and shake it. She loved for me to massage the very back corners of her mouth where her upper and lower jaws connected. She seemed to enjoy this more than fish. Sometimes, with each perfect act, she would raise a massive pectoral flipper, clearly indicating to me that she wanted me to grab onto it. As I held on, she would swim on her side with that pec up until I dropped off. Then she'd come back at me with the opposite pectoral flipper up and I'd grab it to make another circuit around the pool with her. Her mother, Kasatka, loved to do exactly the same thing. We motivated the whales to perform by giving them the flexibility to solicit the type of rewards they preferred. You could hear how excited they were by the vocalizations they produced throughout.

Play fulfilled some of the deeper needs of the orcas. I was aware even then of how boring and sterile their captive lives were. In the evenings, they would float in limited space, almost never having access to all the pools in Shamu stadium, usually restricted to just one or two. There, barely able to move, they'd wait for the next day's training sessions and Shamu shows. Young orcas have so much energy and curiosity—I could sense the desperation sink in when they finally realize their fate is to be one of repetitive performance and routine. The job of a good trainer is keeping the lives of the whales as interesting as possible. Even if you performed for food, how happy could you be if you were fed the same salmon and mackerel time after time? For a human, it would be like eating nothing but boiled chicken breast at every meal.

I know from my experience with the whales that they were motivated by a greater variety of reinforcement. There is a practical reason to make play and creative interaction part of a whale's curriculum and reinforcement. What would happen if you had an emergency and didn't have fish with which to reward a whale and you found yourself with an orca that always worked with a trainer with a bucket of food? You're stuck with no leverage with the whale. You have got to train your whales not to focus on the food. You actually condition a whale to be more relaxed when they aren't single-mindedly focused on what's in the bucket. This is when the quality of your relationship comes through. Psychological reinforcement can take many forms. Takara loved for you to drag her by her tail flukes along the perimeter of the pool—a backbreaking exercise for a trainer. You could hear her excitement in her vocalizations. Orcas can sense affection and they can return it.

Before waterwork becomes a completely lost art, let me leave a record of what it entailed. Orca trainers had to reach three increasingly complex levels of skill in the water to remain at Shamu Stadium. With each level came a greater understanding of SeaWorld's orcas.

The Behavioral Review Committee (BRC) had the final say on who got to go into the water with the orcas. Some trainers promoted to Shamu never got to the point where they were allowed by the BRC to do waterwork at all. In California, the BRC was so strict it specified which trainer was allowed to get into the water with which whale. The committee divided waterwork into three different levels. Level 1 comprised the most basic behaviors. Level 2 included the more advanced behaviors such as the haul-outs, surf rides and some spy hop behaviors (variations of which include hugging, sitting and standing on the whale as it rises vertically with its body almost entirely out of the water). You couldn't perform in shows unless you had reached the second level.

Only after you provided evidence of full proficiency in levels 1 and 2 were you allowed to perform the signature behaviors of the show: the hydros and rocket hops. Your fitness was key. Not every trainer who got to Shamu Stadium got to the third level. In fact, few did. And if they didn't, they eventually were moved out of Shamu.

As the trainers moved through the levels, each developed his or her own style and strategies about the work. My fellow trainers and I disagreed about some techniques. When I was working through a new set of behaviors with the whales, I wanted to challenge the orcas and let them solve problems, to prospect for a solution to a training challenge. Most of my sessions lasted no more than 10 to 12 minutes—though I also made sure to throw in a longer or shorter session now and then for the sake of variety.

My style was to nurture the whale—to let them know that I was on their side. If a whale I was working or swimming with was being exceptional during a performance, I would just let the music play, avoiding the show pressure to hurry the whale along, just hanging out and swimming with the orca, rubbing his or her belly with my feet. The entertainment department managers would always complain when I did this, saying I was holding up the show. I'd tell them off, saying my job was to take care of the whale. My managers, of course, always told me "John, you need to work on your interdepartmental skills." I didn't care for that or the entertainment department's management. I cared for the whales.

A good trainer is always varying the type of reinforcement for the orcas. They are incredibly smart and aware that you are taking the time to reward them properly. If a trainer is always rushing whales to the rear pools immediately after a show, throwing fish into their mouths automatically, without making eye contact, the whales sense you are treating them perfunctorily—and they will remember that. I always tried to add the extra rub and eye contact that said thank-you—and that made a difference. These are the kinds of details that took your relationship with a whale to another level. I've always believed and taught that the stronger your relationship with a whale, the more layers of protection you have in the event that whale becomes upset. This can help prevent an aggression or can help you safely get out of one. Of course, no matter how strong your relationship is, it does not guarantee that the whale will not slip into the dark side. SeaWorld's history proves that we will never be able to predict orca behavior completely—certainly not aggressions.

4

"IN THE CARE OF MAN"

How do killer whales sleep?

At SeaWorld, we taught the whales to be comfortable at night in various combinations—all together or alone. SeaWorld's orcas generally sleep motionless on the surface of their pools. But Corky, who was born in the wild, would take a breath, descend into the depths of the pool, stay there for about three to five minutes then come back up to breathe again.

We call it sleep, but it isn't exactly what humans do. We lose consciousness when we retire to bed. But only one half of the whale's brain switches off when it sleeps because in the wild, the marine mammal has to remain conscious to breathe in the ocean and to be aware of the many hazards that may approach. Even a sleeping whale, floating still in captivity, knows what you are up to if you wander by. They are always hyperaware about what goes on in their environment.

The various SeaWorld parks have their own policies about sleeping arrangements for their whales. In Orlando, the whales that usually performed together, slept together. The Texas facility almost always put all its whales together each night. California varied the groupings: sometimes, all of them were gathered in the same place; at other times, the whales were mixed and matched, sleeping in different pools so they could get used to each other and the experience of being in diverse locales; sometimes, we'd slowly wean individual whales away from their companions and have them learn to sleep by themselves.

San Diego's reason for diversifying sleeping arrangements was practical. It produced a more relaxed orca, one who accepted, without being stressed, being placed in pools with any combination of other whales, or even being able to sleep alone. Whales who had not been trained to sleep alone would be distressed if, all of a sudden, they had to be separated from the rest of their companions. The distress would only aggravate their frustration and lead to more problems. There were also occasions when a whale would have to travel alone—for example, when shipped to another park.

But training an orca to sleep by themselves is a difficult endeavor because killer whales are so social. We had to get an individual orca used to solitude a half-step at a time, sharing sleep times with another whale in shorter and shorter intervals before the other whale was completely withdrawn. In the end, the whale would finally be comfortable alone. Some whales took to this better than others. Some would emit worried vocalizations as they went through the anxiety of separation from their companions.

How long do whales need to sleep? At SeaWorld, we set up an arbitrary rule at all three Shamu Stadiums that eight hours of total darkness should be scheduled for the orcas and that no sound should disturb the whales during that period. All construction work on the site had to stop; and rehearsals for the shows the entertainment department wanted to stage were halted. Lights out were mandated at a certain point each night so that the whales got the eight hours. In SeaWorld San Antonio, where I rejoined SeaWorld, I was a Senior 1 Trainer with the authority to cut the lights no matter who needed the stadium grounds. Sometimes the construction workers or, more often than not, the entertainment department's management was adamant about trespassing on the orcas' bedtime. It often provoked a fight.

I let whoever wanted to cross me know that they weren't calling the shots in that situation. I was. We had a corporate rule to protect the whales in this specific situation. The show doesn't have to go on all the time for them. Give them their sleep. Even the corporation realized that and invariably came down on my side in any quarrel with the entertainment department. After all, SeaWorld didn't become a $2.5 billion company because of sequins and choreography. It was built on the backs of captive killer whales.

One of the catchphrases of SeaWorld's ideology is that the animals in its collection benefit from being "in the care of man." And, for visitors, the physical appearance of the parks is impressive. The pools of SeaWorld are gigantic—if you are a human being. Including the filtration system, San Diego has 6.2 million gallons of water in its combined orca pools, or close to the volume of ten Olympic-size pools. San Antonio has 4.5 million gallons. Orlando has 5.9 million. What we call the med (short for medical) pool—a shallower transitional area for moving whales between larger show areas and where we could tend to some of their needs—is only eight feet deep, a few feet deeper than a lap pool in a nice urban gym. But all of that water is a drop in the bucket compared to the killer whales' natural habitat. It is like putting a whale in a bathtub—squeezing down the orca to human scale to benefit the profit motives of SeaWorld Entertainment Inc.

Orcas cannot easily maneuver in the med pool—and yet the show business side of SeaWorld has forced the trainers to use it as a staging area for Shamu Stadium spectacles. For a human being, it would be like being stuck in a doctor's waiting room except that the waiting room is a closet without a ceiling, exposing the top of your head to the hot sun. Regularly whales have had to wait in that pool for 15 minutes before, 30 minutes during, and sometimes 15 minutes after a performance, their giant dorsal fins put at even greater risk of drying out. That is not just a once-in-a-while occurrence. There are as many as seven shows a day, each running about 25 to 30 minutes, and some whales perform in all seven. If they aren't waiting to go on to perform, they may be placed in the eight-foot-deep med pool as they wait to be featured for park guests who sit at the back poolside tables of the Dine with Shamu restaurant, an area where visitors can eat as they watch the orcas swim. I regularly saw one or more whales in the med pool for hours at a time. I fought to stop it from happening, sending an email to the general manager raising the Animal Welfare Act and questioning the legality of forcing the whales into the shallow med pool. Management was not happy and I lost that battle.

Humans cannot replicate the ocean. The 30 whales currently owned by SeaWorld must make do in the microcosm of the marine park's facilities. It is a paradoxical empire: the chemically processed water in the pools is purer than that of the ocean, but it is not anywhere near what is natural for the whales; the orcas cavort for the crowds but they do not get enough physical exercise because there is not enough room to allow them to swim normally. These whales live lives of quiet desperation and intense boredom. It is the kind of ennui that can be fatal—to both whale and human.

Orcas can be only so accommodating. Their intelligence and emotions are as mercurial as humans', if not more so. You have to be able to be sensitive to the way a whale is feeling if you want the whale to stick with you. Being inattentive to their feelings—and their acute sensitivity to environment and their complex relationships with other whales—can be potentially deadly.

My frightening encounter with Freya—the first and only time in my career I was truly unnerved by killer whale aggression—arose from several factors. It took place in the south of France, where I was working with the whales of the Marineland in Antibes, an invaluable overseas assignment that I began in 2001 after rising to a senior level in SeaWorld San Diego. One of the keys to understanding Freya is her relationship with her son, Valentine—Val for short. It isn't quite what you'd expect of a human mother-child interaction. It is one of social dominance—and human trainers have to pay attention to the sociology of orca families in order to understand why they choose to behave the way they do.

Val was just six years old when I got to work and swim with him. Born in captivity, he was enormous and beautiful, with an impressive head and, at that time, a great tall straight dorsal fin. Freya had been captured off the coast of Iceland in 1982, when she was one or two years old. I imagine she must remember what it was like to be free, to be able to swim for hundreds of miles a day, unconfined by the tight walls and shallowness of concrete pools.

She was also female, which meant that she had social precedence over any male orca. Killer whale society is matriarchal; the dominant female has command authority over all the whales in her familial unit. In marine parks, from what I have learned by observation and experience, it is a prominence that is earned by will and by force. You cannot say "no" to the dominant female orca with impunity; you do not deny her the rights and privileges of her rank.

Just before Freya turned on me, I had a training session where I swam with Val in one of the back pools of the stadium. His mother was in an adjacent pool with the gate closed, separating her from Val and me. The young male did so well in training, mastering the behaviors I wanted to inculcate in him so quickly, that I decided to reward him with playtime in the water. During this period when I was with Val, I noticed that Freya was watching us intently from her pool; I thought she was enjoying the sight and decided to include her in the playtime. That would also allow her to interact with Val, part of our overall strategy to get them used to performing together in public. Mother and son were having trouble with that.

I got Val to propel me through the water, foot-pushing me with his rostrum, toward Freya's gate. I touched her from over the top of the gate and fed her some fish—signs we had taught her in training to mean she and I were going to begin our interaction. I continued to swim with Val on his side of the gate—another sign that whatever Freya and I were going to do would also have to involve him. I continued to touch and feed her repeatedly as I swam with Val.

As part of this process, I swam off with Val, getting him to perform certain behaviors or just playing with him. At the same time, I'd ask him to go back and forth toward the gate of Freya's pool, steering him with my foot on his rostrum or having him pec-push me to her gate. Or I would ride on his back as he carried me at the surface around the perimeter of the pool and approached his mother at the gate. All of this was done to make her feel comfortable with what I was hoping to get her to do: to work with the two of us.

At the point I believed she was ready to collaborate, I dived into her side of the water and, when I surfaced, asked one of the trainers on land to throw me a few fish—herring and mackerel—so I could reward Freya immediately as she approached me. That was when the trouble began.

After surviving the encounter and analyzing the incident, I realized that Freya was nursing a grievance. She did not like the fact that Val was receiving so much attention while she was stewing behind her gate. She was the dominant whale, after all. In previous sessions, when we were attempting to get Freya and Val to perform together, she would try to race ahead of him and displace him in the water to take precedence. When a solo trainer was having fun with another whale—and Freya wasn't part of it—she would become jealous. If they were in the same pool together, she would move up and crowd out the other orca to take up the attention from the trainer. Once I figured that out, I paid her the right amount of attention—more than just fish and a touch, offering her real interaction—as I trained the subdominant whales simultaneously. She learned to accept the fact that I worked with the other whales—not just her. But the relationship required constant maintenance.

Freya was a challenge, always out to remind you of her rank and, sometimes, taking offense at the subtlest of slights. But, after my encounter with her—the biggest and most serious aggression of my career—we figured out how to work with each other. You might say that I trained her. But that would be generous. More accurately, she had made certain that I had learned the right way to treat her. Once that was established, the monster would become an angel to me. But now I know: monster and angel can be one and the same.

Food is the edge humans have over the captive whales of SeaWorld. The orcas know that. SeaWorld says it uses food to reinforce and reward the whales for performing the behaviors that go into the Shamu Stadium spectacle. The corporation insists that it never inflicts corporal punishment on the animals. It also says that it never deprives them of food for not obeying or learning fast enough. The first part is true because it is physically impossible for humans to use pain to teach the whales a lesson. It would be ineffective. Elephant trainers using their hooked prods to keep the pachyderms in line have the advantage of being able to maneuver on land and being nimble on their feet; humans have nowhere to stand—or run—if they had to use physical punishment against a whale. When you are in the water with an orca, she or he holds all the cards.

The overpowering reality, however, is that the whales of SeaWorld are completely dependent on human beings for food. The orcas get not only nutrition but hydration from the food they eat. The huge marine mammals do not "drink" to get the liquid they need to stay alive. They can only hydrate by absorbing the water content of the fish they eat. Even if food deprivation was rarely used, the whales know all too well that it is a constant possibility.

SeaWorld says that its animals receive all of their food regardless of how they perform throughout the day. This is false. The corporation would like the public to believe that withholding food is a practice relegated to the past. The reality is that it was still happening even as I resigned in August 2012. I know of whales whose food base usually ranged from 180 to 250 pounds per day being restricted to as little as 59 pounds of food. The records reflect this wasn't just a single-day abnormality. It was carried out over multiple days and multiple weeks and with multiple whales. Those orcas did not get the amount of food calculated to maintain their weight on any day of that entire week.

There are only a couple of situations in which it is acceptable to withhold food from whales: if it is a matter of health or a medical situation; or if the whales simply refuse to eat, even after the trainers have tried multiple times to give them all of their food. The records show no evidence of those conditions; the whale's food was withheld for behavioral reasons—that is, to make sure the whales performed to SeaWorld's expectations.

The deprivation I am referring to is vindictive and more insidious. In accordance with SeaWorld policies, trainers have reduced the amount of fish that a whale needs to eat daily—sometimes by more than two-thirds—to remind the orca who provides sustenance at the marine park. It is not done often and it has a mixed record of effectiveness. But it has been one of the trainer's options for making sure a whale understands that it is best to cooperate. Because SeaWorld meticulously documents the lives, health and constantly shifting psychology of the orcas, the company has kept records of depriving whales of fish to make them behave or perform to the standards set by the trainers. But because such a form of "behavior modification" would sound barbarous to human audiences, the practice has been kept secret. It would not be good for business to say that the stars of the show were not given food in order to make them perform. But it has happened. I have been part of inflicting the policy myself at the request of a supervisor.

Imagine the situation in human terms and the closest institution that comes to mind is a prison, where the inmates are completely dependent on the guards and the system to provide them with the basic needs of life: food and water. It is a terrifying and depressing metaphor for trainers who love the whales and who feel responsible for them. Why? Because in the analogy, even if the prisoner-whale decides that it likes some of the guards better than others, in the end, they are all still guards, part of the same system that oppresses them. You can be a prisoner and genuinely like a specific prison guard—and that prison guard may genuinely like you—but that doesn't take away the fact that you're in prison.

There are usually—but not always—observable precursors to aggression. Some examples are when the muscles on a whale's back tighten, when their eyes are opened wide and strained, when you hear certain types of vocalizations. You have to be alert to when whales drop their heads or avoid making eye contact or when they pull away from you. An erection in a male whale is another precursor to a likely incident of aggression, the consequence of sexual frustration, which occurs quite often in captivity.

But many other precursors of killer whale aggression can be subtle. To its credit, SeaWorld is assiduous in documenting every human-whale interaction not just to monitor the orcas' health but to detect whether a whale is on the verge of an episode that might prove dangerous to trainers. As illustrated by what I could describe as Freya's "jealousy" over her son Val, a whale may become aggressive because of a history or pattern of events, not just because of something happening at a given moment.

The trainers were supposed to report everything. Every time we called the whales over to begin an interaction it was documented—even if it was just to feed the orca. You'd have to note down how long the interaction lasted, if anything out of the norm happened—how well the whales performed the behaviors we asked them for, how many were correct or incorrect. Which trainer was working the whale? How much food was the orca fed? Was any medication being provided at the time? Were the whales perhaps exhibiting the most recognizable precursors associated with aggression or illness? Were there any other indications that a whale might be in the middle of a social altercation with other whales? This may in popular terms be described as quarreling, though it is much more complex than that—and is always a sign of potential aggression. Did a whale eat well or slowly or refuse food? You'd have to write down whether the interaction with the whale was part of a learning or a training session, a show, playtime or relationship session, exercise, or whether it was what we called "husbandry"—collecting urine samples or dentistry or veterinarian work. (We used the acronym HELPRS as shorthand for the interactions we'd get into with the orcas—husbandry, exercise, learning, play, relationship, show.) We'd rate the whale's responsiveness on a scale of zero (the poorest) to five (perfect behavior). If a whale had a poor session or show, the assessment was communicated to all trainers who were approved to work with that whale. Repeated poor behavior could indicate something else was happening with the whale—perhaps something health-related.

Watching for patterns helped. But the dynamics of a whale's relationship with the other whales in the park could also change rapidly and contribute to aggression. Trainers had to be constantly vigilant to make sure working conditions remained safe for all. The social dynamics among the whales changed constantly—which whales were getting along or not getting along could shift within minutes. At the bare minimum, there was always an apprentice trainer on hand whose job was to observe the whales when the more experienced trainers were not poolside. In the beginning of my career, apprentices and trainers would be assigned to 4 p.m.-to-midnight and midnight-to-8 a.m. shifts to make sure the whales were constantly monitored. Toward the end of my career, the night shifts were given to a security guard. That apprentice's job would be to alert a senior trainer or supervisor if sexual activity was observed or certain whales were fighting, which could influence our plans for which whales to use for shows.

Sometimes, a whale would choose not to participate in a session or not to come over when called. If it was the dominant female, the other whales would more often than not choose not to participate as well. The dominant female orca had the power to shut down the entire group of whales at Shamu. The subdominant whales would not risk being raked by her—that is scratched or cut deeply by a whale's teeth, like the wounds that might be inflicted on flesh by a rake—by choosing to work with the trainers. Sometimes, you had no choice but to give the orcas time to work out whatever communal killer whale issue was vexing them. Trying to press the matter could potentially produce an aggressive incident. For the sake of peace and safety, the show did not always go on.

In San Diego, where whales were provided more diverse types of rewards, there were on average only two cancellations a year. But in Texas, there were years when the show was cancelled an average of once every week.

Being a trainer was hard work, and it didn't mean I was exempt from the scut work. Everyone had to do their share scrubbing buckets. Meanwhile, trainers had to work in as many as seven Shamu shows a day. I had never been happier or prouder in my life.

But there was more to learn—much of it painful—and the most important lessons were life-changing. The trainers would have their doubts and frustrations about the conditions under which the whales lived. We knew how assiduous the company was about monitoring whale behavior and that registered in our minds as significant proof that SeaWorld cared for the orcas. If our faith in SeaWorld as a corporation wavered, we would always come back to the tenets of the theme park—that what it was doing was for the greater good of the species.

For most of us, this was our dream job. We were never going to rock the boat. Not about pay. Not about the danger. We loved the whales we worked with. There was also fear: many of us chose not to speak out about the conditions at SeaWorld because management might assign us away from the whales, sending us to Sea Lion or Dolphin or even to work at Bird Stadium—which is fine if that's what you wanted. But working with birds was not my dream job—nor that of many of my colleagues at Shamu. There was an even worse scenario: we might lose the dream job entirely. In public, we remained believers; in private, we discussed our misgivings.

I adore the whales of SeaWorld. I have learned, however, to give voice to my doubts—because they are more than doubts. At the height of my career in San Diego and San Antonio, I knew how fragile the whales were and how much care had to be taken to make sure they were healthy. But as the years passed at the marine park, it became evident that the whales were not happy or well-adjusted, much less thriving.

The fact that we monitored their behavior so carefully for aggression meant that something must be wrong with the conditions of their confinement. If the whales out in nature were harmless to human beings, why then did we have to be so wary of their moods in captivity? Why did we have to worry about orca aggressions?

I also came to another realization as I trained the stars of SeaWorld. The whales were motivated to perform in shows for two reasons: it gave them more opportunities to be rewarded with food and it provided them with a temporary escape from their horrifically sterile lives in captivity. They were bored.

They wanted to perform because there was nothing else for them to do. They were prisoners in the park, relegated after the shows to their cramped tanks—some only eight feet deep—clanging against the gates out of frustration. I tried to alleviate this by making their learning sessions as exciting and different as possible, trying to buoy the spirits of these magnificent beings so that they could perform the magic that enthralled SeaWorld's millions of visitors.

That was the goal of every interaction the trainers had with the whales—to try and make the session as varied and different as possible to give the orcas a momentary respite. And yet, we all knew that no matter how hard we tried, no matter how creative we were in a session, as soon as it ended, the whales would go right back to their shell of an existence, floating motionless in the pools, dealing with the monotony of captive life, bored out of their minds. The magic of SeaWorld was always grounded in this hard reality.

5

ELEGY OF THE KILLER WHALE

The biblical Leviathan is often imagined as a whale, the most enormous creature in God's creation, so immense that scripture scoffs at humans thinking they might somehow overcome him. "Will he make supplications unto thee? Will he speak soft words unto thee? Will he make a covenant with thee? Will thou take him as a servant for ever?" However, SeaWorld and the marine parks of the world have made Leviathan, as embodied in the orca, their captive—the greatest predator of the ocean has been reduced to a poor and desperate prisoner.

Visitors to SeaWorld's Dine with Shamu restaurant in California and Florida get to see the whales underwater by way of windows cut into the pool (there is no such cutaway pool in Texas). It allows nontrainers to come within inches of the magnificent orcas, separated from them only by see-through panels. Through the partitions of the close-up pool, the whales seem to be as curious about the humans as the humans about the orcas. But the humans may also get close to some curious, if not bizarre, behavior by the whales themselves. For example, there is the matter of eating paint.

The whales peel the paint off the pool's inner walls with their teeth. To those who witness the behavior, it looks as if they are nibbling on the wall or the floor of the pool. They are trying to occupy themselves, stimulating their enormous jaws and great intelligences with obsessively meticulous work. One whale in SeaWorld San Antonio, Unna, went at the wall paint with such a frightening vigor that she bloodied and bruised her jaw. She would strip so much paint off the floor of the pool that I had trouble figuring out where I was while performing with the whales underwater, all the familiar geography of the pool having been transformed by Unna's peeling. Trainers working with whales during Shamu Stadium's spectacular numbers needed to know with absolute precision where they were in the pool. You had mere seconds to spot one of the three large square drains that help you position yourself beneath the surface and give you a sense of perspective as you steer the whale. You don't want to triangulate yourself and the whale inaccurately, explode out of the water and catapult yourself into the glass. Spotting the cues could be difficult because of the paint-peeling habits of the whales. Unna, specifically, would pick at the paint almost as if she were trying to paint an image of a drain, replicating its shape and contours. She had a real talent for paint stripping.

Boredom manifests itself in other ways. Whales will rub their faces against the wall or sometimes bang their heads against the sides of the pool. Some orcas even develop eating disorders similar to human bulimia nervosa. Killer whales, longing for stimulation, have learned to regurgitate food just to keep themselves busy. Older whales sometimes even teach younger whales the disgusting practice.

Health problems can also arise from these habits of boredom. When whales regurgitate their food, digestive acid surging the wrong way from the stomach destroys the sensitive lining of the esophagus. When it reaches the mouth, the reflux damages the enamel of the orca's teeth, which is already weakened by the friction from the whale's teeth grinding against the concrete walls.

Almost all the whales in SeaWorld wear down their teeth by obsessively rubbing them on the ledges, floors and stages of the pool. Sometimes, a whale can break off a tooth in the process. But some whales rub and bite and chew at the walls worse than others. Eventually, pinholes form in their teeth. The trainers leave them alone as long as they can. But you can't ignore them forever. If not addressed, the pinholes may form abscesses that attract bacteria, and the resulting infection could kill the whale.

To treat this problem, the trainers have to, first, manually drill the tooth—which is known as a pulpotomy—then irrigate invasively, flushing the tooth two to three times a day as a preventative measure, as the vets offer directions. The veterinarians, for all their medical knowledge, aren't trained in how to be safe near the whales, so the trainers have to do all the close-up work, especially the dentistry. We have to condition the whales to let strangers get close to them in order to allow the vets to touch them. That only happens after we have helped immobilize the whale by bringing them into the med pool and raising the mechanical floor so that the orca is artificially beached. Then we jam a 2 x 4 block of wood into the very back of the whale's throat so it doesn't bring its jaws down on the veterinarians.

Drilling a tooth that is already causing a killer whale pain is risky and places the trainer in a vulnerable position. Only the most experienced trainers perform pulpotomies—and even then we go it slow. Imagine a child on his or her first trip to the dentist. Then imagine that kid is an orca. The whale doesn't know why the procedure is happening, just that the experience is painful.

But it has to be done. Killer whales grow only one set of teeth in their lifetimes—and so all effort must be expended to preserve them. The consequences for not doing so are enormous. An orca may eventually become so uncomfortable from the swelling and pain of its dental problems that they may just stop eating, which would result in lethargy and illness and, very quickly, death. Trainers have to desensitize the whale to the idea of accepting a drill—and that takes weeks or months of training. We slowly approximate the pressure of the drill, each time rewarding the whale before we finally have to perform the actual dental procedure that will open the tooth up and allow the bacterial inflammation to erupt and clear. The whales—like most humans—hate dental work. They shut their eyes when we have to irrigate their teeth and drill out the pinholes which have developed.

For the rest of the whale's life, you will need to pump daily doses of hydrogen peroxide solution into the tooth to keep it from getting reinfected and to make certain the drilled hole is free from blockage. On average, trainers drill and then irrigate 10 to 14 teeth for the whales who need it. It is the rare whale that doesn't. Probably because of their temperament, Kasatka and Takara had perfect teeth. They were the exceptions. Their good strong teeth made them particularly fearsome to whales who might challenge them. Being raked by Kasatka and Takara was bloody and painful.

As mighty as they appear, killer whales become fragile creatures in the artificial world of marine parks. In captivity, they face so many miniscule but potentially catastrophic risks. Tiny bacteria growing in a dental cavity might bring down the apex predators of the ocean. Several whales may have died of infections stemming from holes drilled into their teeth; it was most likely the cause of the infection which killed Kalina—the original "Baby Shamu"—who was born in 1985 and died in 2010. Two whales have died as a result of mosquito bites—Kanduke, who came down with St. Louis Encephalitis in the Florida facility; and Taku, who fell victim to the West Nile virus, in SeaWorld Texas. One influential peer-reviewed scientific paper on the deaths by two former trainers—John Jett and Jeffrey Ventre—said that mosquitos were often seen "accessing the dorsal surfaces of captive orcas in Florida." These are hazards orcas never have to face in the wild.

Splash was a star-crossed whale—and his misfortunes were exacerbated by captivity. He was born in 1989 at a Canadian marine park before being sold to SeaWorld San Diego in 1992. There was always something wrong with him. He kept getting into unlucky scrapes. Once, he was playfully rough-housing with Takara; they were pushing and tossing each other in the water. Unfortunately, someone forgot to put the protective barrier over the pool gate's hook, which latches the gate in an open position, and Splash hit it and ripped a large piece of flesh out of his lower jaw. He looked like Frankenstein's monster.

But he had much more severe problems. He was epileptic—a condition never documented in whales in the wild. To control his seizures, we treated him with phenobarbital, a barbiturate for convulsions. He also had severe digestive problems, including ulcers, for which he was medicated and that were probably caused by stress. In 2005, at the age of 15, he died of a perforated ulcer, succumbing to what must have been peritonitis—that is, the toxins of his digestive tract spreading into his body cavity to cause massive infection. A veterinarian told me they found hundreds of pounds of filtration sand in his stomach. Sand is used to purify the pool water and the filtration system, which in this instance, had malfunctioned and sent the grit directly into the pools. Splash had then spent hours each day sucking in the sand at the inflow, swallowing it out of boredom. The rough granules, found in all the chambers of his stomach, would only have worsened the pain of his ulcers. It may have led to the perforation of the lining of his intestines—and even caused the peritonitis that killed him.

He was another paint eater and had terrible teeth from rubbing them excessively against the pool walls. He also had the misfortune of having multiple teeth drilled by a trainer who virtually destroyed the crowns. It is no surprise then that Splash was one of the more unpredictable and potentially aggressive orcas of SeaWorld. And because of his lethargy and his illnesses, you never quite knew how his frustration was going to manifest itself.

Splash often seemed to be in a haze, a likely side effect of the many drugs he had to take. At 15, he was also at a difficult age—the point at which young male whales are sexually mature, dealing with surging testosterone and other hormones, which contribute to aggression. You definitely do not want to find yourself swimming with a killer whale with an erection.

During one show with Splash, I remember diving into the water and rolling on my back, which is a signal to the whale to roll over as well before swimming underneath to scoop you up on his stomach in a ventral position. The whale then swims along the perimeter, carrying you along. But when Splash picked me up, his penis was already out and fully erect, many feet in length. Luckily, he allowed me to step off him at the main slide-out area. I rewarded him with fish for letting me get out. But given his arousal, I could not risk swimming with him. I gave him a signal to swim to the back pool where he was received by another trainer. I then went on with the rest of the show, performing with a different whale.

I had another strange experience swimming with Splash one night. Not only was it completely dark but it was even harder to see because a fog machine had blanketed the surface of the pool with mist for theatrical effect. Splash and I were supposed to move underwater, out of sight of the audience, and then surface magically in the middle of the pool. With the lights out, I sent him from the back pool to the front silently and underwater to swim around the pool's perimeter. I then dived in to meet up with him in the middle, swimming through pitch-black water. I could not see anything.

Whales have the advantage of echolocation and, during performances, they use it to find the trainer as they course their way through the pool. When they use it, you can feel the vibration of their sonar. You can hear it as it reverberates in your chest, so even if you don't see the whale, you can sense its presence. Killer whales use these sound waves to identify objects in the water with absolute precision. Their sonar even allows them to make out the internal organs of the creatures they are searching for. In the wild, orcas can tell if a seal they have been pursuing is tired or injured because their sonar allows them to sense the heart rate and breathing of their prey. It helps the whales strategize the final kill.

But as I swam through the pool that night, I could not hear or feel Splash echolocating on me. He was completely silent and it was eerie. I knew that a 5,000-pound sexually mature male orca was swimming toward me but why couldn't I hear or feel his echolocation? Why was he silent? What was he doing? More importantly, what was he thinking about doing?

These concerns ran through my mind as I swam, trying to detect invisible clues. And then, boom, I was nose to nose with Splash under the water. My adrenaline levels must have been off the charts. He could well have been thinking of doing something aggressive and violent. He would have known I had no idea what he was up to. I am grateful that, in the shadows of that pool, he decided he would behave and we proceeded to complete the rest of the show without any problem.

Splash may have been one of the unluckiest whales I have ever worked with. But he had the good fortune to have a protector: Orkid. She wasn't the dominant female at SeaWorld San Diego. That was Kasatka. But she was always on the cusp of challenging Kasatka for the crown. For some reason, she made herself Splash's guardian—and also his partner in crime.

Every time Splash had an epileptic seizure, Orkid, who was just about a year older, would be there to bring him back to the surface to breathe if the episode occurred at the bottom of the pool. She would lead him away from the hard walls where he could hurt himself as his seizure caused him to lose control of his body and flail against the concrete. She would sometimes put herself between Splash and the wall to keep him from injuring himself. There was no incentive for her to do this. She did it because she cared for him.

Orkid was by no means virtuous. She was one of the more dangerous whales we had in San Diego. She was as smart as Kasatka but had a devilish streak in her as the many birds that flew into the park learned all too late. One day, a mother duck and her seven ducklings wandered into the Dine with Shamu pool. No whales were in that pool at the time—but they had access to it because the gates were open. As soon as I saw the ducks hit the water, the other trainers and I scrambled to make sure the whales were called over to another pool and the gate closed behind them. But it was too late. Orkid was in the Dine with Shamu pool within seconds. She made her way there completely underwater. The ducks were never aware that she lay in wait under them. The enormous whale slowly sucked the ducklings under and into her mouth, swallowing one by one until only the mother duck and one duckling were left. It is a testament to the precision of killer whales that they can do such subtle and undetectable work—and also proof of how nefarious they can be. We managed to wave the surviving birds out of the pool before Orkid got to them as well. It was impressive to see a 6,000-pound orca work so stealthily and with such speed. Orkid did all of this without causing a ripple on the surface. But the other trainers and I felt very sorry for the poor mother duck searching desperately for her babies.

Orkid, Kasatka, and Takara were experts at making sport of seagulls—animals that are not typically orca prey in the wild. Among the three of them, they could easily catch and kill ten of the gray-and-white birds a day. During some training sessions, I'd be in the water with the orcas and, as we submerged on a practice run for a specific behavior, we'd swim right by a dead bird that a whale had killed without anyone noticing. Takara was particularly creative at enjoying her seagulls. She would nibble at the carcass, carving it up with the skill of a sculptor so that by the time she presented it to you when you asked her to retrieve it, it was just the wings attached to the bird's heart, a morbid piece of jewelry, something Hannibal Lecter might find attractive.

Orkid and the other orcas had an especially bizarre way of luring seagulls for the kill. They would regurgitate some food to attract the birds but remain calm and steady, floating on the surface, lulling the birds into a false sense of security as they bobbed on the water next to them. When a gull finally convinced itself that there was no danger, the whales would grab the bird in their jaws, drag it around the pool, pull it under water and let it go to splash helplessly at the surface. The whale would toy with the poor creature in what humans would describe as a sadistic manner. A kind of ritual would ensue: the orca would let the gull struggle free every now and then, allowing it to recover a little from its dunking in the frigid waters. But, at the very moment the bird thought it was dry enough to finally flap its wings to fly away from the pool, the whale would snap, grab it and drag the poor gull under once again. The whale would do it again and again until the bird was exhausted. Or the orca got bored. Then the whale would kill it.

We eventually trained the whales through approximation to give us back a bird—alive. In the beginning, you had to accept the fact that the whales would come over with a dead gull. But as you trained the orcas, they'd bring back an injured one and then eventually a live and uninjured bird. They would choose not to kill.

Still, the whales almost seemed to wait for opportunities to misbehave. Splash and Orkid worked with each other in a Bonnie-and-Clyde way. You had to watch them carefully because they could be up to no good. They once victimized a young trainer—with horrific results.

The trainer, Tamarie Tollison, was working as a spotter at the Dine with Shamu close-up pool. When a trainer is spotting in that section of SeaWorld, he or she typically works alone because they are not interacting with the whales, just spotting both the whales and the park visitors. You have to make sure that park guests don't try to put their hands in the water or interact with the orcas directly, or throw anything into the water. You just have to patrol the area and keep things orderly—and make sure the visitors and the whales stay apart.

In any event, trainers—even the most experienced ones—are never allowed to interact with whales alone. Everyone needs a spotter to watch their back. However, while sitting by the gates in the pool, Tollison began to make physical contact with Orkid. Tollison repeatedly placed her foot on Orkid's rostrum as well as in the orca's mouth and on her tongue. All this took place as Splash floated beside Orkid, watching.

Clearly Tollison had no idea of Orkid's history of "baiting" a trainer by soliciting contact in some fashion. If a trainer responded, Orkid would strike or grab at him or her. Orkid was doing just that with Tollison in full view of SeaWorld visitors enjoying their meals and watching the action in the pool. Later, when I reviewed the video, I knew what was about to happen. I knew Orkid well.

Orkid closed her mouth on the trainer's foot and would not let it go. Tollison tried to reach down to give Orkid a signal to release her. But the whale refused. The trainer whipped around and desperately grabbed the gate to pull herself out of the whale's mouth but she was no match for the power of the 6,000-pound orca. The whale ripped Tollison from the gate and pulled her underwater. As Tollison plunged into the water, Splash joined in and bit her arm, crunching and compound fracturing it. Both Orkid and Splash then took turns pulling and holding the trainer underwater.

Terrified park guests began to scream for help and soon other trainers rushed to the area. A video camera that a visitor left behind in the panic recorded the incident—including Tollison's voice as she struggled to the surface as Orkid toyed with her, every now and then shouting from the water, "Somebody help me!"

At this point Robbin Sheets, a very experienced trainer, arrived. He attempted to call the whales over by slapping the water. But they refused and continued to drag Tollison under. Robbin, however, had presence of mind. He knew who these whales had to answer to, the dominant female. He asked another trainer to take the chain off the gate to the pool where Kasatka was penned up. He wasn't about to introduce another whale into the chaos; he just wanted to make Orkid and Splash think it was going to happen. Taking the chain off was part of a sequence of actions that we had consistently trained the whales to recognize as always leading to the opening of a gate. And Splash and Orkid knew that behind the gate that day was Kasatka.

In terms of the social hierarchy at SeaWorld San Diego, Kasatka has always been more dominant than Orkid—certainly more so than Splash and all the other whales in San Diego. Once the chain to Kasatka's gate was taken off, Splash and Orkid knew that the number one orca in SeaWorld was in play—a social and hierarchical factor they did not want to calculate into their troublemaking. They let the trainer go.

Tollison was very badly hurt, with multiple broken bones and a lot of bleeding. She was injured because two whales saw an opportunity and they seized it. I believe she is alive today only because Robbin Sheets knew how to manipulate the social hierarchy of whales—and let Kasatka's awesome power influence the outcome.

What Robbin did was also a perfect example of the value of a trainer's experience. These situations are never described in any rule book. It takes years of working with the whales to have the confidence and awareness to know what to do when whales cross over into the dark side.

Kasatka and her daughter Takara are built the same way. Their most eloquent similarity is the steely musculature of their jaws. I sometimes wonder if that is what has made them the dominant forces they are in whatever SeaWorld pool they have been sent into. Do the other whales sense the power in those jaws, in the potential for damage they can cause when they rake those they dislike with their teeth to impose discipline? Is that why they exercise so much power over whales almost twice their size?

Kasatka also had near-perfect teeth, and she never rubbed them against the walls. She did not peel paint. She had a straight dorsal fin that had a unique curve to it, not collapsed like those of all the adult male orcas. She and her daughter had rostrums of steel. Think of brand new tennis balls, just out of the can, the kind you can barely squeeze. That would be what a normal killer whale rostrum is like. But imagine a tennis ball with no give to it at all. That is what Kasatka's rostrum is like. Like stone. And so was Takara's.

No one crossed Kasatka. Not even her daughter. Luckily, she almost always let you know when she wasn't happy. The last thing you want is a whale that masks their feelings. With Kasatka, you knew her moods. And the other whales in the park knew too. In true dominant female fashion, she could shut down an entire show if she was unhappy—or if she was jealous that another whale was receiving more attention than she was, or if she was concerned about her calf. I have been in situations that could only be explained as instances of Kasatka imposing her power. I've seen her communicate to a whale out of her line of sight, causing that whale not to accept a reward of fish. I've seen Kasatka get a whale who had just received a big juicy salmon to swim over and pass it to her through the gate.

It was never good to misread or misinterpret Kasatka. I was the spotter for Ken Peters, one of the best trainers in San Diego, during a show in 1999 with Kasatka and Takara. Petey, as we all called him, had an extremely close and trusting relationship with Kasatka. He believed—we all believed—that few trainers could read her better.

But something was wrong during one segment of the show. Takara was slow to respond to signals. Instead of sitting up with her head out of the water so she could maintain eye contact with her trainer, she was dropping her head with her eyes beneath the surface and keeping them on her mother, who was about 30 feet away working with Petey. Takara became so uncomfortable that she split from her trainer and swam out of the front show pool and into the back pool. We knew there was a social altercation going on between the two of them. Still, her mother seemed, to us, completely calm and well-behaved. But in the back pool, Takara was swimming in fast circles, breathing rapidly, clearly distressed about something that had just happened. At one point, she slid out of the pool and onto the scale we used to weigh the whales once a week. She was escaping a negative environment and was emitting vocalizations to indicate she was upset.

Her mother, meanwhile, continued to take signals from Petey, responding to cues and sticking with the sequence in the show. We decided to close the gate to separate the front and back pools. Hopefully that would give Takara a chance to calm down and prevent the situation from escalating. We also didn't want Kasatka to rake her daughter. With luck, we'd be able to reopen the gate at the end of the performance and mother and daughter could be reunited and work out whatever problem they might be having—once Takara was calm.

Lisa Hugueley, who had the same rank and seniority as Petey, walked up to him and said, "You're not still going to swim with Kasatka, are you?"

"Yes," Petey said. "She looks great. She's been 100%."

As his spotter—the guy ready to hit the emergency underwater recall tone—I thought the same thing. I was on stage listening to the discussion right behind them and watching Kasatka at the same time. She appeared to be completely unaffected by what was happening with her daughter, who was still swimming agitated laps in the back pool.

Petey eased into the pool. He began rubbing Kasatka down, waiting for the moment when the music cue came and they'd begin the sequence. At that moment, however, Kasatka abruptly took off and began swimming in fast circles underwater while emitting upset vocalizations. You could see how distressed she was, her back muscles tightening up. With every lap she made at that intense speed, she created a current that pulled Petey closer to the middle of the pool. He quickly realized what was happening. Hoping to position himself at a spot from which he could safely get out when an opportunity arose, he made one slight skulling motion, a small underwater stroke with his hand. Kasatka saw it. She immediately swam at and over him. Petey did his best to deflect her but, even though she wasn't the biggest whale in the park, she was still 17 feet long and weighed more than 5,000 pounds. Every time she disappeared underwater, Petey put his face in the pool. He needed to find her to make eye contact and reestablish control. Eye contact is important in all situations when you deal with whales. During an incident of aggression, it is critical.

Kasatka came up underneath him, her mouth open, lifting him out of the water violently by his butt. The ferocity of her attack carried them both up against the stage. She once again vanished but then turned around. Her mouth was open and she was beginning to try to grab his feet. Petey tried to push away from her. He put his face back in the water, trying to determine where she was before she could rush at him again. I hadn't been overly worried until then. Now, I watched helplessly, fear pumping through me as I imagined Petey being crushed against the concrete stage.

With one lucky move, however, Petey got his right arm on stage and Robbin grabbed it and yanked him out before Kasatka could get at him again. She then started swimming fast laps around the pool. The show was canceled. No one was allowed to get into the water with Kasatka for the next six months.

I learned a valuable lesson that day. Your whales may appear to be completely fine—even when they are not. As the incident involving Takara and Kasatka showed, you need to read the wider context. You should never get into the water with a whale you suspect is involved, in even the slightest way, in an altercation with another whale—even if that whale appears calm and unaffected, as Kasatka did to all of us that day.

(The summer of 1999 made a deep impression on all of us, not just because of the incident involving Kasatka and Petey. During the same period, the body of Daniel Dukes, a 27-year-old park guest, was found lifeless and draped on Tilikum's back in SeaWorld Orlando. The young man had apparently evaded the facility's security to stay overnight, somehow finding his way into Tilikum's pool. The autopsy showed that Dukes suffered a multitude of injuries to head, chest and limbs before he died; and that Tilikum had continued to mutilate the body after Dukes was dead, partially castrating him. In 1991, Tilikum had killed a trainer at Sealand of the Pacific, a marine park in British Columbia, Canada, which owned him until 1992, when the orca was moved to SeaWorld.)

When we were once again allowed to do waterwork with Kasatka in the fall of 1999, I was officially added to her waterwork team. I was honored and excited. She was a difficult and challenging whale, and for my managers to include me in her waterwork team was a testament to their belief that I had the skill and ability to make the right decisions with her and be safe. It was a huge promotion in my eyes. I am prouder of it than almost any other achievement in my career. I loved Kasatka already because I had put so much energy and thought into developing a relationship with her even without being in the water. I had learned what she liked and what she didn't like. I knew how to listen to the sounds she emitted and could tell from them what mood she was in. But having seen how she turned against Petey—a trainer she was close to and with whom she had a long and entwined history—I was also realistic. A lot goes on inside these whales because they are inmates of SeaWorld.

The complexities of life in the close confines of SeaWorld's parks impose what must be something like paranoia on the orcas. And small things can suddenly become egregious insults to them. They are smart enough to plot their revenge quietly, waiting for the right moment to show you exactly how they feel.

Petey taught me some of the most important lessons I learned about Kasatka. It was completely counterintuitive. He said that "you gotta show her you're willing to put yourself in a vulnerable position with her because you trust her." That doesn't mean being irresponsible about your safety. You're always at the mercy of an orca, whether you are on the edge of a pool or in the water. What Petey meant was to focus on the small things that these huge but sensitive creatures notice. Once I figured out what these little touches were, he told me, my relationship with Kasatka would grow exponentially. When I fed her, I would do it slowly, taking my time to make sure she knew I wasn't rushing her. I wouldn't just throw the fish in her mouth. I'd reach in so that her teeth touched the bones of my hands as I put the food in the back of her throat. All she had to do was shut her mouth and my hands would be gone. But she responded well to situations like that. More than anything, it was about slowing things down when you were with her, not rushing her.

As much as you try to read the signs, it may sometimes be impossible to tell when a whale is slipping into the dark side. A strong relationship with an orca is the best way to survive that kind of reversal. Petey would prove that when, in 2006, Kasatka went after him again during a show.

In that incident, she grabbed him by the foot and dragged him underwater multiple times. It was one of the most severe cases of orca aggression against a trainer in which the trainer survived. Only his ability to remain calm and wait for opportunities to try and calm her down—combined with his relationship with her—got Petey out of a potentially catastrophic situation. He was only able to swim out of the pool because Kasatka allowed him to. Petey was fortunate to have the time to give her the opportunity to make the right choice. She could have overwhelmed him but she chose not to go completely over to the dark side. She broke bones in Petey's foot and he suffered ligament damage that required hospitalization and the insertion of bolts and screws to put him back together. But he recovered.

He would always love Kasatka. And I learned to love her myself, for all her difficulty. When I returned to work in Texas and other trainers there who'd never worked with her called her a psycho whale, I would be deeply offended and ferociously defend her. I reminded them that she had chosen not to kill Petey, when she could easily have done so. It is a choice by an orca that deserves human respect.

Like Freya, Kasatka was born in the wild. I imagined that she too must remember what it was like to swim in the boundless seas. I was awed by that fact that she allowed herself to be put under human control. The matriarch of a group of killer whales permits you to tell her what to do, permits you to reward her, allows you to know what makes her happy, what she enjoys. It takes time to build a relationship like that. It is a reciprocal one. You can't do anything with these whales—especially the most dangerous ones—without a relationship that both you and the orca realize is truly give-and-take. Each relationship is different and unique. The whales realize this as much as the trainer does. No two trainers are alike in the eyes of the whale, just as no two whales are alike in the eyes of a trainer.

Petey was there for me when I left SeaWorld San Diego in 2001 to work as a supervisor in France. It was an enormous opportunity: I would be working with whales who had never performed in the water with trainers before. The trainers of the marine park in Antibes had always worked from the sides of the pools, not swimming with the orcas. I would be training both them and the whales.

But taking the job in France would mean leaving the whales that I loved—Corky, Splash, Takara, Orkid, Ulises and Kasatka.

The last day turned out to be tough. I had dissected and rationalized my feelings about leaving the whales of California behind, telling myself that I would form new relationships with new whales in France. I was moved by the support of my colleagues. Many trainers, even those who had the day off, showed up to watch my final show—including many who worked at Dolphin and Sea Lion stadiums, even trainers who had left SeaWorld. Wendy Ramirez, my one-time roommate and fellow trainer, and I did a sequence with Kasatka and Orkid—which can be tricky because historically we'd seen a lot of aggression between them. Petey and Robbin and I did all the bigger waterwork behaviors with Corky and Takara during the final sequence called the "fast action," which included spy hops, the surf ride and, of course, the hydro at the end. I was nervous. With so many fellow trainers watching, the last thing I wanted was to crash on my hydro or fall on my surf ride. But, thankfully, everything went smoothly.

After the show, I still had two hours left on my shift when Petey told me, "Why don't you just hit the showers, man. Just go." When Petey told me that, I realized it was over. I had to walk away from the whales. I tried to buy myself some time and told him I didn't mind staying. But my voice wavered and I began to tear up. "It's ok," he said again, "You're done. Hit the showers."

At this point I had to get out of there because I was losing control quickly and I didn't want anyone to see it. I took off for the locker room and as soon as my back was turned, the tears began streaming down my face. But I heard Petey's footsteps behind me. The faster I walked, the faster he followed. As soon as I got in the locker room I locked the door behind me. Petey was right behind me. I ran to the second door to jam it closed because I could hear him running. But within seconds, he had opened the door. I stood staring in the mirror seeing Petey behind me and I just lost it. I couldn't stop crying; I could barely breathe.

Petey could be rough around the edges and he was not known for being sensitive to other people's feelings. But he locked eyes with me, he put his hand on my shoulder, and said, "'I'm not going to tell you it's okay or try to stop you from crying. I just want to be here with you while you cry." It was one of the most moving and profound things anyone ever said to me. At that time, it was hard to imagine I was going to be okay, because this separation from the whales hurt like hell.

Petey knew what it was like to love the orcas in all their complexity. He knew how much of your life you had to give and how much you received in return for the sacrifice. We loved the same whales. I cried in that locker room until there were no more tears to cry. I accepted it as a death.

After I left San Diego, Kasatka would be put through a separation that would have broken any human heart.

In the ocean, killer whale mothers and daughters typically stay close for life. Kasatka, having been separated from her own mother in the ocean, was especially attached to Takara, her first calf. But as powerful as Kasatka was in the hierarchy of orcas in San Diego, she was powerless against the will of SeaWorld the corporation.

In 2004, senior management decided to move Takara and her daughter Kohana to Florida for breeding and entertainment purposes. On the day of the transport, the trainers first made sure Takara (with Kohana) and Kasatka were in separate pools. They then put Takara and her daughter into the shallow med pool and slowly raised the floor. As the water levels came down, Takara and Kohana were asked to swim into huge stretchers; they were then lifted by cranes out of the pool and onto the truck that would take them to the airport. However, as Takara was hoisted up and out of the pool and loaded into the box on the back of an 18-wheeler, her mother began to emit continuous vocalizations, sounds that had never been heard from her in the three decades of her captivity.

I would learn later that Kasatka's vocalizations continued long after the younger female had been taken away. SeaWorld brought in Ann Bowles, a senior research scientist for Hubbs SeaWorld Research Institute to record and analyze the vocalizations. She concluded they were long-range vocals. Unable to sense her daughter's presence in any of the adjoining pools, Kasatka was sending sounds far into the world, as far as she could, to see if they would bounce back or elicit a response. It was heartbreaking for all who heard what could easily be interpreted as crying.

Kasatka never got over the separation from her first offspring. Three years after they were separated, trainers recorded Takara's vocalizations in Florida and played them back in California for Kasatka. The sound of Takara, however, caused immediate consternation in the older whale, who became extremely agitated, swimming rapidly around the pool and emitting vocalizations that were tight and fast, with rapid breaths.

Long before all trainers were forbidden to do waterwork with SeaWorld's orcas, Kasatka was put off limits, beginning in November 2006. She had become too dangerous for trainers to swim with, as was evident by her incidents with Petey.

Whales do remember. Are they able to forgive?

6

THE NATURAL AND UNNATURAL HISTORY OF THE ORCA

The orcas of SeaWorld have beautiful names, often adopted from the language of cultures that have had centuries of contact with the species. Some project our own romantic notions about the orca onto the whales. Takara is Japanese for "treasure." Unna is Icelandic for "love." Tilikum is Chinook for "friend." Some are matter-of-fact. Kasatka means "orca" in Russian. Some were intended to be fun: Splash, for example. He was born in a non-SeaWorld park that did not have the company's penchant for the poetic and the exotic.

Names are sometimes recycled: Corky is the oldest whale at Sea-World (as well as the oldest orca in captivity in the world) but the name first belonged to an orca from the early days of the marine park, one that died in 1970. Corky would not get to SeaWorld till 1987, along with her companion, friend and sometime mate Orky. The rhyming pair would produce no viable offspring; Corky became pregnant seven times but all her calves died, the longest-lived lasting only 46 days.

Orky, however, would sire a calf with another female, Kandu. Their child was Orkid, not named for a flower but for her father.

Kandu was the dominant female of SeaWorld San Diego in the 1980s, but she died in a horrific incident when she charged Corky in the middle of a show, perhaps in an attempt to emphasize her role as matriarch. As Corky attempted to get out of her way, Kandu suffered a bilateral fracture to her jaw when she engaged with the other whale's massive 8,200 pounds. The impact ruptured one of Kandu's arteries and she hemorrhaged to death on the bottom of the pool. Corky would adopt the motherless and traumatized Orkid—not quite one year old when she swam around her dying mother on the bottom of the pool—and raise her as her own. Corky would never attempt to become the dominant whale; and Kasatka assumed that role in 1990. But in Orkid's name, you can hear the echo of Orky and Corky and a SeaWorld melodrama.

The names we give the whales are solely for human consumption, memory and our need to organize and categorize. Whales cannot really recognize the sounds of the words by which we call them: their vocal and hearing systems, as sophisticated as they may be, are much more attuned to vowel than to consonant sounds. Orcas in nature live in a different cosmos than ours.

Humans have given the species of *Orcinus orca* different appellations through the centuries. At the start of the twentieth century, the *Encyclopaedia Britannica* cited one scientific name for the species as *Orca gladiator,* a reference to the ancient Roman swordsman-slaves that imposed an even more bellicose embellishment to the image of the whales than the ogre-ish *orcus* given to them by the Roman historian Pliny almost 2,000 years ago. The same gladiatorial connotation can be heard in a French word for orca, *épaulard*—with its whisper of *épeé*—a reference to the sharp, blade-like dorsal fins of the orca, visible as they race at the surface of the ocean toward their prey. The Finns, Dutch and Germans also embed swords in their names for the orca: *miekkavalas, zwaardwalvis* and *Schwertwal.*

The French were responsible for a word that was, until the early twentieth century, widely used in English for orcas: *grampus.* It is a strange concoction that devolved from medieval Latin (*Crassus Piscis* or Fat Fish) to old French *Grapois*—with the syllable "pois" linked to the word now used for fish in France, *poisson.* The English further corrupted the sound of the word into Grampus. Herman Melville used it in his classic novel *Moby Dick,* published in 1851, to refer to orcas.

It was not until the twentieth century that the word "killer" began to receive wider usage in connection with orcas. It had always been a nickname, originating with Spanish sailors who called it *asesina-ballenas,* "killer of whales," for the murderousness of the species when it attacked larger cetaceans. The Danish word for orca also reflects that voracious nature: *spaekhugger,* the one who cuts into the blubber (*spaek*) before the whalers can get to it. In Japan, the kanji ideogram for orca, pronounced "shachi," is particularly telling: it is a combination of the character for fish with the one for tiger. It is also the name given to a mythical creature, with a vaguely tiger-like head and the torso and tail of a fish, that can be seen decorating some of the more elaborate traditional temples of Japan.

Myth and reality have always mingled. We can only speculate about the rise in popularity of the name "killer whale" after the bloody First World War. It had been in use since the eighteenth century but became the predominant term for orcas as the twentieth century coursed its way through unspeakable violence. "Killer whale" began to be eclipsed by "orca"—a word used even by the Spaniards, who originated the assassin nickname—in no small part because of SeaWorld and the immense success of its human-orca Shamu spectacles. The world began to see the animals in a different light.

And yet that perspective, as positive and as much of a corrective as it is to the image of the orca as vicious murderer, is founded on the lives of whales who do not live in their natural environment and whose behavior and psychology have been completely warped by captivity. SeaWorld has not turned them into gladiator-slaves—as that old Latin name indicated—but in a way they are performing prisoners. They may still have the intelligence of their relatives in the wild, but they have been transformed so completely that they may never be able to return to nature.

In their appearance and in their biology, orcas have essentially been orcas for more than eight million years. They evolved into the sleek black-and-white masterpieces of predation long before *Homo sapiens* arrived on the scene.

They descended, like the rest of the whales, from a terrestrial mammal called Pakicetus (named for Pakistan, where its remains were first discovered). The forerunner of the great mammals of the sea—of the blue whale, the sperm whale, the orca, the beluga, the dolphin—may have looked very much like a wolf with hooves; oddly enough, its other living descendant appears to be another aquatic mammal, the hippopotamus. Whales evolved from Pakicetus about 50 million years ago. Toothed whales diverged from the main line after that; and then the dolphins split off from the toothed whales around 20 million to 30 million years ago. The largest of the dolphins, orcas descend from toothed whales. All whales belong to the order cetacean—dolphins, orcas, the toothed sperm whale and the toothless blue whale. And their ultimate common ancestor is that strange creature, Pakicetus.

One feature of whale evolution should humble humans. Our species may pride itself on the size of our brains but orcas, dolphins, the great whales and other members of the cetacean family have been "big-brained" for a much longer time, evolving those relatively large sizes about 35 million years ago. Contemporary cetaceans achieved their brain sizes 10 to 15 million years ago. Our ancestors did not evolve their large brains until about one million years ago. As Dr. Lori Marino, an expert on the cetacean brain notes, "This puts into perspective how little time humans have been able to claim to be the most encephalized species on the planet." And, she adds, "It isn't clear that we—or anything else—will be able to survive 10–15 million years of the human brain!"

Alone of all the mammals whose habitat is the sea, orcas have developed the dramatic swordlike dorsal fin that cuts through the water as they dash toward their meals, looking like black-sailed corsairs catching the wind to speed toward booty. The forces of evolution seem to have favored those huge fins for engineering reasons. The dorsals help regulate the enormous energies generated by the speeding orcas—who can swim in bursts as fast as 30 miles per hour—by shifting the warmth away from the center of the body to the extremities so that the killer whales don't overheat. Like the equivalent fin in sharks, the dorsal allows the orca to navigate sharp turns and quick changes in direction. No one, however, really knows why males have larger dorsal fins. They may well play some role in gender relations—like the plumage of peacocks or the puffed-up feathers of a male turkey. Perhaps dorsal fins with the most flair help attract the females who are at the top of the orca social hierarchy.

Just as the dorsal fin seems engineered to help killer whales keep up their speed without overheating, the orcas' black-and-white coloration may have evolved to help them hunt. Fish and other mammals swimming below the whales would look skyward and miss the orca above them because the whales' white bellies blend into the refracted white light of the sun. Similarly, potential prey swimming above the whales would not detect the orcas below them because the black pigment at the top of their bodies would mask them in the darkness of the deeper sea. And the orcas can turn their eyes every which way to find their prey, seeing what lies above as well as below.

In many ways, the rationale behind the black-and-white coloration may be similar to what it is for pandas—to blend in with the environment. But panda coloration is defensive—they can hide in the snow, for example—while orca colors are offensive, allowing them to sneak up swiftly on their prey. The white patch around orca eyes may serve another purpose entirely. Some scientists speculate that they allow calves, who swim alongside the adults, to keep track of their mothers. That lateral perspective also allows whales to tell which way the family or pod is traveling.

Orcas live in what can be called tribes, or better yet, ecotypes. At least ten distinct groups exist, some so separated from each other by time and distance that some experts argue that they constitute separate species. The groups chase different prey and vocalize in distinct ways, like mutually incomprehensible languages. The white eye patches may have slightly different orientations and sizes depending on the ecotype as well. But all share the same knifelike dorsal fin and the general white-and-black coloration (though some ecotypes are tinged gray or sometimes a bit yellow, because of microscopic parasites). However, even with the ubiquitous dorsals, the orcas are not identical: there are variations in the slant, and individual whales can be identified through photographs of their dorsals. No two whales are exactly the same in appearance.

The orcas in SeaWorld and its associated parks are descended from whales originating from disparate parts of the planet. The Pacific Northwest and the waters off Washington State and British Columbia are the ancestral home for some. Corky was captured in this area on December 11, 1969. Other whales, like Kasatka and Tilikum, can trace their origins to the north Atlantic and the area around Iceland. Takara's father, Kotar, also comes from the area around Iceland. Takara herself is the result of a liaison between Kotar and Kasatka when Kasatka was loaned to SeaWorld San Antonio in the late 1980s.

Then there are the whales who were born in captivity to orcas from different oceans. Health-plagued Splash was the offspring of Gudrun, a female from the Atlantic waters off Iceland, and Kanduke, who came from the Pacific Northwest. Splash would never have had that kind of parentage in the wild because it is highly unlikely that the populations that produced Gudrun and Kanduke would ever have intermingled. Like her pal Splash, Orkid's parentage is also Atlantic and Pacific. Both were hybrids without a natural social identity.

Among the various ecotypes, the whales of the Pacific Northwest have received the most scientific scrutiny and therefore provide us with the bulk of what we know about the life cycle of a killer whale. Out of this oceanic grouping, there are two large divisions that have been studied in detail: the Northern resident population, which is spread generally around British Columbia; and the Southern resident community, present in the same region but with members found as far south as the coast of California. Even though they traverse the same waters, the Northern and Southern communities of killer whales do not interbreed. Some scientists like Dr. Naomi Rose, a prominent marine mammalogist and an expert on orcas, suspect there have been Romeo-and-Juliet-like trysts every so often, but generally the

Northerners and the Southerners are the Capulets and Montagues of the orca world. Matches between them are taboo.

Both the Northern and Southern resident populations are made up of clans and pods and families. Each family is led by a female, forming the basic unit of orca society. Everything in the family revolves around the matriarch. Even when her daughters become adults, their own families stay within reach. No one is ever more than a mile apart.

Matriarchy—and age—establishes order and authority. Below the matriarch, older brothers lord it over younger brothers, for example. And while older brothers may also have precedence over younger sisters, they treat them with great deference. Daughters who have set up their own families defer to their mothers when everyone gets together.

Everyone in the matriarch's immediate court stays close to her physically, surrounding her like a queen bee in an oceanic hive, a few body lengths away. Her circle includes all her offspring younger than five years old—male and female—as well as her adult sons. In some of these families, male relations of the matriarch's own generation or older—brothers and uncles—are part of the entourage. Sometimes nephews—the sons of deceased sisters—are part of the group.

Males have no status apart from their mothers or an equivalent female. At the death of a matriarch, her sons will join the families of an aunt or sister or niece, just to maintain social status and a place in some communal hierarchy. Completely orphaned orca males may sometimes try to band together, but studies have shown that such associations are short-lived, lasting no more than four years at most. Pity the male orca with no female relations. He is shunted aside in whale society, very quickly pines away and dies. SeaWorld has basically forced motherlessness on many of its male orcas. It is these males who are often the outcasts of the societies that emerge among SeaWorld's orcas, subjected to vicious and repeated attacks by the other whales.

What about mates? Males come from outside the family structure, visit to mate and then swim away to rejoin their mothers. Unlike in SeaWorld, there is no known instance of mother-son mating in wild orca communities. In SeaWorld Orlando, Katina mated with her son Taku, resulting in the female calf Nalani. Kohana was bred with her uncle Keto twice. This is an instance of what appears to be a taboo—strictly reinforced in the wild by generations of matriarchs—that has broken down in the confines of captivity. Orca communities seem to have traditions and practices that are more than instinctive and are taught by older whales to younger ones. The incest taboo between fertile females and their sons appears to be one of them.

It is intriguing to see how the females reacted to their offspring by incest. Katina, who had previously been a caring mother to her other calves, resisted accepting Nalani. Meanwhile, Kohana—who was unnaturally young when she was first impregnated—rejected both of her calves, the second one dying within its first year.

Orcas' sense of community is bolstered by what we might call language. Matriarchal groups that send out the same kind of calls and various sounds that make up vocalization—that is, families that speak the same "language"—form a pod; pods that communicate in the same dialect go on to form what scientists call a clan. The clans combine into populations or communities—the Northern and Southern in this case. In that greater definition, language becomes secondary. Some clans in the same population may not be able to speak the same language and yet they know they belong to the same community and, thus, interbreed. Somehow, they recognize the common line of ancestry, unerringly telling Northern apart from Southern. Genetic field research has confirmed this.

To complicate the survey of orca society in the Pacific Northwest, another group of killer whales shares the same waters as the Northern and Southern residents. Whale researchers call them transients—as opposed to residents. While the residents tend to eat fish—salmon, for the most part—the transients mostly chase after other marine mammals. They travel in smaller family groups, so much so that people consider some of them to be solitary killer whales. But even when transients travel alone—as many do—they continue to associate with the matriarchal groups that produced them. Their choice of prey determines the size of their packs. Unlike salmon and other immense schools of fish that resident orcas can scoop up as a family—and which provide a big gulp of calories at a single go—the transients go after whales, dolphins, seals and sharks, which must be hunted solo, that is, one at a time. Except maybe for sharks, their prey are also smarter, requiring more energy to hunt down. It is more efficient—in terms of caloric pay-off and effort—to share even a large shark among a small band of two or three whales. Or better, to dine alone. Family reunions can happen later.

If a blue whale—the biggest animal on the planet—suddenly comes into range, perhaps six or seven transients will join in to bring it down. But all the orcas really want to eat are the whale's tongue and blubber. The attacks are cruel in human eyes: orcas will not kill a large whale outright, merely rip out its tongue during the attack, feasting on it as the huge animal swims off to bleed to death. Sometimes, transients will eat only the fat of the animal because that's where all the calories are.

The largest toothed cetacean is the sperm whale, but its teeth are only used for gripping, not biting. In contrast, transient killer whales are surgeons. According to Dr. Rose, an orca researcher she knows once came upon a porpoise slaughtered by a killer whale with such precision that its internal organs had popped out of a small incision near its gut area. That incision had been perfectly made with teeth after a well-targeted ramming blow. The macabre seagull jewelry that Takara created in SeaWorld comes to mind.

Orcas in different environments have developed distinct hunting skills. Killer whales in Norway will work together to surround herring, shepherding the large schools of fish into tight little globes of swirling fish before stunning them en masse with their flukes for a feast. In Patagonia, at the southern tip of South America, orcas hurl themselves onshore, beaching on purpose in order to drag sea lion pups into the sea. It is a behavior that is passed on from generation to generation. Orcas—transient or resident—will do what it takes to eat what they want. Even if that meal is on land. But not all whales learn the lesson perfectly. Orcas have stranded themselves on land and died as a result of this hunting tactic.

SeaWorld recognizes the importance of the matriarchal whale and has used those dominant females to keep order in its marine parks. But consider this: these whales originate from different parts of the world and from families that communicate in distinct dialects. Dr. Ingrid Visser, who has studied the orcas off the coast of New Zealand as well as those in the North Pacific ocean, says, "The culture and behavior of wild orcas vary greatly throughout the world, just as with people who hail from other nations." Gathering them in the quarters of even the biggest of aquatic theme parks is like squishing people who speak different languages into a single jail cell—for years. Perhaps they will figure out how to communicate. But what more often emerges is a horrible caricature of what happens in nature—where whales from other pods are chased away with the threat of violence. In the confines of SeaWorld, there is nowhere to swim away to escape and so violence is not just a threat but often a consequence.

In the mid-2000s, SeaWorld of California brought in a senior research scientist from the corporation's affiliated research facility to study the vocal patterns of Corky and Kasatka and find an explanation for why Corky was so often brutally attacked and raked by Kasatka. The scientist discovered that neither Corky nor Kasatka could replicate each other's vocalizations—that is, their dialects. That was determined to be a contributing factor to the hyperaggression incidents that took place between them.

Aggressive behavior does exist in the wild. When residents and transients cross paths in the waters of the Pacific Northwest, unfriendly pushing and splashing takes place, usually with the residents—who travel in large groups of up to 200 whales—chasing the transients away. Researchers have also recorded incidents of aggression within resident pods, when a male strays from his matriarchal family and tries to join another. The local matriarchy's male "enforcers" then shoo the intruder away, sometimes sandwiching him between them to escort him out of their territory.

According to Dr. Rose and other researchers, raking with teeth— so ugly and bloody in SeaWorld—is used only by very young resident calves, who don't know any better, and is discouraged by the matriarchs. The reigns of terror imposed by dominant females at SeaWorld are unknown among the pods of the Pacific Northwest. The more loner-like transients show greater evidence of raking. It occurs more often among the orcas in the waters of New Zealand. Dr. Ingrid Visser, who has studied the killer whales in that country, speculates that the raking occurs because orcas from the Antarctic have strayed into the territory of local whales. As Howard Garrett of the Orca Network, a nonprofit opposed to killer whales in captivity in SeaWorld and elsewhere, says, "Groups put together in captivity are likely to have unresolvable relationships and exaggerated tensions that are often demonstrated by rakes, sometimes deep rakes."

In the expanse of the oceans, orcas acquiesce to what seems to be the natural order they have inherited at birth. The confrontation between Kandu and Corky in 1989 would never have happened in the open seas because they would have lived in widely separated pods: Kandu in the North Atlantic near Iceland; and Corky among her relatives off the Pacific coast of Canada. You have to wonder how they even communicated with each other, if at all. Did Corky even know that Kandu was trying to tell her who was boss? And did Corky's lack of response just infuriate Kandu even more, so much so that she charged her and broke her jaw and bled to death? In captivity, adult orcas may use their teeth more often because they don't know how else to get their way with the other whales.

The original generation of captives has now produced orcas that know only captivity—a cluster of animals that, I imagine, communicate with each other in some strange amalgamation of their original dialects. "These whales were interbred and produced hybrids with no conservation value and with no natural identity," says Dr. Deborah Giles, a biogeographer with the University of California, Davis, who spent nine summers studying the orcas of Puget Sound.

The potential for frustration, strife and lashing out only increases once you throw in the fact that the orcas of SeaWorld have to figure out how trainers—who supply all their food—fit into the calculus of their hierarchy.

Dr. Rose has an accurate but tragic assessment of the plight of Sea-World's orcas. "I personally think," she says, "all captive orcas, whether caught in the wild or born in captivity, are behaviorally abnormal. They are like the children in *Lord of the Flies*—unnaturally violent because they do not have any of the normal societal brakes on their immature tendency toward violence. Children can be very violent, but under normal circumstances, they are socialized to suppress that violence and channel it productively as they mature."

Suppressing violence is problematic for those orcas, Dr. Rose says. "In captivity, all the orcas are 'feral' children—they had no adult orcas to socialize them properly. Human trainers, especially those who have no knowledge of wild orca behavior, are not adequate substitutes." None of the original captive orcas were mature enough to take on the full role that matriarchs play in the wild. They only had distant and instinctive memories of what their mothers were like.

Dr. Rose points to the experience of farmers in Africa who would cull fast-growing elephant populations that wandered into farms and villages and caused extensive and costly damage. At first, the cullers would kill only the adults. They would, out of a sense of pity, allow the young to survive. However, the young would grow up without adult supervision—and not know how to behave as adults, becoming even more violent than their elders. In a horrific strategy, the cullers have since learned to kill all the elephants in a group. "I believe a similar problem afflicts captive orcas," says Dr. Rose. "Their 'childish' levels of violence and aggression are not socialized out of them by normal adults. The only adult orcas they know were either caught when very young themselves or were born in captivity. They simply grow up without being properly socialized. The captive whales that are not violent are simply that way inherently—their innate personality is not aggressive. Those that are violent were never properly socialized."

For most of my tenure at SeaWorld, I thought of Naomi Rose as the enemy. She is one of the most prominent marine mammal scientists in the world and she had very little good to say about all the hard work

118

we trainers were doing with the orcas. The champions of SeaWorld—everyone from public relations spokespeople to officials of the company to true believers among the public—believed she had betrayed her scientific neutrality to become an advocate for changes that would completely up-end the way our enterprise worked. The company openly mocked her research. Her criticism always raised my anxieties about the future of SeaWorld—my job security—and, like any true believer in the mission of the organization, I never gave her or her science a chance.

Why should I have? I loved the whales I worked with more than anything and was certain that no one knew them better. The trainers and I were with them every day, sometimes for 12 to 14 hours a day. I knew everything they needed: I knew how each whale stood in the social hierarchy at SeaWorld and was aware of how to manage those relationships to keep altercations down. In all of this, there was discipline and love. I didn't need some scientist to tell me what I knew better than almost anyone else on earth.

When we were finally on the same side—after I left SeaWorld and when I was promoting the documentary *Blackfish*—we had a spectacular clash. She had watched as I taped extra segments for the documentary DVD and she was not happy. She told the director, Gabriela Cowperthwaite, that I was glamorizing the life of a killer whale trainer as I discussed my relationships with Kasatka and Takara, and that this only helped SeaWorld's case. If anyone didn't see the film, she said, they could think that my sound bites were promotional spots for my old employer.

I was outraged and confronted her. How dare she tell me how to describe my life's work with whales that I loved? No one was going to dictate how I was going to talk about Kasatka or Takara or whatever whale I wanted to describe. These were some of the deepest and most magnificent relationships I've had in my life.

Yet I was also aware that what I observed at Shamu Stadium was not the natural habitat of orcas. That was the world Dr. Rose knew all about. She and her colleagues had spent much of their lives observing the whales in their natural habitats. She was the expert in how they lived in the oceans, where they were free. Her point about the DVD extras was a valid one. If someone had not seen my other interviews, the sound bites would appear almost entirely like promotions for Sea-World and killer whale captivity. That's why telling my story in its entirety is so important to me. What was the point of fighting? We both agreed on the horrors of captivity. It would be months before we communicated again but by then we had both calmed down. When we spoke at a press conference in California in early 2014, we embraced. We were united as allies in the campaign to save the orcas of SeaWorld.

And so, while writing this book, I finally asked her, "What is a day in the life of orcas in the open sea like?"

She laughed. "There is no typical day," she said. "There are no SeaWorld routines. Every day is different—certainly for resident orcas in the Pacific Northwest."

She and her colleagues watched orcas for four seasons on a 15-foot Avon inflatable craft and for one season from an observation station on a cliff in Johnstone Strait on Vancouver Island in British Columbia. In the mornings, on the boat, they might spy on a family of orcas engaged in a kind of water ballet: the matriarch in the middle, the adult males flanking the unit like bodyguards, all of them breathing almost in unison, with a calming regularity. "It's really quite beautiful to watch them," she says. "They take three to four breaths every 10 to 12 seconds or so." Then they take a shallow dive for two or three minutes. They return to the surface before diving again. They typically don't go very deep into the water in this state—the closest they come to sleeping. In fact, says Dr. Rose, "The dorsal fins of the adult males

Me and Corky performing a hula pec-ride in a show at SeaWorld of California
Credit: Melissa Hargrove

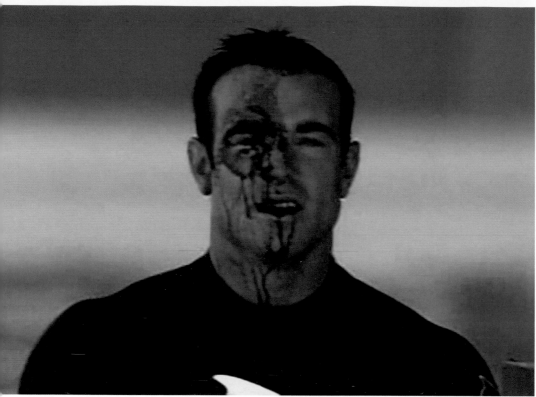

Injury sustained performing a fast foot push stage slide with 8,200 pound Corky during a show at SeaWorld of California
Photo credit: Blackfish *(2013)*

Me and Takara during a night show at SeaWorld of Texas, 2009

Performing a stand-on spy hop in a show with Corky at SeaWorld of California
Credit: Melissa Hargrove

Performing a rocket hop with Corky during a show at SeaWorld of California
Credit: Melissa Hargrove

Playtime session with Takara at SeaWorld of Texas, 2012
Credit: Daniel

Playtime session with Takara at SeaWorld of Texas, 2012
Credit: Daniel

Me and Takara performing a hula grab-on in a show at SeaWorld of Texas, 2009

Performing a surf ride with Takara during a night show at SeaWorld of Texas, 2009

Me and Corky during a show at SeaWorld of California
Credit: Melissa Hargrove

Me and Corky during a show at SeaWorld of California
Credit: Melissa Hargrove

Takara during a playtime session

Hugging and kissing Takara at SeaWorld of Texas, 2012
Credit: Daniel

do not entirely disappear below the surface." The state is not quite what we call sleep because the orcas are not inert. But neither are they fully awake. Researchers call it "resting."

When I heard this, I thought of Corky and how she spent her sleep time—submerging every few minutes. What we described as against "the norm" of the other whales at SeaWorld was absolutely natural. She had been born in the wild, after all.

While resting in their family huddle, the whales are almost certainly in physical contact with each other, their pectoral fins touching underwater. They are not swimming in place but moving forward slowly with each dive, their flukes pumping subtly to propel them forward. The flip of their tails is so gentle that if they come up against a stronger-than-usual current the whales may actually float backward.

Usually, there is one member of the family who remains fully awake—the designated watchman. Unlike SeaWorld, where we force the whales into solitude and dark silence for about eight hours, an orca family in the open ocean might rest for around two hours or maybe as briefly as 20 minutes. Usually, it is the matriarch who decides when it is time for everyone to become fully conscious.

When she issues that order, the coordinated calm and almost perfectly synchronized breathing is disrupted and the family once again becomes a collection of individuals. Yet the submersions and emergences retain much of their balletic choreography as they travel and search for food. Only when they start to socialize do the whales break their coordinated pattern and each begins to do his or her own thing—vocalizing, socializing, darting about, swimming beyond what had seemed to be the tight fin-touching bounds of the resting family.

As they begin their search for food, the whales remain within one to ten body lengths of each other. They move forward in full wakefulness with the same kind of motions as resting: they dive as they push ahead, taking two or three short dives before a long deep one and then repeating the pattern. But these dives come at a faster pace, the whales moving forward at a speed of about four to eight knots. Though the respiration pattern is similar to when the whales are resting, the deep dives now take them completely beneath the surface. Their tall dorsals vanish entirely as the dives grow longer—perhaps 30 to 60 feet. They have the capacity to travel up to 100 miles a day at eight to ten knots. But that wouldn't be an ordinary day. Typically, they will probably range about 20 to 30 miles before stopping and doing something else. "Sometimes," says Dr. Rose, "you will see a pod traveling very fast— up to 15 knots. They can move in short bursts at 25 knots or so. It's hard to know what the rush is. It doesn't happen often."

When looking for food—"foraging" is the technical term—the orcas will sometimes head to a regular spot where they know the fish congregate searching for their own food. At other times, they are searching for new sites where prey might be available. The orcas pounce, the fish flee and the whales give chase.

Usually, the fish have no chance. "Orcas can turn on a dime," says Dr. Rose. "They can double back on themselves, breach, use their tails to lob or smack schools of fish, stunning them." From the Avon inflatable craft, Dr. Rose and her fellow researchers would sometimes see an oily slick appear on the water. That's all that would be left of a large, fat salmon that was just devoured.

The boat provided Dr. Rose and her associates with a panorama of killer whales' real lives, on a stage immensely bigger than any Shamu Stadium. Even at night, they'd be able to see orcas foraging, because the whales would excite bioluminescent zooplankton in the water. The chase for food would be visible in the darkness. "The large Chinook salmon would glow a pale green while the orcas would blaze a bright green where their white patches were," says Dr. Rose, "You could see the small faint green streak shoot out from a kelp bed into the center of the strait and a big green comet go after it." From a hydrophone in the water at the base of a cliff, Dr. Rose and the researchers could hear the orcas constantly echo-locating and vocalizing loudly and rapidly. The resident whales, she says, produced "tons of chatter when foraging" for fish. (Dr. Rose explained that transients, in contrast, stalk their prey in silence because the animals they are usually hunting are mammals, who are much smarter than fish. Transients only vocalize after a kill. I wonder if that may explain Splash's silence during that night show.)

Foraging usually takes place irregularly throughout a day or week. About four times a week, when the orcas have foraged to their fill, they may settle into socializing, milling around and keeping within a smaller space. They swim a bit then "double back, almost aimlessly sometimes, as they interact," says Dr. Rose. Mothers gather with their calves for play dates. Mature females hang around together. "I like to think they are gossiping." Younger females might "babysit" a younger sibling or even someone else's calf. "Practicing motherhood," explains Dr. Rose. Older male siblings and other older male relatives, like uncles, also babysit, but mothers only allow them to watch over siblings or nephews and nieces. Young calves are never left in the company of adult males from outside their matrilines. At SeaWorld, the father of a one-and-a-half-year-old calf attempted to breed with her after the mother was shipped to another park in the corporation. (That calf, Halyn, died in front of my eyes in June 2008. She had caught an infection that caused brain swelling. She was only two-and-a-half years old.)

The males also hang out among themselves. "The equivalent of guys getting together to smoke cigars, drink beer and watch football," says Dr. Rose. Older, sexually mature males may swim off for a few hours, sometimes a day or two, to mate with females from another family. The younger males will experiment sexually—among themselves or, startlingly, with the "grannies." Orca researchers have never seen sex between fertile male and females of the same family. But young adolescent males will have sex with post-reproductive females of the same family. Those females—since they can't get pregnant anymore—don't seem to mind that the young males are sexually awkward. It seems to be part of the learning process.

Orcas and dolphins (and human beings) are among the rare species that appear to enjoy sex. They will mate even if there is no possibility of reproduction. In other animals, sex isn't really desire: it's more like an instinctive hormonal drive. Killer whales like to have sex—though, like human beings, there are some very strict parameters about who they have sex with. There are, however, no prohibitions against homosexual trysts; male killer whales in the wild and in captivity have been seen entwined, their erect penises exposed.

Female killer whales are also among the few mammals that go through menopause. Most female mammals tend to die soon after they are no longer able to reproduce. Not so with orcas and human beings. What is the evolutionary purpose of post-reproductive survival of female orcas? Perhaps, as the dalliances between young males and the grannies may show, they help socialize and train the next generations. Researchers believe it maximizes the reproductive success of sons, by giving them social status and introducing them to what might in human terms be called "eligible" females through their mothers. They may also pass along valuable knowledge, such as where the best foraging sites are located.

Socializing takes place on the family level and on the superpod level—when families belonging to the same population get together. That kind of reunion, sometimes lasting four or five days, is spectacular, says Dr. Rose. "There will be breaching and tail lobbing and spy-hopping and cartwheels and playful pushing and shovings and pec slaps. And they will all be vocalizing like mad." Among the Southern residents, two pods of whales may face off in long lines, then swim slowly toward each other and, when they meet, begin to vocalize.

Mass grooming may take place too. Northern residents rub on pebbles about a dozen feet below the surface off two beaches in Johnstone Strait. The underwater slope of these beaches is perfect for the whales to pass over the rocks and scratch and slough their skin. Dr. Rose says you can see the dorsal fins of the adult males from the surface as they are giving themselves this dermabrasion therapy. The ritual occurs about once a week for some groups but maybe only once a season for others.

Orcas in the Antarctic have made epic swims northward to South America or Africa perhaps just in order to molt. These aren't migrations, because the treks aren't seasonal. The 8,000- to 9,000-kilometer round trips take 40 days and appear to be primarily for the purpose of removing skin that won't slough off in the cold polar waters. The white areas of orcas who haven't molted for a while start to appear brownish.

In SeaWorld, the trainers have to groom the whales daily. We went at it with our bare hands and fingernails and with large brushes. After the sessions, my hands and nails looked as if they had been spray-painted black. There was so much dead skin to remove.

How long do orcas live? It is a controversial question because SeaWorld contends that its whales live as long as or longer than wild orcas.

A research paper published in 2005 by the Canadian Science Advisory Secretariat (CSAS) on the Northern resident orcas concluded that female orcas have a mean life expectancy of about 50 years; the statistic for males is 30 years. That is different from the maximum estimated life span. Females are believed to be able to achieve 80 to 90 years, perhaps more in some rare cases; males a maximum of 70 years. SeaWorld points to calculations that its whales have a mean life expectancy of about 46 years. Dr. Rose disputes the validity of that figure because, even though SeaWorld has owned 67 orcas over the last half century, that is not a statistically large enough group to extrapolate a meaningful life expectancy figure for its whales.

Howard Garrett of the Orca Network says that the 2005 paper has been rigorously researched and is a great resource for statistics about the Northern and Southern residents from about 1973 to the early 2000s. He notes, however, that the resulting estimates for life expectancy may be skewed by the fact that the pods in the area were subjected to shooting and even target bombing for decades before the study. The Southern resident population was also the source of whales for marine park shows in the 1960s and early 1970s, the paper notes, "which undoubtedly reduced its size and altered its sex- and age-composition." Indeed, the Southern residents have never truly recovered from the ravages of those decades. They are the only endangered population of killer whales in the northern hemisphere and are protected under the Endangered Species Act. (SeaWorld likes to say that they own only five orcas captured in the wild. More accurately, they have owned 32 killer whales captured in the wild throughout the company's history, only five of whom have survived.)

As a trainer, I will leave the interpretation of statistics to the experts. All I have is my own experience. I know how long the whales at SeaWorld lived: 36 have died, 50 if you count stillbirths and miscarriages. Looking at the lives of those 36—which include orcas who were born and died in SeaWorld as well as orcas that were already a certain age in the wild before being captured—the average life span was only ten and a half years. If you add in the stillbirths and miscarriages, that average life span drops to seven and a half years. Among the calves born in SeaWorld who survived more than ten days, the average life span is only 8.8 years.

SeaWorld likes to point to Corky, who is 48 years old and is the oldest killer whale in captivity (there are arguments that Lolita, a solitary orca at the Miami Seaquarium, may be slightly older). When she dies, her longevity will pull up the average—but just by a bit. The rest of the whales at SeaWorld will have to live a long time to be able to bring the averages anywhere close to the mean life expectancy that the CSAS study calculated for orcas in the wild.

Of the 67 orcas SeaWorld has owned, only two males have lived past the study's mean life expectancy, debatably low at 30. No female, not even Corky, has yet reached the mean life expectancy of 50.

7

TREASURE

I knew Takara was somewhere in the pool, because my face felt as if it had been buzzed by a hummingbird. But it was not air that fluttered by me; it was sound waves traveling through water, reverberations caused not by a tiny bird but by a 5,000-pound orca. Takara was quite literally telegraphing me—bouncing sonar from within her head toward and off my body. She was doing it to identify who I was and to find out exactly where I was swimming underwater. But there was more to the vibrations than recognition. Takara emitted sounds that told me how excited she was to see me and how prepared she was to perform one of her favorite acts with me in the water at SeaWorld.

She swam at great speed from the back pool of the stadium to where I had just dived underwater in the show area, out in front, surrounded by an audience of several thousand people in the stands. In the water, as she raced by me, she had seen my hand signal for the specific routine and she was ready. She then swam past me, circling over to the other end of the show pool, where she rose out of the water to take a preliminary bow before the spectators. Then she submerged deep to race back to where I was. Her objective: to rise directly and vertically in front of me, elevating herself high enough but not completely out of the 36-foot-deep pool in an explosive pop—all without making physical contact with me. The trainers called this behavior an "Alien" because it reminded some of us of the scene in the movie where the embryonic monster pops out of its human host. Takara performed it with perfect precision. The audience erupted in applause.

Takara is a princess—albeit an accidental one. Her mother, Kasatka, is a veteran of the entire SeaWorld empire, traveling from California to Florida and Texas. Kasatka has also become one of the most socially dominant killer whales in SeaWorld since her capture off the coast of Iceland in 1978 when she was a year old. She was certainly the most dominant whale during my time in California. After one of Kasatka's cross-country sojourns in 1990, trainers in San Diego found out she was pregnant. It caught everyone by surprise. Breeding had not been on Kasatka's schedule—and no one was sure who the father was. According to company legend, Kasatka and a younger male named Kotar managed to mate despite being separated by a steel gate in a pool at the SeaWorld in San Antonio, Texas. Eighteen months after that encounter, Takara was born on July 9, 1991.

Her name means "treasure" in Japanese but we all called her "Tiki" for short. Like her mother, she can be identified by the black freckle in the white patch over her left eye. She has another birthmark: a brown patch on the tip of her lower jaw that can only be seen close up. Tiki is mischievous and among the toughest and smartest of the 20 killer whales I have worked with in my career. Our lives intersected again and again. I love her so much.

Sweetness has nothing to do with why I adore Tiki. I love her because she's strong, she's smart and she's tough—and she's a spoiled brat who knows when it's time to behave. Like the most attractive person in the room, she knows how to manipulate everyone around her. She gets her way. And that's because she had a mother who taught her how to be the boss.

Kasatka, as I have described earlier, may not have been the biggest whale in SeaWorld, but no one messed with her. Tiki was constantly by her mother's side, so none of the other whales dared to upset her. She was often her mother's sidekick in terrorizing the other whales, usually by raking them—which can be as superficial as scratching other whales with their teeth or as severe as cutting them and causing gashes and lots of bleeding. She could also swim so aggressively against the other orcas that they had to give way, sometimes launching out of the water and into the air with astonishing force, literally rammed out of the pool.

SeaWorld would eventually put Takara's talent for taking charge to administrative use. The San Antonio trainers saw that their whales were growing desultory and unresponsive because they lacked a female orca dominant enough to keep discipline in the small tribe. Trainers often rely on the ruling female in a group to discipline the other whales. But in San Antonio, the closest animal to a top whale in the hierarchy was male. His assertion of dominance—which was not natural to the matriarchal orcas—sent the whales' social structure in San Antonio into freefall and chaos. And so, in 2009, the corporation decided to send Takara from Florida (where she had been moved after she was separated from her mother) to Texas. She slammed her way into dominance almost immediately, in fact, on the very day she arrived.

The princess whale came to town with pomp and circumstance. She was flown in on a military C-130 aircraft. It was the only way to transport her mega-poundage plus the water in her container—a total of 35,000 pounds. I was the Texas trainer who went to pick her up at the San Antonio airport at 4:30 a.m., and, after a crane lifted her box out of the C-130, she traveled to the park in an 18-wheeler escorted in front and back by the police. Her enormous, perfectly straight black dorsal fin stuck out of the top of the truck, a surreal sight on a road in inland Texas.

After getting her to the park, we lowered her into the shallowest of the four pools—the eight-foot-deep med pool. She came over to us right away to take food, a clear sign that the trip had not upset her. It is not uncommon for whales to be so traumatized by transport that it takes days before they regain the comfort level required to eat. Because of their size, orcas need to eat constantly or else face the possibility of illness and death. To complicate things, Takara was at that time seven months pregnant. She needed food.

It was her third pregnancy and she knew from experience—and from her mother, Kasatka—that she had to eat not only for her own sake but for the sake of her unborn calf. I was certain there were other things that weighed on her. Since her separation from Kasatka, her calf Kohana, just three at the time, had been taken from her and sent to Spain; and, when Takara was moved to Texas, her three-year-old son Trua remained in Florida. But because she was doing so well physically, we quickly opened the gate of the shallow pool to give Takara access to one of the two big and deeper back pools. Two male orcas, Kyuquot and Tuar, were in the pool adjacent to Tiki's, with the gates closed to separate them from her. They were, however, aware of her presence and decided to give her a noisy and intimidating welcome, slamming themselves against the gates to Takara's pool.

Most other whales would have been cowed by this reception. The sound and shaking that emanates from steel gates battered by 5,000-to

8,000-pound orcas is terrifying. You can feel the ground move. Two gates led to Takara's back pool; Kyuquot was slamming one, Tuar the other.

Tiki wasted no time. She swam to each gate and slammed it right back, even harder. The clang was unbelievable and, to human witnesses, humbling. The males never slammed her gate again. Whales can bend steel with the force of their bodies, sometimes reshaping the bars so dramatically that a human diver can swim right through the crevice created. After every episode of whale misbehavior like that, SeaWorld had to use a crane to take out the massive steel gates. Then, we'd drive the crane over the damaged metal to straighten it out, returning the gates to their original shape before replacing them in the pools.

To solidify her position as Queen of San Antonio, Tiki followed up on that slamming session with swiftly applied and almost Machiavellian intelligence. She sized up the social situation in the pool. Kyuquot, the largest male, had the three other whales—Unna, Tuar and Keet—subordinate to him. Being pregnant, Takara knew she couldn't take on four whales. But she had a strategy. She was aware that Unna, who was usually quiet, and Keet, a male she had known at another stadium, were already effectively subordinated to her. All she had to do was remind the rambunctious male duo that their first run-in with her was not an anomaly. She chose to divide and conquer.

First, she took on Tuar. Immediately upon being let into the same pool, she raked him violently, leaving a huge gash across the top of his head. He was devastated and terrified of her. In a later session, when I called the whales over, I asked Tuar to position himself beside her. He did, but throughout he had his pectoral flippers tucked in defensively, a clear sign of nervousness. He knew who was boss and did not dare touch Tiki for fear of offending her even more. For her part, Takara paid him no mind, focusing her attention on me, like a duchess who refused to be bothered by the riffraff.

After that, she dealt with Kyuquot—or Ky, as we had nicknamed him. He was much bigger than she was—more than 8,000 pounds to her 5,000; and we had initially kept them apart because we weren't quite sure how he'd respond to her after the gate-banging incident. Her pregnancy also made her more vulnerable. But eventually, they had to come together. If she was concerned about him in any way, she did not show it. Instead, she raked him with her teeth, again and again. He did not fight back. It was painful to watch him bleeding. He swam as fast as he could to try to escape from her but he did not fight back.

You can't prevent raking because the whales have to eventually perform and swim together—and the dominant whales will impose their will on the other whales the moment they feel the need to enforce discipline. Sometimes, raking can be so bad we have to call in the veterinarians to give antibiotics to the injured whale to prevent infection. But Ky would never question Takara's authority. He had accepted that she was the boss. She could wound him if she wanted to. These are the kinds of rules that orcas in captivity live by.

I have always been drawn to the power and the intelligence of whales like Takara, Kasatka and Freya—and how those two qualities come together in the way the orcas deal with humans like myself. My experience with Takara was unlike anything else in my life. We don't know enough about cetaceans to define what "whale-ness" is. In my dealings, I think it is a combination of mental acuity, hypersociability and an innocence that is both childlike and savage. And mysterious. Always, mysterious.

But there are things that whales do that allow humans to guess at the emotional parallels they have with us. Motherhood, for example, is one relationship that humans and whales share. Like her own mother, Takara was an intense parent, exhibiting all the self-sacrifice and tireless work we associate with ideal human moms.

In the early morning hours of January 7, 2010, after nearly 18 months of gestation, Takara went into labor. I rushed to the stadium and saw her resting on the surface. Her belly faced me. The tail flukes of the calf were already out of the womb. We could tell that her offspring was female because we could see the calf's two mammary slits ventrally. I saw the look on Takara's face and knew she was incredibly uncomfortable. The last few weeks of her pregnancy had been difficult but she continued to put on good shows, even though she was hundreds of pounds over her normal weight. Out of concern for her safety and that of the unborn calf, we had canceled certain routines that required her to spin around and slide out onto shallow water. But, even as she got bigger, she continued to perform, with no letup in the behaviors we asked her to do.

Within 45 minutes of my getting to the stadium pool, her labor was over. She gave birth right in front of me. Takara immediately started directing her approximately 300-pound newborn, leading her to the surface to take her very first breath. Her daughter would be named Sakari, which we picked by vote (it was my choice). It was a Japanese word for apex, the paramount position of orcas in the oceanic food chain. Tiki began to nurse Sakari within a few hours.

In the afternoon, Tiki passed the placenta, again right in front of me. Trainers have to be on hand for this epilogue to birthing because the mother can sometimes have problems expelling it. The ideal is to remove it from the pool as quickly as possible for the safety of the mother and calf because the placenta is filled with bacteria, which can attract organisms harmful to the whales. Sometimes, when a whale has produced a stillbirth, she will then become very possessive of the placenta, believing it to be a calf. Often, the mother may view the placenta as part of her and the calf. Removing it can then be dangerous. Fortunately, this was Tiki's third birth, so she knew the drill. She even pushed the placenta in my direction after she passed it.

Physically, removing the organ remained quite the task. The placenta weighed between 60 and 80 pounds. I needed the help of another senior manager to get it out of the pool. We draped our bodies over the six-foot-tall clear acrylic panels to reach into the water to pull the placenta over and out of the pool. The faster you take it out, the better—and not just because of health hazards. The placenta is absorbent and sucks in water with every second, growing heavier and heavier.

In the wild, as Dr. Rose described, orcas never stop moving even when they sleep. But for nearly three months, Takara's swimming took on a kind of anxious energy—and she did not allow herself to slow down, even to pause to rest. She did this to keep her calf from accidentally bumping into some part of the pool's wall or floor. But there was another exhausting reason for this nonstop motion: it takes orca calves about three months to master the motor skills required to suckle without swimming. That is, they do not automatically know how to nurse while staying afloat and at rest. What appears to be simple—being still—is a learned behavior in captivity. In the wild, mother and calf are in perpetual motion; that is their natural state. But staying motionless is a skill that orcas have to learn in order to survive in artificial pools.

And so, as the calf learns to keep still, the mom needs to be in constant movement. To get the perpetually circling Takara to eat, we had to reach out and extend our arms into her mouth to throw handfuls of fish to her as she passed us in the pool, refusing to stop.

Once Takara was confident enough in her calf's motor skills and coordination—and the calf had learned to pause in the water—Tiki rested, absolutely exhausted, floating on the surface as the youngster nursed at her mammary slits, which lie toward the end of her belly where her body starts to taper toward the tail. Takara nursed Sakari for about two years and taught her everything about being a dominant female whale even as she protected her daughter from smacking into the wall and making sure the other whales did no harm to her.

While it is highly unlikely that another whale would try to harm the calf of a dominant female, the possibility should never be discounted. In one instance in Japan, adult whales grabbed and pulled the calf of another orca through the steel bars of a gate separating them from each other, tearing the young orca apart in the process. In any event, Takara made sure no injury came to her calf. It was probably another incentive for her to establish her dominance in San Antonio immediately upon arrival—with enough time for her authority to sink in before her baby arrived.

I was overjoyed when SeaWorld moved Takara to Texas in February 2009. I had returned to work at SeaWorld San Antonio in March 2008. I had loved working with her and Kasatka when mother and daughter were in San Diego. Tiki was always a character, even when she was a calf. Like a human kid, she would break from a training routine to watch what was happening on television—in this case, Sea-World's jumbotron. She liked looking at the screen so much we would give her time to watch the images (which often included herself in replay) as a reward for a good training session. I knew Tiki and her mom so well I could read their moods from the sounds they vocalized through their enormous skull cavities, emanating as various types of clicks and whistles. Every mood of the whales was represented by a different-sounding vocalization; there are subtle ranges among the sounds themselves to reflect how strong each mood is. Learning these complex vocal patterns takes years but, with experience, you can make an accurate assessment of the whale's emotional state.

The sounds are complex and we may never learn to decode whale-talk. But you can sense the whale's moods through the sounds it is making. I can recognize the vocal patterns that represent joy or excitement or enthusiasm. We know that others are sexual. And then there are those that the trainers pay close attention to: the sounds of annoyance that are harbingers of aggression or hostility. This secret, almost undecipherable language provided a glimpse into the inner life of whales.

By the time Tiki came to Texas, we had been apart for close to eight years. Would she remember me? Some experienced trainers believe that whales forget humans within a year after they stop working together. I know it isn't true. Killer whales have long memories.

I have first-hand experience of how good Tiki's memory is. In SeaWorld San Diego, we trained her on a behavior we called a "zipper." It required the whale to swim swiftly around the perimeter of the pool and then break the surface of the water in specific positions while still swimming fast. But when Tiki moved to Florida, the trainers in Orlando used a different signal for the zipper, replacing San Diego's finger-touch and visual command with an entirely different visual one. When I was reunited with Takara in Texas, I decided to see whether she would remember the signal we had used together in California. I touched her side with two fingers and slid them across her body, asking her for the zipper. It had been five years since she left San Diego but she recognized the signal immediately and performed the routine perfectly in her first attempt.

That Takara could remember and interpret something as insignificant as a light touch from a trainer she hadn't seen in years was evidence that all orcas are able to remember complex and intimate relationships that involve innumerable little cues and interactions that number into the thousands. The relationship between whale and trainer may not be composed of the subtle, interpersonal nods and gestures human beings use to express their feelings, but they have their own depths. I believe the whales notice everything, that they invest all stimuli and memory with what humans can interpret as feelings.

Takara—like all killer whales—also can tell one trainer from another. That can be good and bad, because the whales learn to play favorites and discriminate. I knew early on that I was one of her favorites. Sometimes, a whale prefers one trainer to another for completely random reasons. Perhaps it's the way you look at her or the way you carry yourself. Or even the sound of your voice or the way your hand moves when you give them signals. We discovered, for example, that Kasatka and Takara and, to an extent, Freya preferred male trainers and would sometimes snub—or barely tolerate—women who were assigned to work them.

But often, a whale prefers one trainer to another for more complex reasons. It lies in the way the trainer chooses to interact with the orca. I am a big believer in the power of touch. You can communicate everything in the way you touch your whale.

Tiki loved playtime with me. I'd toss balls and enormous flotation devices into the pool and have her toss them back. She'd do it with vocals indicating delight and excitement—sending these massive objects, some weighing hundreds of pounds, into the stands, launched like missiles, sometimes damaging the bleachers and walls and anything in their way. The force would sometimes bend steel bars or knock chunks of concrete off. If her projectile toy hit you, it was unlikely you'd just get up and walk away. Takara knows all about having fun and when she frolics it is a spectacle of things flying in the air—including trainers she'd happily but carefully flip into an adjacent pool. She knew who she liked to have fun with—and who she cared for.

Normally, performing in the water with Takara is a rough ride; she's strong, explosive and fast and expects you to be able to handle the physicality of it all. In October 2009, I and another San Antonio SeaWorld trainer were performing a synchronized routine with Takara and Keet during a show. The aim was to submerge with the whales to the bottom of the pool, 40 feet under, and then get the whales to pull up. Once their tails cleared the bottom, the animals would kick in and, with us standing on the tips of their rostrums, they'd push to the surface at an immense speed, simultaneously exploding almost completely out of the water with us standing atop them like human-cetacean jack-in-the-boxes. In SeaWorld lingo, it's called a double stand-on spy-hop.

For this act to succeed, Takara and Keet had to be perfectly in sync and we trainers had to keep our equilibrium precisely as the animals sped up to the surface. In this case, however, Takara was much faster than Keet. That meant that when she got to the bottom of the pool, she had to wait for him to catch up to coordinate their ascent. When a whale stalls out like that underwater, it affects the trainer trying to keep himself or herself attached to and balanced on the orca. Because of the way water and gravity work, the human's body will begin to float during the wait, moving out of position because the momentum has stopped. That's what happened to me in the brief time it took Keet to catch up with Tiki. Once they were lined up, Takara whipped up her powerful flukes and the sudden burst of power caused my left foot to shift slightly on her rostrum. That was the beginning of disaster.

I immediately knew I was in trouble when my left foot—my dominant one—shifted off its spot. The thought flashed through my head that I should abort the behavior and break off from Takara. But I convinced myself that I had enough balance to make it. Wrong. She got to the surface with such force that my left foot washed completely off her. It made me lean forward. Tiki was aware something was wrong. In the video of the incident, you can clearly tell that she is trying to stop. You see her arching to try to avoid me. But it was too late and, as I fell forward right as we broke the surface, her rostrum—with more than 5,000 pounds behind it—slammed into my side and sent me into the pool like a rag doll.

Right away, Takara began to echolocate on my entire body—it felt just like the hummingbird buzz, but I could tell these were different. Her sonar was almost like thought. Takara had, during a previous waterwork show, approached me with echolocation and I could hear and feel it in my chest like I normally did but then it became different. It caused a snapping sound—like that of a rubber band—that I could hear but also feel at the top left side of my brain. I have never experienced anything like it before or after. Later, I joked with other trainers that she was stealing my thoughts and reading my mind. Maybe she was.

As I tried to regain my senses in the pool after the collision, Takara sent out her sonar while "sharking" me, that is swimming around me in a circle at the surface with her perfectly straight dorsal exposed. It wasn't because she thought I was prey. She was trying to figure out how badly I was hurt.

The wind had been knocked out of me but I managed to float to the surface. I motioned a thumbs-up to my control spotter on land, pretending I was fine so they wouldn't emergency recall Tiki away from me. I needed her help. I had fallen right into the middle of the pool and I knew I didn't have the strength to make it back to solid ground without her help.

As she continued to echolocate on my body, I gently snapped my fingers underwater, signaling her to swim in front of me. I placed both hands on her rostrum as I tried to catch my breath. Then I gave her a signal for a pec-push from the show area to the edge of one of the pools in the back. Suddenly, this roughest, toughest princess of SeaWorld became the gentlest of rescuers. I never even felt her pectoral flippers touch my feet as she began to glide me to safety. She then gave me a pec-push step-off onto the back pool's ledge, smoothly coming underneath me to lift me high enough as I floated that I barely needed to exert any effort to step off her pec and out of the pool. That last move was a behavior she was never trained for. She was aware of how important I was in her life; and she wanted to make sure I would be safe.

I arrived in the emergency room in very bad shape. The staff performed CT scans to test for internal injuries. When Takara's rostrum slammed into me, the impact compressed my rib cage, breaking several ribs and injuring soft tissue both in the front and back. The ER doctor would tell me that an impact of that magnitude could have easily stopped my heart. For about a month, any physical contact caused incredible pain and made it impossible to get comfortable or even to lie down without agony.

I learned one important thing from the incident: Takara treasured me as much as I treasured her. The greatest compliment I ever got in my career came from several young up-and-coming trainers. They told me that what they wanted most out of their careers was one day to have a relationship with an orca as strong as mine was with Takara.

8

GETTING WITH THE ARTIFICIAL PROGRAM

I was beyond excited to be a member of the special team that was as-sembled one spring morning in 2000 in San Diego. I was still a rela-tively junior member of the Shamu Stadium orca-training squad. But I had been assigned to be part of what everyone on staff described as a historic event: the first artificial insemination of a female killer whale in the world. I felt as if I were a scientific pioneer.

The project had been years in the making, starting sometime in the 1990s with the first attempts to collect semen from a male orca. Now, in April 2000, after about six months of training, Kasatka had been sufficiently desensitized to the invasiveness of the procedure, making it possible for us to carry it out the way it had been mapped out step-by-step in advance. Her hormonal readings indicated that she would be ready to ovulate precisely that morning. The sperm had al-ready been flown in from Florida, where it had been harvested and stored.

SeaWorld has had a successful orca-breeding program since 1985. But the corporation decided that artificial insemination would increase the number of orcas in the parks at a faster rate. It was, management explained, a way to sustain the company's killer whale population. If not, the whales would have died out or suffered from inbreeding, because only orcas in close proximity would be able to mate. Flying the orcas around the country on C-130s or similarly sized aircraft is extremely expensive; and you have to be sure that the orcas you pair up will actually want to mate. A mismatch would be a huge waste of resources. (SeaWorld could no longer diversify its orca population with new whales from the wild because it had stopped capturing orcas due to a public outcry in the 1970s.)

The solution was a program of artificial insemination. It would allow SeaWorld to ship sperm to a park where a female orca was ready to ovulate. Veterinarians and trainers could track her readiness through the levels of hormones in her urine and blood. We could even follow the development of the ovum in her fallopian tubes via ultrasound.

Getting Kasatka ready for the introduction of an alien tube into her body took six months. The procedure required her to roll ventral, that is, to be on her back, with her blowhole, through which she breathed, underwater. She would have to hold her breath for as long as 10 minutes; and she would have to get used to trainers and vets touching her genital area and injecting air into her cervix to open it up for the eventual introduction of the tube. How do you get a whale used to doing all of that without her reacting badly? What do you do when that whale is Kasatka—one of the most dangerous in the SeaWorld system?

She was already trained to roll over ventrally and have her dorsal fin pointing down to the pool floor. That was part of the repertoire of behaviors we taught all whales to get them ready for physical

144

examinations or for playful rubdowns. A trainer could just give her the signal and she'd roll onto her back. That was only the first step, however.

In the wild, orcas can stay underwater for as long as 12 to 15 minutes, if they have to. It's a matter of choice as they go about their lives, feeding and foraging and swimming freely. In captivity, for Sea-World's purposes, we have been able to train the most well conditioned whales to hold their breaths for approximately ten minutes. We would start Kasatka slowly, rewarding her first for two minutes of holding her breath, then two and a half, then three and so on until we got to the goal of approximately ten minutes—all the while making sure she knew to keep absolutely still. The small increments were important because she was supposed to learn not to wiggle or move through the ordeal. If we had started her at ten minutes, she would have displayed discomfort—and that would be harder to train out of her. So we went slowly—that is, like all trained behavior, we approximated it, step by step. Every time she succeeded, we rewarded her with fish or something else she really enjoyed. The project was extremely important to SeaWorld and we needed the whale to feel the process was a positive experience. We were likely to have her go through it again and again to produce calf after calf. She had to learn to feel rewarded by it.

Next, we had to get her used to being touched in a sensitive part of her body. You can tell a female orca from a male by two additional slits in the genital area. These are the mammary glands where her calf will nurse. The third slit shields the vagina (the same slit in a male orca hides the penis, which is not visible except when it is erect). While Kasatka was ventral, we'd have trainers she trusted by her side, touching her pectoral flippers to reassure her that everything was fine. Their presence signaled that she was in safe hands, that they were watching out for her no matter how strange the proceedings were. That helped keep her calm. One trainer would then start to manipulate the area, gently pulling apart the vaginal walls, as slowly as possible, reassuring her each step of the way to let her know that this is what we really wanted her to do, that it was part of the behavior we required of her.

In retrospect, the process sounds barbaric: using behavioral training methods to get a hugely intelligent animal to submit to being artificially inseminated for the benefit of a corporation. But that didn't cross my mind during the months we trained Kasatka for the procedure. I believed it was for the good of the killer whale population.

I was one of the few trainers assigned to Kasatka's team to train her for the procedure. We spread the vaginal walls apart a little, the first step in conditioning her to be able to accept the tube of sperm that would be injected in there on the day of the actual insemination. We used a small lubricated plastic tube—no thicker than a ballpoint pen but flexible—to figure out the pathways of her vagina. Each female orca is different—never exactly like the anatomy textbooks diagram. We needed to know how she was structured to avoid causing any internal damage the day we introduced the larger, more important tube into her to send sperm toward the ovum. We slowly got her used to larger and thicker tubes.

To simulate the actual tube, we used a soft plastic proxy of the same dimensions; it injected air into the whale's cervix just as the real device would. We had to prepare her for that as well. Because the insemination would be performed by a veterinarian—and not a trainer—we had to get Kasatka used to a stranger joining her trainers. The veterinarians don't have relationships with the whales and they know better than to just step over the protective barrier and insert something into a 5,000-pound killer whale without the animal being properly conditioned to accept their presence and their intrusion. It is extremely rare for SeaWorld veterinarians to be next to the trainers with the whales. Usually, they are on the other side of the wall that separates the pool and its immediate perimeter from the rest of the stadium. We had stand-ins playing the part of the vet, making that role a variable part of the training so Kasatka would know that someone she was unfamiliar with would always be part of the process.

For Kasatka, the air in the cervix was the most difficult part of the training. She kept her eyes closed every time we practiced it. To help keep her comfortable, we had Takara nearby in the same pool. It was important that she could sense her daughter's presence. She and Takara were inseparable and we knew we had to have the younger female close. She would be by her mother's side on the day of the procedure itself.

As we practiced, the vets monitored Kasatka's urine day by day to find out when she would ovulate next. They tracked her luteinizing hormones as well as her progesterone and estrogen levels. The veterinarian, Todd Robeck, who would perform the actual insemination was on site in San Diego. But the sperm had been flown in from Florida where Tilikum, the donor, was based. The whole process would come down to the one moment when she started to ovulate. Via sonogram, we would know when the ovum was about to drop and practically to the minute when to inject the sperm. Everything had to be right. Everyone had to be ready to work efficiently and precisely. You couldn't waste the semen that had been excruciatingly difficult to harvest in the first place.

If preparing a female killer whale for artificial insemination was a complex choreography of sonograms and chemistry, taking semen from a male orca was, well, sensitive and dangerous. Tommy Lee of Mötley Crüe—a supporter of People for the Ethical Treatment of Animals

(PETA)—infamously accused SeaWorld of "having someone get in the pool [with Tilikum] and masturbate him with a cow's vagina filled with hot water." That isn't how it's done. Though it wasn't too far off from the way SeaWorld first tried to do it.

The first would-be donor was Kotar (whose alleged through-the-gate tryst with Kasatka in San Antonio produced Takara). The attempt was made in the early 1990s. After training him to roll on his back and basically keep his blowhole underwater, the team in San Antonio began to manipulate his penis to produce an ejaculation. That was more than the orca was willing to put up with. He raised himself up with a fury at the abuse and turned an open jaw toward the trainers at work. That hands-on strategy of sperm collection was rethought.

The trainers then devised an unlikely but ingenious approach to collecting sperm from male orcas without having to manipulate their penises. They would associate the procedure with sex—by having a whale that the potential donor orca was sexually attracted to in the same pool, male or female. When the trainers saw the donor had a full or partial erection, they would call him over and see if they could get him to slowly associate the process they were initiating with "sex in mind." Then step-by-step, in session after session, the constantly rewarded whale would incrementally learn to produce an erection.

The orca's penis is not visible unless erect. But when aroused, it cannot be missed. It is pink with some white coloration and four to six feet long. But getting a male trained to produce an erection is only one step toward getting him to ejaculate. A whale has to guess that is what you want him to do. It requires the orca to do what trainers call "prospecting"—trying out several possibilities to find out what results were needed to gain reinforcement or rewards from the trainers around him. At first, there was a lot of thrusting, which the trainers wouldn't reinforce. The usual result of a next attempt would see the orca producing urine. We didn't want that either. Eventually, through leaps of the killer whale imagination, there would be some semen but combined with urine. That sperm sample is unusable because it is contaminated. With luck and even more careful reinforcement, the orca would finally produce pure semen. It is astonishing proof of the orca's control over its physical functions—able to produce semen without friction, almost entirely by its imagination, coaxed along by behaviorist principles.

(One precaution taken after the sperm collection procedure: the trainers who got a male orca to produce an erection were never allowed to work with that whale in the water because the whale most likely would associate them with sexual arousal, which was almost always a precursor for aggression.)

A good harvest was 50 cubic centimeters of semen—or just over three tablespoons. The goal, however, was to get larger and larger volumes because the fluid was so valuable to the corporation. The sperm was collected in a plastic bag attached by an elastic band to the base of the orca's penis. The container was completely sterilized and could not come into contact with the pool's salt water—or anything that could possibly contaminate and kill the precious sperm. Immediately after ejaculation, the bag would be rushed by a trainer to the veterinarian lab, where the sperm would be frozen. Every second counted because the moment the spermatozoa were out of the orca, they would begin to die.

Not all male whales could produce semen this way. It required a special kind of killer whale mentality. SeaWorld has been trying to train Ky—who was born in 1991—for years; and he still does not fully understand what he needs to do to satisfy the trainers.

But three whales were particularly accommodating in the quest for orca sperm: Ulises, Keet and Tilikum. Of the three, Tilikum has been the most prodigious. He has produced 17 calves in less than 20 years, through both natural breeding and artificial insemination. Five have died. SeaWorld probably got 25 to 50 semen samples from Keet that are totally viable and could produce offspring. They remain frozen in storage. Though he was amenable to the procedure, Ulises did not produce viable sperm, according to lab results shared with the trainers. At least in the beginning. After Tilikum killed Dawn Brancheau in 2010, SeaWorld claimed that Ulises' sperm was successfully used to impregnate eight-year-old Kalia in 2013. I'd like to see DNA proof of that.

Let's get back to Kasatka.

For much of the six months of training Kasatka for the procedure, I stood at her genital region to condition her to the tube. But most often my role was to be in control of her, asking her to roll over, line up parallel to the wall and give me her pectoral flipper so I could help keep her calm and reassured. On the day of the procedure in April 2000, her hormone levels indicated she was about to ovulate. All of us on her team were present as she lined up parallel and laterally to the wall. Then she was given the hand signal to roll over, which she did while looking at her trainer, taking a deep breath. A simple finger point underwater at her eye level toward her tail flukes let her know that we wanted her to place her tail on the water-covered ledge of the pool. Then, just as in training, we grabbed her pectoral flipper, waiting for her to be completely relaxed. Part of her tail was by the pool wall to keep her steady, in a straight ventral line, her head upside down in the water, pointing toward the middle of the pool. Nearby was her daughter Takara, under the guidance of other trainers so she remained a calming presence but not a disturbance to her mother.

All the conditions were optimal. When I rehearsed Kasatka for the procedure, my job was to hold her pectoral flipper. If her tail flukes began to come off the ledge, I could put my hand underwater next to her eye so she could see me point down to her tail flukes. She'd know to readjust and make sure her flukes remained steady. If she closed her eyes (as she often did during practice), I would run my finger down the side of her body for about a foot's length, beginning at her head and trailing toward her flukes. That would be a signal to make the same adjustment and to stay steady.

During the actual procedure itself, it was the call of the trainer in control of Kasatka when to signal for the other trainers and the vet, Todd Robeck, to step over the wall, and whether they should proceed or get back behind the wall for their safety if something in Kasatka reflected a change in her behavior, that she wasn't comfortable, or perhaps some precursor to aggression.

Meanwhile, the trainers and the vets were tracking the ovum via ultrasound equipment on her lateral side, on the area of her body known as the peduncle, in the genital area. When the egg was on the point of dropping, the trainers spread open her vaginal walls. And up over the wall that separated us from the public areas of the stadium stepped Dr. Todd Robeck, SeaWorld's no-nonsense "reproductive specialist." He was responsible for impregnating Kasatka with Tilikum's sperm. No one messed with Dr. Robeck. And, if you did, he would let you know loudly that you were in his way. The tube would be inserted as Robeck had instructed.

Every now and then, Kasatka would lift her head to try to get a better look at what was happening but she remained calm otherwise. Still, every time she moved while Dr. Robeck was at work watching the monitor, he'd shout, "Get her to stop."

The large lubricated tube that would deliver the seminal fluid was inserted. It wasn't as big as a male orca's penis but it had the same shape. Air was also injected via the tube to open up Kasatka's cervix, expanding it even as the tube pushed forward to the best position to get the semen to the ovum when the egg sac burst. That happened moments after we injected the sperm into her. The tube was carefully pulled out of her and most everyone stepped back behind the wall. We were still holding on to Kasatka's pec and trainers were at her tail flukes.

As Dr. Robeck packed up his equipment, I and the other trainers turned our attention to Kasatka, who had rolled right-side up and was breathing normally as she was bridged for being correct over the entire procedure. We praised her, reinforcing her for being a good girl. We wanted to make sure she knew this was a big deal for her and for us. We got her food, we rubbed her down, we played with her, we made sure she was fine. The vets could do what they wanted. I wanted to make sure Kasatka was feeling good about herself and that she was physically okay.

We had to wait a month for the results. But the procedure proved successful. After a gestation period of 18 months, Kasatka gave birth to the calf, Nakai, in 2001. It was the beginning of a whole new and lucrative enterprise for SeaWorld. They called it Genetic Management.

I was very proud at the time of my part in pioneering the artificial insemination (AI) program at SeaWorld. Diversifying the gene pool of the whales was a lofty and scientific goal. The AI program certainly seemed to be a way to do it.

But I soon found out that the welfare of the whales was hardly uppermost on SeaWorld's agenda. According to the newspaper *U-T San Diego*, Dennis Spiegel, president of International Theme Park Services, a Cincinnati-based leisure consultancy, said a study by his company put a price of about $15 million to $20 million on each of

SeaWorld's killer whales. The AI program has produced at least five calves in the 15 years it's been in place—and the sperm trade between SeaWorld and at least two other parks around the world must bring in an unknown but large sum of money as well.

Little has been done to improve the facilities for the same whales that are worth tens of millions to the corporation. I was acutely aware of this in SeaWorld of Texas, where I spent the last four-and-a-half years of my career. Despite a constant clamor from trainers, the pools there remained the same, unchanged except for the sets that came and went with each more expensive Shamu spectacular. Instead of more space, the whales had to endure the cacophony of construction mandated by the entertainment division.

In that period, SeaWorld of Texas did not repaint the front show pool after the whales pulled the paint off the walls out of boredom. SeaWorld says it put back $70 million into the killer whale pools in all its parks. Very little or nothing of which went toward improving the living conditions of the whales. The company did not enlarge or build additional pools for the whales. Most of the money has been spent on adding emergency equipment and a lifting floor to a back pool in each park. In fact, the lifting floors took up three feet of space from the bottom of each of those pools, further shrinking the orcas' environment.

According to SeaWorld's public financial disclosures, it is a $2.5-billion company making hundreds of millions of dollars in profit annually. So why was it that the pools had not been improved since the 1980s? Florida and California got additional close-up pools in the early 1990s—Texas never did—but those were mostly to drum up more revenue by attracting Dine with Shamu customers who would be able to see the whales through glass. It was not meant to give the orcas more space. Only in August 2014 did SeaWorld declare it would expand its pools, an announcement that occurred after its stock price plunged 33 percent in one day in the prolonged public furor in the wake of the *Blackfish* controversy.

Through the 2000s, the AI program moved forward. Immediately after Tilikum killed Dawn Brancheau in February 2010, we were told of a corporate directive that all viable orca females were to be impregnated via artificial insemination, as fast as we could, and again and again. Some of us began to have doubts about the ethics of it all but kept quiet. We complained but management knew that they had a certain power over us: we loved working with the whales.

The breeding program—both artificial and not—was cruel. In the wild, mothers and their calves—even as adult offspring—are never far apart. Mothers and daughters are especially close—as I learned with Kasatka and Takara. I was in France pursuing my career in Antibes when SeaWorld separated them, but I heard of the trauma.

The company denies separating mothers and calves, and when a mother and her offspring are assigned to separate parks, SeaWorld explains that the calf has been weaned. But orcas are unlike other animals. A calf is always a calf, no matter how old the whale becomes, it is always its mother's son or daughter. An entire social hierarchy is built around this parental relationship.

However, to diversify their orca gene pool and repopulate their parks, SeaWorld moved its fertile female orcas around in a country-spanning breeding program. Worst of all, they would impregnate—whether through artificial means or natural breeding—females that in the wild would be too young to breed. Or just as bad, they would impregnate the females so soon after they had given birth that the orcas—already young and not yet fully developed—would have little time to physically recover from the difficulties of pregnancy. In the wild, female orcas calve only every four to five years. They do not usually start to breed until they are about 13–15 years old. SeaWorld

154

exacerbates the conditions of captivity by rushing and telescoping the orca's rhythm of reproduction. In the wild, motherhood is not just a biological function; it is a highly socialized one as well. As Dr. Rose and others have shown in their studies, mother orcas teach their daughters how to parent. In SeaWorld, there are only a few free-born females to remind the younger born-in-captivity generation what to do when they calve.

Takara again helped me to see this horrific aspect of captivity and unnatural breeding for what it is. She was the second female orca at SeaWorld to be artificially inseminated, becoming the mother of Kohana, a female, also via Tilikum's sperm. In 2004, as I described, SeaWorld sent Takara and Kohana from San Diego to Florida, separating them from Kasatka and what was left of their natural matrilineal grouping. In 2006, the corporation took three-year-old Kohana from Takara and sent her to the SeaWorld-associated Loro Parque in Spain's Canary Islands. Takara and Tilikum were then bred to produce a male calf named Trua. Takara was separated from Trua when she was reassigned to the Texas park in San Antonio. At that time, Trua was just three years old. Takara was seven months pregnant again when she was transported to Texas in early February 2009. That was when I caught up with her.

I was ecstatic to see her. But I knew what she had been through. She had been taken from her mother, then she had her first calf taken from her and then she herself was removed from the side of her second calf. By the time I was reunited with her in 2009, she had been impregnated three times.

Takara's life was one of serial separations from her mother and her children, and the fate of her daughter Kohana in the Canary Islands was an ugly, dysfunctional mess. Within five years of her stay in Loro

Parque, Kohana had given birth twice—and twice had rejected her calves. Her second rejected calf died within its first year. Kohana was too young when she was separated from Takara to have fully learned what orca motherhood entails. She was still a child herself.

At first, I thought the news and the stories were merely sad. I continued to believe they were an aberrant part of a well-meaning program. That changed when I was reunited with Takara in San Antonio.

Takara reminded me of what I considered some of the best years of my career: working in San Diego with her mother Kasatka. When she arrived in Texas, I saw how hard she was laboring. She came heavily pregnant from Florida yet knew how to adjust to the conditions immediately. She was resilient and showed her take-charge attitude right away, slamming her authority into those two males who tried to intimidate her. When she gave birth, she was a great mother to Sakari, her calf, as well—protecting her from the walls as she exhausted herself swimming protective circles around the pool.

But SeaWorld saw Takara as a baby machine. Within one year of giving birth to Sakari, we started preparing to artificially inseminate her again, this time with the sperm from Kshamenk, who lived alone in a marine park in Argentina. We monitored Takara's urine after she gave birth to Sakari to track when she was ovulating once again. That happened, as expected, 18 months after Sakari was born. There is usually a six week interval between ovulations so we had that amount of time to fly staff, equipment and semen to Texas to be part of the procedure to impregnate her once again. I winced. She had just been through a difficult gestation. And now SeaWorld wanted her to endure another 18-month pregnancy? What if we lost her the same way we lost Taima, who died in 2010 at the age of 20 of placental hemorrhaging as she was trying to give birth to her fourth calf?

Nevertheless, everyone in Texas went into overdrive so we could catch the ovum in six weeks. I was the trainer who was to be in charge of her—in control, in behaviorist terms, to make sure she stayed calm and the procedure went like clockwork. I wanted to make sure she got through the procedure as safely and as comfortably as possible.

In late July 2011, we put her through the same procedure that we first used on her mother more than a decade earlier. As with Kasatka, I held Takara's pectoral flipper, rubbing her down and talking to her in barely a whisper. It was a near carbon copy of what I had done with her mother. But the difference this time was instead of the praise I whispered to Kasatka—what a good girl she was for making history for SeaWorld and all that—I just kept telling Takara, "I'm sorry. I'm sorry. I'm sorry."

Except for my emotional reversal, everything was the same. Once again, Dr. Robeck—who flew in from San Diego—was on hand to perform the actual insemination. Once again, we had to wait a month to see if she had become pregnant. She did. But by March 2012, her progesterone levels had dropped to the point where the veterinarians were certain she was no longer carrying a calf. No one could explain what happened. Takara was less than halfway through the gestation period but the fetus had vanished, reabsorbed, it seemed, into her body.

I told everyone how happy I was that she was not going to have another calf. Management was upset with me and did not want me to go around undermining company policies, especially with younger staffers. But I couldn't keep my feelings to myself. I was also incensed because I knew they were soon going to want to put Takara through the process again—and that they were eventually going to take Sakari away from her.

Julie Sigman, a SeaWorld supervisor whom I greatly respected at the time, took me aside. "John," she said, "you are a leader at Shamu

Stadium. I cannot have you telling everyone that you're glad she's not pregnant and we shouldn't be doing this to her. We have a moral responsibility to diversify their gene pool." That was the gist of her long talk with me. It put a spell on me and I was once again a loyalist. Her words took my anger away and I reverted to my old self as an obedient subject of the SeaWorld kingdom. I even thanked her for reminding me of the mission, telling her that no one had ever explained the situation to me that way before.

Within 24 hours, however, the spell was broken. "What the hell just happened to me?" I said to myself. I realized what my responsibility really was.

I've been around this industry for a long time and I have strong views shaped by experiences with these whales, experiences that few other people share. I began sputtering. Our moral responsibility is not to diversify the gene pool of these orcas. We took these whales from the ocean and put them in a captive situation and now we are breeding them because we want more whales in our collection in order to make more money. Our responsibility is to make their lives better, not to impregnate them again and again in an abnormal way.

I was angry at myself. I had finally realized what the corporation was going to put Takara through and had converted from a true believer in SeaWorld into a rebel with a powerful cause. Yet, Julie Sigman turned me around. If I could allow myself to be re-brainwashed so quickly, how much easier would it be to fool the public?

"We recognize the importance of the family bond," Chuck Tompkins, the corporate vice president of animal training, told the press. But I have done the math: 19 calves were taken from their mothers in SeaWorld's history, including Kasatka and Katina, who were captured from the wild and thus, wrested from their mothers.

Only two of the 19 separations were medically necessary, most likely because the mothers—abnormally young themselves—became excessively aggressive toward their calves. SeaWorld likes to point out that Kasatka is now living with three of her offspring. They do not care to say that Takara (and her daughter Kohana, Kasatka's granddaughter) were taken from her and shipped to Florida. And that Kohana was subsequently taken from her mother Takara and shipped to Spain and then bred unnaturally young. Kasatka's daughter Kalia was artificially inseminated at the age of eight. That would have never happened in the wild.

My anger over this treatment of the whales as baby-making factories would become a big factor in my decision to leave SeaWorld for good in August 2012. There were more reasons. My body was exhausted from the many times I'd physically been injured by the whales. And my soul was battered because I was coming to the difficult realization that as much as I loved the whales, love alone was not going to save them.

Even before all that, I—and everyone else at SeaWorld—had to deal with the terrible events of December 24, 2009, and February 24, 2010.

9

THE DARK SIDE

You have been abducted by aliens. You have some memory of the world you were born into but it is all a haze. There are others like you nearby and no one knows how to get away. No one has any power. Authority is wielded by the strange little creatures who dart in and around you. They are in command. You do not understand their language and they do not understand yours. They communicate with you in signals. They are your sole source of food and they only feed you when you obey. They prick and prod you. They take your fluids. Or they insert fluids into you. They breed you. But you don't ever see your progeny. At least not for long. And you have no say in the matter.

Alien abduction has been part of contemporary mythology for more than half a century. Some people believe it has happened. I used to sit around with fellow orca trainers and laugh about it. And then I'd riff and say, "Well, it has happened. Except we are the aliens and the whales are the abductees."

So you are an orca in SeaWorld captivity. As a highly intelligent, extremely emotional being, you immediately know who will keep you alive, if not make you happy. The trainers feed you—and they feed you more when you do what they want. But they also try to control your every action—from sleeping to playing to resting to what you do with the other whales who share the pools with you. You like some trainers more than others. You actually enjoy some of the acts they ask you to perform. You learn to recognize the signs they use; to a large degree, you can tell what they want you to do. But the humans watch your every move. And you know why. They are afraid of you. But they are the only ones who can keep you alive. You want to escape but have no way to do so. Beyond the walls of your pool is an expanse of air and concrete. And, again and again, sometimes seven times a day, screaming people.

So you have to behave. Until you can't. Perhaps the other whales are daring you to do something. Perhaps the memories you have accumulated as you have learned to survive are no longer viable. Your emotions shift. You move toward the dark side. And then, suddenly, an opportunity comes for revenge. Will you take it?

Sometimes, even the most well-behaved of captive orcas have their moments when you feel they may be on the verge of crossing over to their dark side. One time, I had just finished swimming with Corky during a show in San Diego. She is one of the more easygoing of the orcas, despite her size and love of speed. She's seen all kinds of trainers—good and mediocre—and knows how to deal with them. After I swam with Corky for the entire show, Petey asked me and another trainer, Amy, to hang out in one of the small areas of about waist- to chest-high water on either side of the main stage of the front show pool. Called a slide-over, it's where the orcas slide up during shows to interact with trainers. They can even slip from the front to the back pools via the slide-over. Petey wanted to bring Corky and Splash into the front show pool after we had sent them to the back following the show. As part of the psychological conditioning that constantly went on in the California park, Petey wanted these two orcas to swim past us without turning around, desensitizing them to our presence so they wouldn't be distracted from the desired behavior—swimming past us to meet up with Petey at stage. The uninitiated members of the public—at this point, the stadium was clearing out—may not even have suspected training was going on but everything in San Diego was part of a regimen, of getting the whales used to doing tasks with precision, being focused and not being distracted by extraneous stimuli.

No sooner had Petey set control with Corky and Splash—getting them to chin up at stage—than Corky split off and swam at high speed toward the spot where Amy and I were standing, waist deep in water in the slide-over area. We didn't have a chance to take a few steps back to get out of the way before she had slid up between us. She turned to her left and scooped me into the pool. I was no match for her 8,200 pounds. Using her rostrum, she began to gently push into my chest while vocalizing. I would have been alarmed but her vocals were not fast and tight. She did not seem to be upset. Still, she continued to push me along the perimeter of the front show pool. Corky ignored multiple hand slaps and an emergency recall tone by Petey. Finally, she responded to one of his hand slaps. She dropped away from my chest and dived straight down and underneath me as she swam back to the stage area. Once Petey felt he had tight control over her, he told me to swim out of the pool.

What was going through Corky's brain? She wasn't upset enough to appear aggressive and yet what she was doing was out of her norm and definitely unacceptable. It is alarming any time a killer whale departs from the control of one trainer to pull another into the water—and then ignores emergency recalls and hand slaps. Management decided not to write up what had happened as a corporate incident report—a record of an aggressive act—because Corky did not seem agitated enough. But to this day, I wonder. She would later be part of a few more incidents, clearly closer to aggression, including turning on my friend Wendy who was in scuba gear in the pool in full view of Dine with Shamu guests watching from the underwater viewing area. Corky pushed Wendy with such speed and force she couldn't turn to her left or right, fearful that the orca might crush her against the artificial rock formations in the pool. Again, this was not considered aggressive enough to be written up as a corporate incident report.

It may seem that SeaWorld set the bar quite high for incidents to be classified as acts of aggression. But when OSHA, the federal agency that looks after worker safety, was investigating the company in the wake of Dawn Brancheau's 2010 death, the company had to turn over 100 incident reports from 1988 to 2009, a dozen of which recorded injuries. If OSHA had gone back just a year more, to 1987—before the marine parks were sold by Harcourt Brace Jovanovich to a division of Anheuser-Busch—it might have seen three more major incidents in which trainers sued the company. On June 15, 1987, Joanne Webber had her neck broken after a 6,000-pound killer whale hit her during a difficult behavior called a "human hurdle" in which the orca has to perform a bow over a trainer. The force thrust Webber to the bottom of the 40-foot pool. There appeared to be more concern over SeaWorld property than over getting her immediate care. According to the lawsuit Webber would file, she was made to walk 50 feet to an enclosure and was told to remove her wetsuit so that emergency workers wouldn't have to cut through it and damage it. Because she was unable to comply, SeaWorld personnel allegedly forcibly took the suit off Webber. According to the *Los Angeles Times'* account, Webber was then told to dress in civilian clothes and walk 200 yards to the ambulance, rather than have the emergency vehicle come to the stadium. As a result, she lost 50 percent of the side-to-side motion of her neck, her lawyer said in the *Los Angeles Times.* Her injuries reportedly included fractures to the first cervical vertebrae and contusions to the skull and scalp, with bruises to her left arm and shoulder. Three months earlier, Jonathan Smith was hospitalized for nine days with internal bleeding and organ lacerations after being involved in a double waterwork aggression with the orcas Keanu and Kandu, who were nicknamed the "twisted sisters" and who took turns dragging him along the bottom of the pool in their jaws. According to a report in the *Los Angeles Times,* he suffered internal bleeding and a six-inch cut to his liver. His lawsuit, the paper said, alleged that SeaWorld did not properly inform him of the "dangerous propensities of killer whales." On November 21 of the same year, John Silick suffered internal injuries and a crushed pelvis after he was slammed by an adult male killer whale that had breached the water, landing on Silick while he was riding another whale. The three trainers settled out of court; and they all agreed to gag orders. Nevertheless, Webber's lawsuit, as cited in the *Los Angeles Times,* had already raised the issue of SeaWorld whitewashing the dangers posed by captive orcas. It alleged that the whales were "likely to attack and injure human beings."

In any case, under cross-examination during the OSHA case, Chuck Tompkins, SeaWorld's corporate vice president of Animal Training overseeing all parks, was asked about several events between 1988 and 2009 that did not appear to be part of the official incident reports turned over to the government. As the judge noted in his decision, "SeaWorld failed to document several known events of undesirable behavior by killer whales when working with trainers."

The judge quoted Tompkins as saying "We missed a few" to account for the lapses.

No one really knows what goes on in an orca's brain. But magnetic resonance imaging (MRI) of a killer whale brain, extracted from a recently dead specimen in the wild, may provide us with clues about how their thoughts and emotions are wired. Dr. Lori Marino, a professor of cetacean neuroscience at Emory University who studied the orca MRI, points out that the killer whale neocortex is more convoluted—that is, wrinkled—than the human brain. "The neocortex wrinkles because that is the way volume increases in a skull of fixed size," she explains, "like wrinkling up a piece of paper to fit in a small space." This increases the actual surface area of that part of the brain, meaning that there are more neurons and brain cells there. The neocortex is where problem solving and information processing occur. It is also linked to the limbic system—which in the human brain governs long-term memory, emotions, sense of smell and how you make decisions—by way of a distinctive paralimbic cortex. "All mammal brains have paralimbic systems," says Dr. Marino, "however, the orca paralimbic region appears more developed and defined than the same region in other mammals, including primates." The orca's insular cortex too, she says, "is very wrinkled." That indicates that the brain devotes "a lot of tissue to that area." "All of these highly elaborated cortical and neo-cortical regions point to a very sophisticated brain." Since those parts of the brain are "involved in consciousness and awareness in humans and probably all mammals then we can infer that this part of the brain is, at least, part of the foundation for a sophisticated level of self and social awareness in orcas."

That may help explain the hypersocial nature of the killer whales and how they can cooperate and coordinate so well in the wild, with the ability to plot out hunting and feeding strategies to snare schools of fish or seals or larger whales. It may also help explain how they organize themselves into families and pods and can recognize members of the same clan. It could well allow them to store all sorts of rules: whom to associate with, whom to mate with and at what point of their life cycles these events take place. Dr. Marino says that the killer whale's highly elaborated neocortex "allows the orca to make conscious choices about who to eat and who to fight with. It's not just a 'flip the switch' reflex." It is how, she says, two different orca populations can share resources in the same area with a minimum of conflict. "It is by choice. And you need a big neocortex to control your instincts like that."

The idea that the orca neocortex gives it the capacity to make conscious choices is both poignant and sobering. In combination with the orca's elaborated paralimbic system, the neocortex may be evidence of how integrated emotions and consciousness are for the killer whale—and how emotions dominate the orca's life. Emotional pain for whales—because it is so much part of their social existence—might then be of a higher magnitude than for human beings. It makes it almost possible to apply the word "mourning" to the fact that male orcas can often waste away and perish after the death of their mothers—the dominant centers of their social existence. I was told by trainers in Florida that Tilikum exhibited what they described as mourning behavior after he killed Dawn.

Conscious choice, says Marino, also means that aggressions in captivity are not predatory instincts "gone haywire." The attacks on trainers or fighting between orcas in a marine park are deliberate acts of aggression—a matter of choice. If an orca goes after a trainer, it is not playing, says Marino. "Given that the neocortex is intimately linked with the limbic system," she says, they probably "got angry enough" to act out. It is a conscious act, she explains, not a reflexive one.

The aggressions that I and other trainers have had to deal with rarely occur among the wild adult orca populations from which Sea-World's killer whales trace their descent. From what Dr. Rose and other researchers observed, only young whales among the resident populations in the Pacific Northwest appear to rake each other in the wild. These young whales don't know any better and have not yet been fully instructed in the way of orca behavior in the family unit or pod.

Dr. Marino says she would love to be able to compare the brains of captive orcas to those of wild orcas. "But," she says, SeaWorld and other marine parks "despite saying they are supportive of research, would never turn over a deceased dolphin or whale for that kind of examination." She suspects that the differences would likely be seen in the areas of the brain that respond to chronic stress, such as the hippo-campus. Like all mammals, killer whales' Hippocampal-Pituitary axis helps them to regulate stress. Chronic stress can lead to an impairment of that axis in humans and other mammals, including whales. "When this happens, the hippocampus structure in the brain starts to shrink, affecting memory and emotional regulation," says Marino. "The im-mune system starts to go." For the orcas of SeaWorld, the sources of stress are everywhere—from boredom to the constant training for shows for which the whales have to perform behaviors precisely right to be properly rewarded. Many of SeaWorld's whales had elevated and chronic stress levels reflected in their blood work; many were medi-cated for ulcers.

The whales we train at SeaWorld and other marine parks do not have the familial structure to help them learn the rules of their origi-nal pods and clans and families. When the dominant females in the park resort to raking to impose their will on the rest of the pack, the comparison shouldn't be to orca family units in the wild. In this case, they are acting more like prisoners thrown into the same cell, with all the dysfunctions that come with human incarceration—and with violence as the main way of establishing authority. The conditions in SeaWorld are vastly different from those the whales experience in freedom; and yet their brains are engineered the same way as their cousins in the wild and must wrap—or warp—around the realities of captive existence. That extends to rationalizing or socializing the true yet unnatural dominant presences in their lives—the trainers. I've always wondered how the orcas socialize us into the way they look at the world from their cramped, watery prisons. If we can anthropomorphize them, how do we look when they orca-ize us?

Could it be that, in the process of trying to integrate trainers into their already dysfunctional social hierarchy, orcas in captivity may be more dangerous to humans than orcas in the wild, who have no reason to pursue people as prey? Howard Garrett of the Orca Network believes that may be true. "I think," he says, "they do tend to try to socialize the humans to fit into their structures, which inevitably results in tensions because the humans have to maintain their control and dominance, which are totally foreign to the whales unless coming from their grandmothers or other matriarchs."

Sometimes, you get a sixth sense of that shift in emotion. I remember one particular night with the whale I love most, Takara. I had been swimming with her during the last show on a Saturday, and once it was over, I helped move her back out to the front show pool where the plan was to have her sleep alone. After the gate was secured, I signaled to my supervisor Steve Aibel that I was going to get back into the water with her to rub her down, which would reinforce and reward her for coming back out to the front pool. As I eased into the water with her, she was calm and relaxed but something seemed off. I had an ominous feeling. I looked to Steve and the expression on his face—and the nod of his head—let me know he was sensing exactly what I was thinking: "Get out while you can." Steve and I both felt the energy shift and believed that Takara was beginning to show signs she might prevent me from leaving the pool. She knew the last show of the evening was over. There would be fewer trainers around to assist in a rescue. I did not give her a chance to act on what I feared was on her mind.

When I left the United States for France to train orcas that had never worked with trainers in the water, Mike Scarpuzzi, the vice president of zoological operations at SeaWorld in California, warned me "to go slow with those whales. Those whales are a death waiting to happen." If anyone knew about how quickly orcas can turn, Scarp would. I considered him a brilliant behavioral strategist and respected his work tremendously. I took every behavioral word and theory that came out of his mouth as gospel.

He was not happy to see me leave SeaWorld. No one in San Diego was. But I needed to do it for the challenge. Few people at SeaWorld knew that, when I flew out to the south of France for five days in February 2001, it was to interview for the position of Supervisor of Killer Whale Training with Marineland Antibes. But word got out as soon as I returned. The community of trainers is small and news travels fast.

The French wanted me as quickly as they could get my work visa ready. But I told them I couldn't start until after the summer for two important reasons. One: I was still loyal to SeaWorld and did not want to leave them short-staffed at Shamu Stadium during peak season. Two: I wanted to see the birth of Kasatka's calf, the first progeny of the artificial insemination program and whose inception I attended as a trainer at Kasatka's side.

I thought management would appreciate that. But Scarpuzzi was angry. He told me, "Since you've decided to take all the years we've

170

spent developing you to another park, we've decided to move you to Dolphin Stadium for the summer before you leave." But I stood my ground. I told him it didn't make sense. Why would he send me to a stadium where I did not know the animals? There was no one to replace me at Shamu.

Of course, I realize now that I was making his very point. Trainers with my level of experience are rare and I would be difficult to replace. But I was so angry I told the French I was going to join them immediately. Scarpuzzi would eventually relent and say I could stay at Shamu for the summer. But it was too late. I had already notified France so I gave my two weeks' notice anyway.

Scarpuzzi nevertheless gave me a glowing exit review. He told me he believed that I had done a great job with the whales in California; he also said that because of my success with Kasatka, he believed I was ready for the massive responsibility of training the orcas in Antibes. And that's when he told me to be cautious. I was going to get firsthand experience in how whales learn to deal with the intrusion of trainers into their waters for the first time ever.

For killer whales in captivity, change often provokes aggressive behavior as they try to assimilate what is happening around them. The French whales were used to working with their trainers stationed at the sidelines of the pool. I was joining another American, Lindsay Rubincam, a former SeaWorld trainer at Texas and Florida whom I admired, to work in the water. But by the time I arrived in May 2001, there was already evidence that the French assignment was going to be difficult. While in the water, Lindsay had been struck so hard by the female whale Shouka that she was hospitalized with internal bleeding. Before that, Val, Freya's son, had swum directly at her while thrashing with his mouth open, a well-recognized precursor for aggression. There was a lot of work to be done to make sure the whales learned the new rules being imposed on them.

In terms of behaviorist psychology, this is called a context shift. We had one advantage: the best time for a context shift was when the whales are discovering a new environment. The Marineland stadium in Antibes was newly built (the whales and the trainers who cared for them had been in another, much smaller facility for years). Lindsay and I knew the orcas were going to test the boundaries. The whales always did when novelty was introduced in SeaWorld; the orcas in France would not be any different. It was going to be tough and dangerous. Lindsay and I expected episodes of aggression from the Antibes orcas both in and out of the water.

When I first called Lindsay about working in France, she was so enthusiastic she ran the request up the chain of command in Antibes and got them interested in hiring me right away. Like me, she had started in SeaWorld of Texas but had left for Florida before I got there. We had met a couple of times in Texas when she visited. She had been trying to get the French program off the ground by herself for a year. She had a staff of French trainers, who didn't have the experience required to get into the water with the whales. The French had a slightly mystical philosophy about training orcas, describing the trainer as a "whale healer." Lindsay and I were going to have to work hard to get them on the behavioral science program.

In France I would be swimming with killer whales during the day in a beautiful new stadium right on the Cote d'Azur and living in an apartment with views of the Mediterranean from my living room and bedroom windows. I was just 27 and earning double my salary as a senior trainer at SeaWorld. I even fell in love with a famous French singer of Algerian descent, with whom I would have the most significant relationship of my life.

As beautiful as France was, the Antibes facility had severe short-comings. The pools had no chilling system. In the winter, the water temperature was fine, but in the summer, the warmth made the whales lethargic. The heat also increased the bacteria levels—and the chances for infection. There were no scales to weigh the whales. Lindsay, the trainers and I had to eyeball the whales to guess whether or not they were putting on or losing too much weight.

At SeaWorld, we would have problems with eye burns from an excessive amount of chlorine in the pools. The chlorine solution used was many times stronger than household bleach. The water at Shamu Stadium was also treated with two types of caustic substances: ozone, meant to control bacteria that might contaminate the pool but which has a destructive effect on all living organisms and tissue, including lungs and eyes; and aluminum sulfate, which helps make sure the water is clear but is extremely acidic and, in the wrong proportions, can burn skin and corrode metal. The trainers who swam with the whales would on occasion get eye burns serious enough to require medical attention. Sometimes, they were so severe we could not open our eyes at all. It could take anywhere from two days to two weeks for our eyes to heal sufficiently to allow us back into the water with the whales. Management of the Animal Training Department as well as the Water Quality Department would explain that the whales had foot-pushed us underwater through a "pocket of chlorine" that had not yet dispersed or been properly diluted.

Water quality, however, was far worse in France. One trainer's eyes were so badly burned by excessive chlorine that he had to wear patches over them for more than a week or risk blindness if he exposed them to light. One morning, we came in to work to find sheets of skin peeling off the whales. The system had malfunctioned and had sent chlorine in a continuous stream into the pools throughout the night.

Even the mucus membrane that protected their eyes couldn't stand the intensity of the chemical burn. Their eyes were shut in pain and when we fed them, we had to touch the side of their faces with fish so they would know it was time to eat. The biggest shortcoming of the French marine park, however, was the veterinary staff. SeaWorld had a team of veterinarians in each park to safeguard their multimillion-dollar whales. Marineland in Antibes had only one vet and he wasn't on site or even in France. He lived in the United Kingdom.

As for the French trainers, they looked at Lindsay and me with a mixture of gratitude and envy. They were happy to learn about water-work with orcas. But they realized that it wasn't going to happen right away, that for the first two years it would be just Lindsay and I in the water with the whales. That was hard on some of them because they had known these whales longer than us, in spite of the devotion to the whales that we all shared. Lindsay and I approached the entire process carefully and diplomatically. As soon as we got the whales to accept the new rules of engagement and they began to stabilize in terms of behavior, we slowly introduced the most experienced French trainers to waterwork. There was always a level of animosity underlying the French trainers' relationship with us, in spite of the devotion to the whales that we all shared. After the September 11, 2001, attacks on the United States, Lindsay and I found images of people jumping from the World Trade Center pinned to the walls in the trainer offices. The French trainers had annotated them as if they were judging a diving competition. Lindsay and I were furious but we could never find out which individual trainers did this. No one admitted responsibility. Despite this, I formed great friendships with many beautiful and genuinely wonderful French people, who had nothing to do with Marineland. I miss them and France to this day.

To deal with the challenges in France, it helped that Lindsay and I got along on an almost intuitive level. We were able to read each other's minds with just a look. Of course, we had our disagreements over how to approach the whales behaviorally. But one of the things I always appreciated about Lindsay was that she and I could have a huge argument over behavioral protocols, and then ten minutes later, if I needed something, she'd be there for me. She never held grudges.

I remember one day when I was resisting adopting whale behavior protocols that weren't identical to the California system and Lindsay was insisting on doing things the way Florida did. She finally declared, "It doesn't have to be the California system or the Florida system, this can be our system." That kind of camaraderie helped both of us make the gigantic and dangerous enterprise in France work.

I began this book with my frightening encounter with Freya—Val's mother. I like to think of her as the Kasatka of Antibes. Like Kasatka, she was captured as a young whale off the coast of Iceland and must remember what life in the open Atlantic Ocean was like. Getting her to work with the new waterwork program was one of the biggest challenges for me and Lindsay.

Lindsay and I would together have a scary incident with Freya during a waterwork session. I was working with Freya and Lindsay was working with Val. We were side by side, getting the orcas used to rides along the perimeter in tandem. After we both dived into the pool and had the whales pick us up straddled on their backs, Freya began to displace her son subtly in the water. She did not allow him to keep up with her as they moved through the pool. Not willing to overtake his mother, Val was no longer nose-to-nose with her, falling back a little bit at a time as she asserted her dominance. As the session went on, she began to clearly displace him. Straddling her, I could feel the muscles tighten on her back. She was upset. It was the beginning of a potential aggressive incident.

I began to calculate how to get out of the situation safely. But I was at a disadvantage. Lindsay and Val were on the side closest to the perimeter while Freya and I were closer to the middle of the pool. It would get scarier. Freya began to pull away not just from Val but from the perimeter altogether. I watched helplessly as I got farther and farther from Lindsay and Val. I screamed to Lindsay to get out as fast as she could since I was afraid that Freya might go after Val at any moment. In the past, I'd also seen the dominant whale in a double waterwork scenario go after the other whale's trainer.

Once Freya got me to the middle of the pool she rolled me off her back and then positioned herself in front of me as she emitted upset vocals. I placed both my hands on her rostrum and around her jaws—encouraging her to keep her mouth closed—as I worked to calm her down. At the same time, I saw that Lindsay had been able to step off Val's back to safety in a far corner of the perimeter. Immediately, Freya's vocalizations stopped and she became calm. I bridged her for calming down. She followed all signals and brought me to stage safely with a pec-push. She performed it perfectly. She had chosen not to go over to the dark side.

Eventually, Freya would learn to work with Val in shows. And I developed a strong relationship with her and, like all the dominant females I have worked with, she has a special place in my heart.

Freya was a challenge and the most dangerous of the orcas we worked with in France. But there were incidents of aggression with other whales. One such incident occurred with Shouka, who was born in captivity to Sharkane, a whale captured near Iceland. Once during a show, I dived into the water and gave Shouka the signal to swim beneath me to pick me up for a straddle ride around the perimeter of the pool. I turned around to look for her only to see her dorsal fin submerge underwater. She then drilled me in the middle of my back, the force of which pushed me under and smashed me up against the acrylic wall in front of the audience. She swam off, vanishing into the water, where visibility was poor because of inadequate filtration.

I knew I had to figure out where she was before trying to swim out, if only to make certain she would not come at me again. I couldn't see her. I called out to the trainers on stage and around the pool, asking where she was. But no one could see her.

Even though I was along the perimeter of the pool, I didn't dare move an arm toward the bar without knowing where she was. Petey's minimal skulling motion, as I mentioned earlier, had infuriated Kasatka because it indicated he was possibly trying to get out of the pool before she would allow him to exit. I put my face in the water again. I looked straight down—and there she was, lying in wait at the bottom of the pool approximately 30 feet below with her mouth open, looking right at me.

It was the look all experienced trainers recognize and dread: a whale at the bottom of the pool that has decided to become predator with you as the orca's prey.

The crucial thing was to see it coming. As soon as I caught her positioning herself against me that way, I pointed at her to let her know that I had seen her. Then what was almost a quantum shift took place: predation was superseded by cooperation, as if the intelligence of the target had somehow affected the intention of the attacker.

Shouka responded by closing her mouth, rising calmly toward me at the surface after I signaled for her to come to me. I blew my whistle to bridge her, to let her know she had done well to shut her jaws and cooperate. At my signal, I put a foot on each of her pectoral flippers and she pushed me toward the stage. When I got there, I gave her all that was left of the food, about 15 pounds of fish. She followed my signals for the rest of the session. But I have no doubt that she was

177

stalking me in the murk. If I had made a move to get out of the water, she would have come at me. There is no beating a killer whale's speed, no matter how close you think you are to safety.

On another occasion, Shouka was giving me a straddle pick-up when she became extremely vocal, her back muscles tightening. It was in the middle of a ride along the perimeter of the pool and so I stood up on her back in an attempt to jump off and onto land and safety inches away. But just as I was thinking of doing so—with only a split second to make the decision—she pulled away from the edge, giving me no chance to escape at all. Jumping into the water was not an option given how fast she could swim. If I had jumped and not succeeded in getting out of the pool, she would have grabbed me and pulled me underwater. So I went down to my knees on her back as she swam to the middle of the pool, all the time emitting short, tense staccato vocals, the muscles of her back so tense that her body was jerking. The moment she had me in the middle of the pool, she rolled over and dumped me off her back. At first, she slowly swam away from me. Then she turned back fast. With her mouth open, she swam right at me. I stuck my legs out straight underwater—a signal for her to give me a pec-push toward the stage. It was a gamble. Would she follow the signal?

She chose to give me the pec-push. I put one hand on her upper rostrum and one on her lower jaw and asked her to close her mouth. She did. I bridged her with whistles every time she did the right thing, motivating her to continue to make good decisions. Once she brought me to the stage and I stepped off, I immediately fed her.

Shouka was a tough whale to settle down. She was about eight years old at the time and weighed an estimated 4,000 pounds—small for a killer whale her age because she had not been properly fed when she was young and her growth was stunted. She had been the first orca born in the Antibes Marineland, before the expansion that led to the hiring of Lindsay and me. The French did not really know how to manage the weight of their orcas and how much to feed them, especially their first calf.

I had another encounter with Shouka that could have been catastrophic. A few trainers and I were in the front show pool, at the stage, feeding all seven Antibes whales together. As I crouched forward to feed Shouka, I looked to my right to see how the other whales and their trainers were doing, just to make sure that there was no evidence of the whales fighting or trying to displace each other. I also wanted to make sure the French team was making the right behavioral decisions with the orcas.

Shouka and I were on stage left, at the end of the line of whales. Just as I looked to my right, she rose out of the pool and grabbed my wetsuit where there was a fraction of slack at my chest. It was an amazing feat: to spot the only place where a body-tight wetsuit had a weakness and then to pinch it precisely with her enormous mouth in an attempt to pull me into the pool. I instinctively shifted my weight backwards, falling into a squat, just in time to pop the slack out of her mouth. If she had pulled me into the pool with the other whales, I probably wouldn't have made it out. At that point waterwork was still a novelty to all of the whales. And among them was Kim, an adult male orca that Lindsay and I knew posed too much of a risk for us—or any trainer—to work with in the water. Given how opportunistic killer whales can be, the odds would not have been in my favor.

Even whales you love will have their moments. I adored Val. But he would rebel too, if in a more subtle way than Shouka or his mother, Freya. At one point, for about two weeks, Val thought it novel to pull me under the surface of the pool by my socks. It sounds funny but there is really nothing amusing about being dragged against your will into the depths by an orca.

It would happen when I was performing a foot-push on him or sometimes as we were face-to-face at the surface. He would sink and grab at my feet. With incredible precision, he would work my sock away from my toes until he had enough slack to grab it in his mouth. Once he had enough slack off the toe, he would grab it and jerk the sock, pulling me underwater. Once I was underwater, he would try to get the sock completely off. That would have been disastrous for me: a large part of the sock ran up my calf, beneath the suit, extending up to my knee. I would have drowned as he ripped my wetsuit apart. I tried to time my breaths so that every time he yanked me under I would have just taken one. But he never kept me under for too long. He always allowed me to redirect him after he experimented with my sock. This happened several times until I taught him that this was not among the approved list of behaviors for orcas in Antibes. I was always grateful that he cared enough to work up the slack from the toes—instead of just grabbing my entire foot. After two weeks, I trained him out of his obsession with this novel behavior and he lost interest in my socks.

In the end, the work in France would prove too risky—not so much because of the whales but because the company that owned the marine park did next to nothing to improve conditions that I said were dangerous, including the murkiness of the water, which made it difficult to make out precursors to orca aggression. My contract was to be renewed annually and I signed on for a second year on the promise that the water quality would improve. When it didn't, I decided that I would not put up with the risk any longer and returned to the United States in 2003.

I was still in France when I met Dawn Brancheau. She was already one of the stars of SeaWorld Orlando. But this was September 2001, and she had traveled to Antibes to visit Lindsay, one of her best friends.

Lindsay had to work and I had time off so Dawn and I spent a day together in the old village in Antibes where I lived in a one-bedroom flat at 25 Rue Aubernon, just 75 steps from the beach. The village was lovely, with cobblestone streets and houses—such as the place I lived—that were hundreds of years old. We were on the sea wall looking out at the Mediterranean on September 11 when I got a cell phone call from my mother. She said, "You will never believe what is happening in the United States." America was under attack. Dawn's husband, Scott, had been planning to join her in France but couldn't because all flights were grounded. Dawn spent nearly two weeks in France, with a lot of time at Marineland.

Although I was not a part of her close circle, Dawn was pals with two of my good friends, Lindsay and Wendy. And through them, we kept track of each other's careers. She had a warm heart and was a great trainer, among the best at SeaWorld. She would, however, become a symbol of the marine park at its worst—and an example of what happens when a whale refuses to come back from the dark side.

My experience in France with orcas unaccustomed to humans in the water only reinforces my belief that while the relationship between trainer and whale can be beautiful, the overall situation—that of captivity—makes the orcas dysfunctional and dangerous.

Every now and then, the public got an inkling of this. An episode of aggression with a trainer could not be hidden, and it frequently made the news. Most of the time, the trainer would laugh it off in public—and the media would move on. But the end of 2009 and the beginning of 2010 brought a double-whammy that the corporation is still reeling from—and which changed my life and my career forever.

It was the morning of Christmas Eve 2009. I was already anxious because Takara was due to give birth any moment. All of the trainers at

Shamu Stadium were on call to rush to the pool to help out when it happened. When my phone rang, however, it was not to ask me to assist at the birth of Takara's calf. Management had just received news about an incident at Loro Parque, a marine park associated with SeaWorld in the Canary Islands in Spain. Keto, a 14-year-old male orca with whom I had worked briefly in California, had just killed a trainer named Alexis Martinez during a training session. Scarpuzzi—whose official title is vice president of Zoological Operations at the California park—was on his way to Spain to meet with the SeaWorld supervisor at Loro Parque, who had been sent over from the California park and reported to Scarp. We were told that the supervisor was so distraught that Scarpuzzi was unable to get details from him over the phone.

For a few days to almost a week depending on the park, as a precaution, all waterwork with orcas stopped at the three US SeaWorld facilities—though trainers, including myself, were back in the pools with the whales before we got any details of what happened. It was imperative for SeaWorld to figure out what had gone wrong. All four killer whales at Loro Parque were owned by SeaWorld and came from SeaWorld's parks and breeding programs. About three weeks would pass before we got the full story.

Scarpuzzi returned from Spain, stopping in Florida, then Texas, on the way to California, to present his findings to SeaWorld Shamu Stadium trainers, showing us underwater and aerial video footage of the incident. It was admirably thorough and detailed. And chilling to watch. We knew how it would turn out, that a fellow trainer would be dead at the end of it.

The training session had started at about 11 a.m. in seemingly normal fashion, with Alexis and Keto going through routine behaviors. Standing on the edge of the pool, Alexis asked the orca to do a "TNT" (as in dynamite), a behavior in which the whale swims from the back pool, underwater and unseen, to the front show pool, where he breaks the surface of the water with his massive tail flukes. Keto did it correctly and he was bridged and called over by another trainer, who asked the orca to slide-out and rewarded him with fish. That trainer subsequently emptied his bucket and filled it with water with which to splash Keto.

The same trainer then sent Keto swimming along the perimeter of the show pool back toward Alexis, who was waiting in the corner. He rewarded the orca with a rub down. At that point, Alexis got into the water with Keto to practice the stand-on spy hop—the same behavior during which I had broken my ribs just two months earlier, when I slipped off Takara. Unlike the hydro or rocket hop—where the whale throws you into the air—in the stand-on spy hop, the trainer maintains contact with his or her feet on the rostrum of the whale as the orca clears almost the entire length of his or her body vertically out of the water. The trainer remains balanced dramatically on the tip of the whale's rostrum as both rise until gravity brings them both back vertically into the pool.

Keto reached the proper height but came up in a bit of a twist, which sent Alexis off balance, and he fell off the rostrum. Because the behavior did not come off successfully, Alexis did not reward Keto. Instead, he issued what trainers call a "Least Reinforcing Scenario" (LRS)—eye contact and a short, three-second pause that teaches the whales that they failed but still have the opportunity for reinforcement if they remain calm. The neutral LRS was developed sometime in the 1980s after whales reacted badly—as in lunging at the trainers—when they received a signal that indicated they had failed.

If a whale responds to the LRS by remaining calm, the trainer may choose to give the orca some kind of reward (in behavioral terms "on a ratio"). Keto was calm; and so Alexis returned to stage with

Keto and rewarded him with a snowball of ice. They then proceeded to try the spy hop again. Keto again reached the proper height but still twisted. Alexis fell off again. Alexis issued another LRS. Keto was called over by another trainer at the slide-out and fed with fish before being sent back for more work with Alexis, who remained in the water.

Alexis grabbed Keto's rostrum with both hands to steer the whale underwater toward the stage for what is called a "stage haul-out." That was when things began to go wrong. Keto started to take Alexis deeper than needed or normal for the behavior. Alexis let go of Keto's rostrum so that he could float back to the surface to give the whale another LRS. But Keto positioned himself between Alexis and the stage.

SeaWorld supervisor Brian Rokeach, who was the control spotter for the session, immediately sensed what was happening and asked for an underwater tone to call Keto back to the stage and away from Alexis. Keto responded, coming toward the stage; Rokeach put his palm facing out as a hand target, a signal for Keto to come to him and rest his rostrum on the palm of his hand. This is one of the tightest forms of control with the whale because the trainer has actual physical contact with the orca. Rokeach would later say that while Keto responded to the hand target, the orca "was not fully committed" and was "big eyed and watching Alexis." Usually, that means that the whale is only barely touching the trainer's hand and its body and eyes are focused on something else. The incident report does not record Keto receiving primary reinforcement—fish—for responding to the hand target, just Rokeach telling Alexis to swim out of the pool.

As soon as Alexis began to swim toward the perimeter of the pool, Keto split from Brian's control and headed for Alexis. The whale grabbed Alexis' leg and pulled him to the bottom of the pool. Rokeach hand-slapped the water in an attempt to regain control of Keto but the whale refused to respond to that most elemental of commands. Rokeach then began to bang a bucket of fish on stage, a signal that food was available for the whale. Keto did not respond. Rokeach attempted another hand slap recall and when Keto refused the third time, Rokeach sounded the emergency alarm. The other trainers scrambled to deploy a large net to isolate Keto in the show pool. Whales—and dolphins—instinctively flee nets. It is the easiest way to prod a misbehaving orca in the direction you want it to go. (After a 2004 incident in San Antonio, nets were always on standby at the three SeaWorld stadiums and at affiliated parks like Loro Parque.) One trainer made sure the other three whales in the area were moved into one of the back pools, making sure there was a vacant one. The gate of that back pool was opened to corral Keto, once the net separated him from Alexis.

During the aggression, Keto surfaced to breathe, leaving Alexis at the bottom of the pool. Then the whale went back to get Alexis, pushing the trainer around the pool before surfacing with his body draped across his rostrum. Rokeach hand-slapped the water again, desperately trying to get the orca to respond and come to the stage. Again Keto refused. Once the net was deployed, Keto swam into the empty back pool. When the trainers attempted to close the gate, however, Keto turned around and wedged his head between it and prevented it from shutting. The trainers had to use another net to make sure he moved away from the gate so it could be secured.

The video that Scarpuzzi showed us is haunting. In one scene, underwater footage shows Keto swimming into camera range with Alexis, who looks alive. It appeared as if Keto was giving the trainer the classic pec-push to the stage. Alexis was looking directly at the lens, his eyes open. But when the video was slowed down, everyone could tell, by the way his feet and hands were loose and limp, and from the expression on his face, that he was gone. As the orca was penned, Alexis' body sank to the bottom of the 36-foot deep front show pool.

With Keto secured in the back pool, Rokeach dived into the pool with another trainer to retrieve Alexis' body. In the video, it took the supervisor only 7 seconds to reach Alexis 36 feet down. But it took him more than 30 seconds to bring Alexis to the surface because the body had filled with water. Rokeach frantically began attempting CPR, rescue breathing and even the use of a defibrillator. Paramedics arrived and took over the efforts and continued to try and restart Alexis' heart on site and in the ambulance. He could not be revived and was pronounced dead at 11:35 a.m.

I wanted to know more. The US trainers had been hearing all sorts of stories while waiting for the official report. At the San Antonio presentation, I asked Scarpuzzi if Keto had crushed Alexis after he pulled him under. Scarpuzzi hesitated, then broke eye contact with me. He looked around the room at the other trainers and said, "We don't know what happened. What most likely happened was that Alexis panicked as Keto grabbed his leg and pulled him under, and he drowned."

Other trainers present during the incident and involved in the rescue attempt would later tell me that there was a massive amount of blood coming from Alexis' body as Rokeach attempted CPR. Blood was oozing all over the stage, they said, everywhere on Alexis' face as well as on the supervisor's—soaking everything. The blood would have been inconsistent with the SeaWorld version of a simple drowning. But never, at any time during this meeting, or in the incident report, was there any mention of profuse bleeding from Alexis' ears, mouth and nose, signs of massive internal injuries.

Scarpuzzi's answer to my question became the standard response from management on the Loro Parque incident from that point forward: Alexis most likely panicked and drowned. In the documentary *Blackfish,* Alexis' girlfriend described what she saw in the morgue: it was as if Alexis' chest had exploded. The Spanish autopsy concluded that the technical cause of death was drowning, but what fundamentally led to it was "mechanical asphyxiation due to compression and crushing of the thoracic abdomen with injuries to the vital organs."

Exactly two months after Alexis' death, tragedy struck again. On the morning of February 24, 2010, I had just finished doing sessions with some of the whales in the back pools of SeaWorld San Antonio when I noticed the general manager of the park and some other vice-presidents and senior management come through the back gate at Shamu Stadium. I knew something serious was going on because visits by the top brass were rare. All of us were soon summoned to the trainers' office where the general manager Dan Decker said, "There's been an accident at the Orlando park and a trainer was killed."

People gasped; some began to sob and bury their faces in their hands. I thought that perhaps a big waterwork act had gone wrong. Maybe a trainer's foot slipped on a hydro or rocket hop, and they fell and broke their back or neck. That was something we were always afraid of. But then Dan said, "It's Dawn and Tilikum and he still has her."

The name Tilikum sent a chill through me—and most likely throughout the room. No one was allowed to do waterwork with him because he and two other orcas had killed a trainer at his first marine park before he was sold to SeaWorld. Then, in July 1999, the corpse of Daniel Dukes, who had secreted himself in SeaWorld Orlando overnight, was found dead, naked and draped on Tilikum's back. I could feel the fear and anxiety rise in the room. "Not Dawn," I said to myself. "It can't be Dawn." She was one of the most experienced and talented trainers in the corporation. This couldn't have been an accident, I concluded even before I knew the details. This was aggression.

Like the best of experienced trainers, Dawn believed in her ability to stay safe with the whales. It was the same kind of confidence I had in my own abilities, the same as those of my most seasoned colleagues. It is a faith that you are committed to the moment you zip up your wetsuit. It's a belief and trust in both your own behavioral knowledge and abilities as well as your relationship with the whale you are working or swimming with. The more experience you have and the deeper and longer your relationships are with orcas, the more protection you have to prevent bad things from happening. That familiarity with the whale often gives you enough time—even if just seconds—to get you safely out of a potentially catastrophic situation. Or else, if things have already turned bad, your relationship with the whale and your experience will help you redirect the orca, allowing the whale to choose to calm down and follow your signals rather than have the aggression escalate. What had happened that had made it impossible for Dawn to get out of this predicament?

The most bone-chilling words Dan said were "And he still has her." It shook me to my core. I could wrap my brain around the fact that Tilikum had killed her. As experienced trainers, we know what these whales are capable of doing. But I was disturbed to hear that Tilikum was still holding on to her and that SeaWorld didn't have the power to take her body away from him. How much time had passed since the incident took place, since emergency efforts were activated, since the word traveled through the bureaucracy to senior officials in Florida and then the broader corporate decision was made to tell trainers at the Shamu Stadiums in San Diego and San Antonio?

I left the office and immediately called Wendy in California. I knew she was close to Dawn and I was worried about how she was going to handle the news. She was devastated and sobbing. She had thrown up when she was told along with the other trainers in San Diego. I then thought of Lindsay in France. She and Dawn were best friends and had been in each other's weddings. Lindsay had also worked with Tilikum in Florida before going to France. How was she going to hear about Dawn? I knew Lindsay still maintained close ties with the Florida park, but with all the chaos going on, there was a good chance that no one would think to call her. I imagined her waking up the next day, checking the computer for news and finding out that way. I tried frantically to call her. Fortunately, her mother had reached her and told her what had happened before my call. But I'll always remember the devastation in Lindsay's voice when I finally reached her. She was furious and wanted to hear about everything. By the time we spoke, many of the details had been revealed to us at SeaWorld. I said they were grisly but she insisted and I understood her need to know.

Dawn had been the trainer assigned to work with Tilikum for Dine with Shamu that day. All the precautions were in place—she had a spotter and she was not doing waterwork with him. As the leader of the team that trained him, she knew Tilikum extremely well, enjoying what trainers call a "strong relationship"—one in which a trainer knows exactly what to do to make sure the orca performs well. At the Dine with Shamu pool, Tilikum went through a couple of behaviors incorrectly but he was still very good overall in behavioral terms. As part of his reward, Dawn walked over to interact playfully with him, laying herself down on the pool ledge, which is only shin-high in water. Some people who have analyzed the incident say that she was in the water. But waterwork is defined as being deep enough in the pool that your body floats. Dawn was not breaking any rules or protocols.

As she lay on her stomach talking with him, Tilikum grabbed her by the arm and pulled her into the water. SeaWorld says that Tilikum yanked her into the water by her hair. But based on eyewitness and video accounts, it is almost certain that he pulled her into the water by her arm when she was lying on the porch platform interacting with him.

Dawn's spotter at Dine with Shamu was a trainer who was senior and experienced enough to be able to work with Tilikum and to call him over in an emergency. But when the incident took place, she was downstairs at the underwater viewing area, waiting behind the glass to receive Tilikum after Dawn, as planned, directed him down the pool to entertain the visitors below. All the spotter saw was the splash as Tilikum pulled Dawn in; she ran back to the pool, but the route back up was circuitous. The only other trainer at the Dine with Shamu pool area was not qualified to work with Tilikum and could only sound the emergency alarms. That brought the other trainers to poolside, including one who was senior enough to work with Tilikum. But all attempts to call the orca over were in vain.

Tilikum struck Dawn several times with his head, seizing her in his mouth as he dragged her under, swimming around beneath the surface with her in his jaws. He had her at various moments by her arm, by the neck and shoulder area, by her hair and by her leg.

The emergency procedures hit a few critical snags. As it was deployed, the net got stuck on the fake rocks that had been added to the pool for entertainment reasons. Meanwhile, the back pools were blocked because they were occupied by the other whales in the park. Agitated by Tilikum's rampage, they were refusing to move from one pool to another, and a separate net had to be deployed to herd them together into another pool, in order to leave one empty specifically for Tilikum. Ultimately, rescue workers and trainers used the net to shepherd Tilikum from the Dine with Shamu pool to a med pool, which was three pools away. This med pool was the only one that had a floor that could be lifted mechanically. That was the only way rescuers were going to be able to get to Dawn. All that time, her body was in Tilikum's mouth; and as the net forced him from pool to pool toward the lifting floor, he grew increasingly upset and possessive of her, shaking Dawn in his mouth, destroying her body.

The lifting floor of the med pool artificially beached Tilikum; he was further immobilized with a net thrown over him. Only then, about 45 minutes after the incident began, were the trainers able to get his mouth open to remove Dawn. By then, she had been scalped, her spinal cord was severed, her ribs broken, and her left arm had been torn off. One poignant symbol was recovered later from the bottom of the pool: Dawn's whistle, the bridge between trainer and whale, our rosary and reminder of the proximity of death.

The initial statement by the Orange County sheriff's office—which has jurisdiction over SeaWorld Orlando—was that Dawn had slipped and fallen into the pool. Jim Solomons, the spokesman for the sheriff, made that announcement after he had emerged from a private meeting with SeaWorld's president, Dan Brown; the corporation's vice president of Animal Training, Chuck Tompkins; and Orlando's curator of Animal Training, Kelly Flaherty-Clark. They stood to Solomons' left as he spoke. None of them attempted to correct him.

Only after park guests who had witnessed the incident started coming forward to give accounts that contradicted the statement did SeaWorld officials issue another version. They said that the sheriff's office was wrong: Dawn had not fallen, but Tilikum had grabbed her ponytail, which he saw as something novel. In effect, SeaWorld declared, it was an act of playful exploration; Tilikum thought Dawn's hair was a new stimulus; he wasn't going after her in an aggressive way; Tilikum did not attack Dawn.

What SeaWorld did not explain at the time was that the whales in the corporation have been desensitized to ponytails. In the intricate process during which SeaWorld's trainers plan out their daily dealings with the orcas, we work through all possible scenarios—including what objects may potentially annoy the whales. Trainers long ago decided that whales must be taught not to pay attention to ponytails, that the hairstyle of the trainer should mean nothing to them. Tilikum, like every whale in the SeaWorld system, had long shrugged off the novelty of ponytails. SeaWorld would not admit to this until it had to provide testimony in court for the case OSHA brought against the corporation as a result of Dawn's death.

The more outrageous part of SeaWorld's account of what happened is its insinuation that Dawn's death was the unfortunate result of a playful encounter and of Tilikum's habit of not giving up objects once he had taken possession of them, clinging to them like a child with its favorite toy. The implication is that Dawn was wrong to wear her hair in a ponytail.

There was nothing playful about the way Tilikum treated her. He destroyed her body, all the while emitting vocals indicating he was extremely upset, according to trainers who were part of the rescue effort, and he refused every attempt to be emergency recalled. Three years after her death, as SeaWorld waged a PR battle against the documentary *Blackfish,* the company sent out a refutation of the film that included the line, "Tilikum did not attack Dawn."

SeaWorld held to that line when OSHA fined it for the Tilikum incident. Challenging the ruling, SeaWorld brought forward their expert witness Jeff Andrews, a former trainer I had worked with in California, to testify that Tilikum—despite a history SeaWorld trainers knew—had never been an aggressive whale and that Dawn had made the mistake of letting her hair float into the water, which tantalized the whale. Tilikum, Andrews said, "didn't really intend to kill Dawn; he was just controlling her movements so that she couldn't reach the surface. . . . The only thing that led to this event was a mistake by Ms. Brancheau. From the moment he pulled her into the water until she drowned, Tilikum was never aggressive toward her."

The judge presiding over SeaWorld's appeal would have none of that. He pointed out that Andrews had never worked with Tilikum, had never questioned eyewitnesses and had not reviewed the final investigation file of the sheriff's department or read Dawn's autopsy report. The judge also said that Andrews had not read Tilikum's official SeaWorld profile, and that he had relied solely on the information given to him by Chuck Tompkins, who was not present when the incident occurred. Andrews had not worked for SeaWorld or with any killer whales for nine years before Dawn's death. Since his testimony, Andrews has been rehired by SeaWorld as a vice president.

We will never know why Tilikum made that decision to grab Dawn or whether he intended to kill her. What every experienced trainer knows with 100 percent certainty is that it was an aggressive act—the very kind we try to avoid by meticulously documenting orca behavior. I never worked in the Orlando park nor have I ever trained Tilikum. But I know what orca aggression is.

There may well have been other factors that contributed to that tragedy, but SeaWorld has said little about them. What has not been explored in the official accounts is the fact that the other whales at the park appeared to have already been agitated before Tilikum grabbed Dawn. A Shamu Stadium show had to be abruptly ended because the whales were displacing each other socially and refusing to come over in response to trainers' signals. The whales in the community of a single park feed off each other's agitation—and that frustration could very well have been transmitted to Tilikum over at the Dine with Shamu pool. The answer may lie in the broader detailed records that Sea-World keeps of whale behavior—not just of Tilikum but of the other whales in the park on the day of the attack. But it may take years—and a lawsuit—to get the company to make the data public.

The deaths of Alexis and Dawn were crucial to waking me to the reality of SeaWorld. The obfuscation over Tilikum's intentions served no one's interests, certainly not the whale's. For some of us within the corporation, it only offered more evidence that SeaWorld was defending him because he was one of the most prolific suppliers of sperm for its breeding program. But SeaWorld's actions also proved that the corporation did not have the backs of the trainers who put their lives at risk for the sake of the whales. Alexis and Dawn loved their jobs and loved the orcas they worked with. But after they were killed, SeaWorld blamed them for their own deaths.

I had seen the dark side of SeaWorld.

10

LOSING MY RELIGION

I admired the way SeaWorld sent Mike Scarpuzzi to all its facilities to explain the circumstances surrounding Alexis Martinez's death in Spain. The video that Scarpuzzi provided us with, as well as his almost second-by-second reconstruction of the horrific December 2009 incident, was crucial to trainer understanding of worst-case scenarios. We could learn from the tragedy—learn more about how to keep ourselves safer in our daily dealings with the whales.

In a disturbing contrast, SeaWorld did not distribute an incident report to the trainers after Dawn died. I asked to see the video that I knew existed because a camera is always on to record what happens in the pools. I was told, "Leave it alone. There is nothing to learn from it." But I wanted to see if Dawn had tried to work through the aggression, to see how she might have been strategizing to get out of the pool.

Did she have time to make eye contact with Tilikum? To try to bring him back from the dark side? Chuck Tompkins finally told me, "John, there is nothing there behaviorally."

I'd get more of the inside story after I visited the Florida facility in December 2011. Every year, each park in the SeaWorld system tries to send one trainer to one of the other facilities. It wasn't really to learn from each other. As is evident from the way Lindsay and I argued over behavior protocols in Antibes, San Diego, San Antonio and Orlando were all very much set in their ways. But it was a chance to get to see what the differences were—and a chance to network. I'd get into a wetsuit and be on stage and poolside, watching how the trainers interacted with the whales during sessions and shows. Being in Orlando also gave me a chance to see how the park was dealing with Tilikum in the aftermath of Dawn's death.

Tilikum was essentially kept in isolation and, even when he was in a show, his presence was limited. I saw him perform with Trua, Takara's son, and the younger orca clearly did not want to be with him, leaving the pool they shared as quickly as he could. Toward the end of my Florida trip, Tilikum fell ill. His blood work came back with worrisome readings and he was heavily medicated with dexamethasone, a steroid that is usually given as a last resort. After I got back to Texas, he fell even more seriously ill and SeaWorld was afraid they might lose him. But he recovered. The talk among trainers, however, was that he had, at one point in his illness, lost approximately 1,000 pounds.

None of the trainers who were working with Tilikum when I was visiting Florida seemed anxious about being in close proximity with him. No one, of course, could do waterwork with him. None of us could with any of the whales since Dawn's death. In the immediate aftermath of the February 2010 tragedy, SeaWorld had voluntarily suspended waterwork with all orcas. But in August 2010, OSHA ruled that SeaWorld trainers had to stay out of the water completely. Sea-World sued to throw out that ruling and a $75,000 fine imposed by the agency.

The trainers who worked with Tilikum all seemed to love him. Right after the incident with Dawn, some had been openly contemptuous of Tilikum, with at least one throwing food at him and yelling abuse instead of carefully feeding him. There was no evidence of that unprofessional behavior when I was on the premises. That says a lot about the trainer mind-set—understanding that, as intelligent as the orcas are, you can't impose your thinking on them.

As a member of the big SeaWorld family, I'd met some of the Florida trainers before; in fact, I'd known some of them for years. As the week of my visit went by, I would hear about what happened on that day as they tried to rescue Dawn. The one story that moved me the most involved a highly experienced trainer named Laura Surovik—and it reflects what I believe about trainers and whales having a bond that not even tragedy can break.

Laura is probably the most experienced and knowledgeable orca trainer in SeaWorld, with 24 years of experience at Shamu Stadium. She had worked with Tilikum when he arrived in Florida in January 1992 and knew him better than anyone else. But as the result of a promotion, to become the second-highest-ranking animal curator in Orlando, Laura had been reassigned to Dolphin Stadium at the end of 2009. She and Dawn were best friends. They wore rings to signify the strength of that friendship. But February 24, 2010, would bring two of the most important beings in Laura's life in fatal conflict. It was like having a good friend kill an even better friend.

Laura was at work on her side of the marine park. She was on the phone with Kelly Flaherty-Clark, the Animal Training curator at Orlando, when Kelly said she'd just been told by Dan Brown, the park's president, that the emergency alarm had gone off at Shamu Stadium. Laura looked at her husband, Mike, a supervisor at Sea Lion Stadium, and said, "I've got to go." She drove to Shamu across the compound. It was chaos when she got there.

"Who is it?" she shouted to the crowd that had gathered.

"Tilikum and Dawn," came the response. "He has Dawn."

Laura ran to the platform at the Dine with Shamu pool. Tilikum had Dawn in his mouth. Laura recalled that Dawn's hair was missing. She saw that the trainers were deploying the net to try to force Tilikum from one pool into another so that they could finally get him to a med pool with a lifting floor. Her heart was racing. She didn't know whether Dawn was dead or alive.

The trainers were able to move Tilikum into a med pool, but it was one without a lifting floor, and so they had to move him on through the linked pools. As she later told a detective of the Orlando sheriff's office in a taped conversation that has been made public, "My first thought was I was very mad that we didn't have that lift station because of this animal we know he's killed two other people." At that point, she still didn't know if Dawn was dead. She was still in Tilikum's jaws. Laura began to pray about what to do next.

Laura saw a Shamu supervisor, Jenny Mairot, being comforted by her husband. She walked over to hug Jenny, who said, "She's gone, Laura. She's gone." At that point, Laura turned and thought for a moment. Another trainer then said, "It seems as though we're exacerbating it." Laura agreed. "Yes, you're right. Let's just calm down. I will get to Kelly."

She asked Kelly Flaherty-Clark, SeaWorld Orlando's curator of Animal Training, if she could tell everyone to back off. "She's already gone and we don't want him to mangle her body." She wanted to preserve the dignity of the friend she loved.

After Clark ordered the rescuers off, Tilikum appeared to relax a bit. Laura then went into the locker room, removed her street clothes and put on a wetsuit. "I had made the decision," she later told a detective of the Orlando sheriff's office in the taped conversation. "I'm getting that body. I'm getting my friend." Her advantage was her years-long relationship with Tilikum. "He knows me," she told the detective.

The orca was finally at a pool with a lift station, and Laura waited for the floor to lift him up, essentially beaching him. She stepped onto the platform and made eye contact with the whale who had her friend in his mouth, shaking the body back and forth. She looked at Tilikum again, right into his eyes, and said in a strong voice, "It's alright, baby. Settle down." She knelt and cradled Dawn's torso while Tilikum still had her in his jaws. "It's alright. Let go," she told him. "Let go." Tilikum seemed to be responding.

The rescuers were once again trying to get a net over Tilikum's head. They had already draped one over his body. "He almost let her go," Laura told them. "Just tuck it around his rostrum and he'll let go." They did and she was able to extricate her friend.

She now focused all her attention on Dawn, looking at her face and bringing the body to a place where no one could gawk as they cut the wetsuit away and tried in vain to use the defibrillator to bring her back. The rescuers realized that Dawn's left arm had been torn off but managed to reopen Tilikum's mouth to retrieve it. Dawn's "sister ring"—identical to the one she shared with Laura—was on the hand of that arm.

After calling Dawn's husband, Scott, with the news, Laura tried to help Kelly Flaherty-Clark move Tilikum from the med pool to isolate him in a back pool once the mechanical lift was lowered. Still in her wetsuit, Laura took a bucket of fish and tried to convince the orca to move into another pool. He appeared to be responding to some of her signals. "Good boy, okay, you ready?" she asked. She slapped the water on the far side to try to get him to move; he looked as if he might. But, ultimately, he refused to leave the med pool area. Laura said it was because he could see that Dawn was still nearby, her body covered in a black blanket only a few feet away from Tilikum on the other side of the wall. "He knew she was there," she told the detective on tape. "That was his possession. Don't try to take that away."

The best trainers know there are no moral equivalencies between humans and orcas. Like Laura Surovik, they give the whales the proper respect and space to be whales under the duress of captivity. Good trainers are sensitive to the subtle danger of anthropomorphizing: while humans and orcas may share the same feelings, killer whales do not think like human beings.

There is another factor to consider. The world was surprised by the gentleness of orcas when they were first captured and displayed in aquariums in the 1960s. But the ensuing decades of industrial-strength marine park isolation has most likely skewed the way orcas look at people—through the painful prism of imprisonment. Whatever remains of that gentleness with human beings—never their prey in the seas—must now be thrown into the social calculus of prisoner and jail-keeper. The repetition and boredom, the lack of freedom to move, the tiny two-legged creatures that control the food supply—all that is like nothing the whales would have had to deal with in the wild. They are no longer really orcas but mutants, genetically killer whales but made up of warped psychologies.

With its careful documentation of virtually every interaction between trainers and whales, SeaWorld is—within the organization—cognizant of the complex relationship between humans and orcas. Yet through the years, its attempts at damage control—not just the way it spun Dawn's death—have failed to explain the difficult reality of captivity to the public. Instead, the script always ends up proclaiming that the whale is never really wrong. That simplistic perspective is a disgusting disservice to the trainers who love the whales and risk their bodies every day to work with them.

After Dawn died, SeaWorld said it was because she had made the mistake of letting her ponytail touch the water, inadvertently attracting Tilikum's attention. After Alexis died, the official line was that he panicked and drowned. Loro Parque—which is supervised by Sea-World—issued a statement reading in part, "This was an unfortunate accident . . . The study of the facts shows that the animal's behavior did not correspond to the way in which these marine mammals attack their prey in the wild, but was rather a shifting of position." This statement made it sound as if Alexis just happened to drown in the pool after he was accidentally bumped by the whale; in contrast, the official autopsy report described the incident as a "violent death" and listed Alexis' injuries as multiple cuts and bruises, the collapse of both lungs, fractures of the ribs and sternum, a lacerated liver, severely damaged vital organs and puncture marks consistent with an orca's teeth.

SeaWorld spins its stories this way to minimize the damage to the corporation and to manage the commercial image of the orca. While acknowledging that the killer whale can be dangerous, SeaWorld keeps the risk within the realm of public acceptability. It would not be advisable—from a business point of view—to admit that a combination of behavioral strictures and cramped quarters have deformed the natural character of the orcas and made them riskier for trainers to deal with.

Trainers instinctively know that reforming SeaWorld potentially means changing the nature of their jobs—and the threat that a new

SeaWorld would dispense with them altogether. Certainly that would happen if SeaWorld ceased to exist. That anxiety works in the company's favor. Whenever an incident of aggression hits the news, SeaWorld can usually count on the affected trainer to support the way the company wants the public to understand the story. I don't blame anyone for sticking with the company line. I too was a loyal corporate citizen and felt I had to do my duty to defend SeaWorld against those who might hurt it—and the whales.

In 2004 at SeaWorld San Antonio, trainer Steve Aibel was involved in a major waterwork aggression incident with Kyquot, Tilikum's son, who was 12 years old at the time. As in the other incidents I've described in this book, Ky had refused a signal for a behavior from Steve, who had known the orca since the whale was two years old. At first, Ky refused to give Steve a rocket-hop; but after he did, he repeatedly swam over Steve, making it impossible for the trainer to leave the pool for several minutes. Aibel was isolated in the center of the pool as Ky went at him again and again, rolling over and under him. At one point, Steve, sounding panicked, told another trainer to "Get me out of here." Fortunately, a trainer was able to yank Steve from the pool. He emerged uninjured and would go on national television with a smile to explain the situation as "no big deal," saying that the young whale was just rambunctious because his hormones were kicking in.

I've reviewed the video of the incident again and again as a learning tool for what to avoid. It is indeed dramatic, with Ky slamming into Steve repeatedly and with the trainer holding on to the orca's rostrum as if his life depended on it. But one important set of factors cannot be gleaned from the incident itself.

For the shows, the rocket-hop had consistently been the last behavior Ky was asked to do before he was sent back to the back pools to be penned up with Kayla, a dominant female. Ky was terrified of

Kayla, who had been raking him up quite badly. From past association, Ky recognized that the rocket-hop meant that he was about to end up with Kayla again. And so he refused to perform it and caused an incident that, at the very least, kept him from immediately joining Kayla. That was, among several other factors, a big underlying cause for his behavior. If hormones had been involved, Ky would have been in a hurry to rejoin Kayla in order to breed.

How do you explain that to the public? Ladies and gentlemen, Ky was terrified by a female whale because in SeaWorld we keep our whales so enclosed that they cannot swim away to protect themselves from other whales who might hurt them with their teeth.

The internal consequences, however, belied SeaWorld's lighthearted attempt to use hormones to explain the matter to the media. After this incident, SeaWorld changed corporate protocol: nets were placed at the ready at the front show pool of every park. Furthermore, it transformed Ky's life forever. To be consistent with the story of a teen whale with raging hormones, he was pulled from waterwork—something he might actually have needed to keep him stimulated because he really was on the cusp of sexual maturity.

Sometimes, when something went wrong, the whale's role in the incident was never mentioned in press releases. One day, my friend Wendy was performing an ultrasound on Orkid in the San Diego park. During the ultrasound, Wendy had Orkid line up on her side and keep the entire length of her body at the surface, straight down to her tail flukes, so that the vets could reach her lateral peduncle area, near her genital area, to place the equipment on her skin for the transabdominal ultrasound. Standing inside the pool area on a ledge covered with a few inches of water, Wendy maintained control of Orkid at the whale's head. At one point, Wendy could feel Orkid becoming "tight" and uncomfortable with what was happening. She quickly told the vets to stop the procedure and step behind the wall, placing themselves safely behind a barrier. Orkid then sat head up in front of Wendy, who delivered an LRS before asking Orkid for a behavior that would have her slide away from Wendy toward another part of the pool. Instead of sliding away from Wendy, however, Orkid struck Wendy with a closed mouth in the middle of her chest, knocking her backward and off her feet. She fell behind the wall, landing on her face on the concrete below the elevated pool ledge. She was briefly unconscious. SeaWorld paramedics called 911—which, of course, attracted the media. Internally, the official incident report would describe what happened as clearly aggressive behavior by Orkid. However, in his statement to the press, Mike Scarpuzzi simply said, "The trainer lost her balance, fell over the side of the pool wall and made contact on the ground with her head." No mention was made of Orkid or the aggression.

SeaWorld would spin a similar story around a painful incident that involved me.

I was swimming with Corky during a show and she was excited about performing. Once she has confidence in the trainer she's working with, Corky, all 8,200 pounds of her, only knows high gear. We would actually have to focus on getting her to slow down on a lot of waterwork behaviors so that we could handle her power. At one point in the segment, I was doing a fast foot-push with my left foot on her rostrum, at the surface of the water along the perimeter of the pool. As we approached the stage, I pushed off just as she launched me forward at the same time. Timing and the angle of launch were critical if I was to slide safely and dramatically across the stage. If I pushed off too soon or if I didn't push off before she launched me, it would spell disaster. What complicated the act this time was that I was supposed to tackle another trainer as I slid across the stage. Sometimes we would do this and play it off to the audience as an accident even though it was scripted. It always got huge laughs and applause.

This time, though, the other trainer saw that Corky was going exceptionally fast along the perimeter. He decided he didn't want to be at the end of what was likely to be a truly hard tackle after Corky launched me forward. He backed out of position; but I was already launched. I slid across the concrete stage with such momentum—perhaps 25 to 30 miles per hour—that my head hit the bottom of the shallow area of the pool on re-entry in the slide-over area. I knew I wasn't going to have an ordinary bump on the head. It sounded bad. Corky was also worried. She began to echolocate on me and became vocal. I asked her for a hand target—to make sure she came to me and my hand. My control spotter, Petey, was still playing the behavior off to the public as an amusing accident. I got his attention and asked if I was bleeding. He looked shocked as he repeatedly told me to get off stage. When SeaWorld issued their public relations statement, it read, "A trainer was injured today when he accidentally dived into a shallow area of the pool." They made me sound stupid. Again, no mention of a whale. I certainly didn't throw myself across the stage at 30 miles an hour.

How much were trainers paid? In 2001, as a senior trainer at San Diego SeaWorld with eight years of experience, I was making $15.45 an hour swimming with the most dangerous whales in the corporation, including Kasatka. That would be about $30,000 a year or, once you adjust for inflation, about $40,000 in 2014 dollars. The adulation of the crowd is one thing but there was nothing glamorous about an orca trainer's pay. When I was rehired by SeaWorld in 2008 after France, trainer pay, even for those of us who swam with the whales, was very low.

I had the advantage of years of experience at SeaWorld—and a willingness to make a lot of noise about things like salary. I can only imagine what other trainers less headstrong than I was could wrangle out of the corporation.

Even the company's moments of apparent generosity were tainted. After Petey's serious encounter with Kasatka in November 2006, August Busch, whose family owned SeaWorld at the time, met with the San Diego trainers. According to friends who were there, one young trainer had the courage to speak up and told him that she had to work two jobs to make enough to cover her living expenses—and do the SeaWorld job she loved. He appeared surprised and asked her how much she made. When she told him, he said he was shocked, adding that he had no idea how underpaid trainers were. He vowed to change it. The result, in early 2007, was a $5 an hour increase for trainers at Shamu Stadium who were approved for waterwork with the whales—a kind of hazard allowance. There was no distinction for experience. Brand-new waterwork trainers who worked with the least dangerous animals and performed only very basic routines only in training sessions were getting the same increase as the most experienced trainers swimming with the most dangerous whales and performing all the difficult acts during shows.

After the deaths of Alexis and Dawn in 2009 and 2010, SeaWorld took the $5 an hour increase away. Since waterwork was now proscribed by OSHA, the company explained, trainers weren't swimming with the whales anymore and shouldn't be paid the extra (at first known as "hazard pay," then, for legal reasons, changed to a "premium"). They seemed to overlook the fact that Dawn was not performing waterwork when she was grabbed, pulled in and dismembered. Meanwhile, the trainers were still expected to drill the whales' teeth and carry out other close-up duties with the orcas. It isn't as if "dry" work is that much less risky. Any time you are over the pool wall with a killer whale, you are at risk of being grabbed and killed.

There was enough of a backlash to that decision that a year and half later, SeaWorld gave that $5 an hour back to us—but only to trainers who had waterwork approval as of February 1, 2011. They had the audacity to call it a raise.

There were so many other things wrong with the way SeaWorld approached compensation. It may seem petty to complain about money when the quality of life of the whales is so dire and appalling. But compensation reflects the way a corporation values its employees and its assets. And if the company didn't care enough for their trainers to pay them well, SeaWorld was unlikely to have moral qualms about exploiting their whales.

I've seen how SeaWorld treated trainers who fell out of the company's favor. One case that still rankles me goes back to the beginnings of my career. When I started out in California, one of the trainers I idolized was Sharon Veitz. She was a pioneer, having succeeded at the male-dominated stadium by being able to do every waterwork behavior with the whales that the best of the male trainers could do. (There are more women now even though there are vestiges of macho behavior in some stadiums.) She had the level of expertise and rank to work with and swim with all the whales, even the most dangerous.

With so much experience came waterwork aggression—and Sharon was a victim of several. In one incident, during a night show, Kasatka grabbed Sharon by the knee to yank her underwater and then, as Sharon surfaced, the orca took her by the foot and pulled her down a second time before swimming off to be with her daughter Takara, who was in a back pool with the gate closed. Sharon could barely pull herself out of the pool because of the injury. During another orca performance, Sharon's knee was severely damaged, with multiple torn ligaments and a fracture requiring months of rehab. As was her right, she hired a workman's comp lawyer—which did not sit well with management when she returned to duty at Shamu Stadium.

Then she had an incident with Ulises. The huge male orca had just rolled her off a perimeter ride and refused to do the follow-through we had taught all whales for that scenario—to swim away from the trainer. Instead, he turned and faced Sharon in the water and ignored the emergency recall tone from the spotter on the stage. Sharon sensed that her window of opportunity to get out was shrinking and decided to climb out of the pool while she could. She was able to hook first her right then her left leg over the glass to allow her to fall over the six-foot-high glass in the front show pool onto the pathway and to safety. Ulises then began to vocalize loudly. Sharon was right to move quickly. Ulises had become aggressive.

Management, however, criticized Sharon's decision. In a memo posted for all trainers to read and initial to show that they had seen it, Mike Scarpuzzi announced her move to Dolphin Stadium: "I feel Sharon has now developed an unhealthy fear of the killer whales. This fear is now affecting her behavioral judgment." The memo continued condescendingly: "Sharon must re-develop her confidence, re-develop her waterwork training skills, re-develop her behavioral attention to details and her behavioral judgments with marine mammals . . . It is also best for our waterwork program with killer whales to have confident trainers who have a respectful fear of the whales and have shown that they are making consistent correct behavioral judgments."

I thought it was a disgraceful way to treat an elite trainer with 11 years of experience who had made a timely decision to get out of the way of a potentially devastating situation. Sharon filed a disability and defamation lawsuit in 1997. It was settled out of court; and, as part of the agreement, she is not allowed to speak of the case.

Dolphin Stadium had its share of accidents as well—and the manner they were handled was the same. My friend Stacy Connery was an orca trainer with 15 years' experience who, after experiencing aggressions and suffering the wear and tear of Shamu Stadium, decided to move voluntarily to work with the smaller mammals. In 2000, she tried to help a dolphin who had swum into a net. In the process of being disentangled from the net, the dolphin swam into Stacy. Stacy was enmeshed for several minutes underwater as the dolphin spun her and the net around and around while it tried to break free. It took more than eight men to pull the net with Stacy and the dolphin out of the pool. She was not breathing when she was pulled from the pool but soon began to do so on her own. She also suffered a spiral fracture to her arm. She hired a workman's comp lawyer—which led SeaWorld to order us not to speak to her or allow her into the back areas of show stadiums or areas where the animals were kept. She sued and settled. The corporation again got what it probably wanted most: a gag order in which she agreed not to talk about the case. In the 14 years since the accident, she has had a total of eight surgeries.

I was constantly battling management over policies involving the working conditions of trainers and the living conditions of the whales. The animosity increased toward the end of my career because I spent those years in SeaWorld's San Antonio facility—where I had begun my life as a trainer but which I had little love for. Neither did the corporation, it seems. Of the three stadiums, Texas received the least financial support and the fewest resources. It did not subscribe to San Diego's philosophies of carefully plotted and all-encompassing psychological conditioning. At the same time, the whales in Texas were out of shape because management had chosen not to expand their repertoire of behaviors or to vary their sessions with enough exercise to keep them stimulated and fit. The conservative mind-set also encouraged the trainers in Texas to consult among themselves rather than reach out to their colleagues in California and Florida if problems arose. Having come from San Diego and having seen what the California trainers were capable of doing, I thought it was a waste that San Antonio did not take advantage of the experience of SeaWorld's California and Florida trainers. I found the lack of imagination in Texas deeply frustrating.

Sometimes, the lack of forethought in San Antonio resulted in ludicrous and potentially dangerous situations. In the immediate wake of Alexis' death, a senior trainer chose to continue waterwork with Keet—the male orca who was performing the synchronized double stand-on spy-hop with Takara when she accidentally hit me—even though Keet had just emerged from an episode in which another whale had aggressively slammed into his gate. Social tension among whales should always be seen as a likely precursor of aggression against trainers. I went over to the supervisor and asked her to get the trainer out of the water—which she did. I thought that choosing to go forward was foolhardy.

Water visibility was extremely poor in Texas. More than once, I lost my place in the pool as the whales and I performed the most spectacular and dangerous waterwork behaviors. I wasn't the only one to whom this happened. I should have refused to do waterwork until the problem was identified and fixed. I pressed on for the love of the whales. But I was increasingly unhappy with the attitude of the people I worked with and with the company that encouraged them to go on that way.

Physically, I was taking a beating from the job.

On the day that Corky launched me across the stage and I lacerated my head, Petey sent me off stage, ended the segment early and immediately joined me to stop the bleeding. Once we got enough blood off my face and out of my eyes, I could see better and managed to walk off, out of the view of the public. I had lacerated my face to the skull above my eye. It took a total of 17 internal and external stitches to close the wound. SeaWorld's doctor in San Diego did an incredible job. I doubt any plastic surgeon could have done better; and I refused the option for one. He put me back together more than once, having treated me years earlier for thoracic strain. I credit him with extending my killer whale training career. If not, it could well have been over by my late 20s.

But the battering would continue. I wrote earlier in this book about how, during a summer 2009 night show, Keet slammed into the middle of my back, on my spine, with his rostrum. My back was not fractured but the doctors did see the damage it had taken from years of being hit by orcas—and also by the heavy lifting and running involved in the job. Getting hit off a hydro by a 7,500-pound, sexually mature male killer whale made me more conservative during performances in the following weeks.

But about two weeks later, Keet hit me again on a hydro reentry. This time, he struck me on the side of my head right in the temple area. I was nearly knocked unconscious. I remember feeling so peaceful I didn't think it was important to surface. But even in my daze, I managed to extend a hand target to Keet and he came to me. With my hand on him, I slowly floated to the surface. Doug Acton, a very experienced trainer I respected, happened to be watching my underwater run. He said he saw my body violently jerk forward as Keet's rostrum hit my head. Doug said that if he didn't see me move underwater a second later than I did, he was ready to signal the control spotter to sound the emergency alarms. The entire left side of my head where Keet's rostrum struck me was so painful that I couldn't tolerate touch for nearly two weeks. Although senior management—all the way up to the curatorial level—was aware of the incident, I was never sent to the doctor.

By the time I was 34, the injuries were beginning to overwhelm me. I had to deal with pain that I didn't have in my 20s. I tried to adjust on my own, by changing the way I approached performing. I refined my waterwork with experience but also to adapt, adjust and compensate for the pain. By 2009, I had injured my knee jumping off a killer whale onto the concrete while performing a surf ride in a show. The knee just never really got better. I sought out multiple medical specialists, including the top orthopedic surgeons in the country. All the while, I never stopped working or swimming with the whales. I just dealt with the pain.

Then, in October 2009, Takara hit me after I lost my footing on a stand-on spy hop. I've described how tender she was in helping to bring me out of the pool. But I had been battered again.

My control spotter had seen everything and, when I emerged from the pool, he kept asking if I needed medical help. I tried to dust myself off but I knew I was hurt and the pain was increasingly intense. My body was tightening up. At SeaWorld's Health Services and then at a hospital emergency room I was subjected to a series of tests—X-rays and a CT scan—to make sure I wasn't bleeding internally. For about a month, it was impossible to get comfortable or even lie down without intense pain. Everything hurt—walking, breathing, bending. Lying down to rest was excruciating. Because of that, I was prescribed high-dose painkillers so that I could actually stay prone to fall asleep.

After about a month, my ribs healed. It was the worst pain I had ever had to deal with in my career. But even after it had subsided, I didn't stop taking the painkillers. I had unfortunately discovered the relief they provided. I had been miserable in Texas for a long time. I felt trapped: I wanted to leave Texas but couldn't abandon Takara. I learned to use the painkillers as a way to cope with and mask my unhappiness. It got to the point where I would look forward to the moment I could leave work and go home to take the drugs. It made Texas bearable.

I knew that the painkillers were a trap. There were truly times when I needed them to manage the pain: they had been prescribed as part of my pain management program for my chronic knee injury. But I also took them for nonmedical reasons. I had always thought addiction involved cocaine, meth, heroin, marijuana or alcohol. I had known people in my life, friends and relatives, who were caught up with those substances. I never thought it could happen with painkillers— and to me.

One day, when I ran out of pills, I decided I didn't want to take the drugs anymore and chose not to get the prescription refilled. Within 24 hours I began to feel increasingly uncomfortable, then in pain, and then physically sick. It was withdrawal. I had become addicted to painkillers and the drugs wouldn't let me go.

I would try to stop. I was foolish enough to think I could do it cold turkey, that it was just a matter of strength or toughness. Friends told me the same thing: look at everything you've done, they would say, you're stronger than this addiction. But they didn't know—and I didn't know—what opiates do to your body. You can't imagine the level of pain and sickness your body goes through as you withdraw from what is essentially heroin. The pain and the sickness got so bad that I quickly filled the prescription to stop the ferocious sickness and pain. It became a vicious cycle and completely overtook me.

Every time I went through withdrawal, pain shot straight to the bone. Every nerve in my body was so sensitive that even a breeze from an air conditioner or fan would be intolerable. I'd turn them off, even if it were 100 degrees outside. The most luxurious sheets felt like sandpaper against my skin. I couldn't hold down food or water.

I attempted to outsmart the addiction by trying different methods of weaning myself off the painkillers. In the end, after failing multiple times to beat my addiction, I sought professional help from doctors who specialized in painkiller opiate addiction. The injuries I suffered at SeaWorld made painkillers necessary: that makes my situation complicated and I am always at a higher risk for relapse. But I have excellent doctors and I follow strict guidelines that allow me to manage my pain and prevent relapse.

The litany of physical breakdown goes on. Since beginning at SeaWorld in my 20s and after performing with the whales at the bottom of the pool, I—like other trainers—would sometimes emerge with nosebleeds. If you didn't drain your sinuses, you also risked infection because of all the water trapped in there. Due to this ritual of clogging and draining, our sinuses would hemorrhage or rupture. As the salt water drained from the sinus cavities, so would chunks of bloody tissue. We were young and laughed it off. But long term damage was being done.

I had accumulated scar tissue in all four compartments of my sinuses from years of being in deep water, with the pressure compacting the nasal cavities as I ascended and descended in the pools, sometimes at immense speeds while attached to an orca. The bones in that part of my skull had thickened from the years of exposure to extremely cold water. In the spring of 2010, I had major surgery in New York City where doctors sawed away the excess bone and scar tissue accretions. I wasn't allowed to board a plane to fly back to Texas for three weeks and, when I returned to SeaWorld San Antonio, I wasn't allowed back in the water for six more weeks. After the surgery, when I had to go for the once-every-three-month swim test, I was worried about how I would hold up, scared it would interfere with my ability to equalize the pressure in my ears, fearful that something would rupture. The surgery proved successful: I had no trouble in the frigid deep waters during the swim tests and during training.

Work remained brutal on the joints. At SeaWorld, apart from swimming and diving, I was always running on cement and up and down stairs, most of the time in just socks with no foot protection as I carried a 30-pound bucket of fish in each hand. The specialists finally diagnosed my problem: I had extensive cartilage destruction in both knees, with my right one being worse. Bone was rubbing against bone in three compartments of that knee. Looking at my MRI and arthrogram results, a specialist for a top pro sports team said he didn't understand how I could still function. His advice was to leave killer whale training immediately.

I was devastated. I wasn't ready to hear or accept that verdict in early 2009. I shopped around for a second opinion, going to doctors throughout the country. After seeing six different top specialists, I found one who said he could buy me more time through therapy and injections of hyaluronic acid every six months to both knees. I also had to follow a pain management program. It bought me about three more years.

By May 2012, the knee pain had become too intense. The gig was up. I was exhausted by the continued battles with SeaWorld management over things I felt were not in the whales' best interests, and directives that put us trainers and the orcas in dangerous positions. I was disgusted by corporate greed and the exploitation of the whales and trainers alike. All that had slowly destroyed my faith in SeaWorld. The disenchantment had increased after I saw how the corporation handled the tragedies of Alexis Martinez and Dawn Brancheau. It was time to go. I took medical leave in May 2012 and ultimately resigned three months later, on August 17, 2012.

I could no longer do my dream job.

11

LEAP OF FAITH

I broke my face, my fingers and my toes. I broke my ribs—twice. I frac-
tured my foot. I destroyed my knees. Scar tissue blocked up my sinuses. I got addicted to painkillers and suffered through excruciating
withdrawal. The list of damage I've done to my body throughout my
career is extensive.

I was devastated when I came to the decision to end my career. I
cried. I cried the same kind of gut-wrenching, uncontrollable sobs I
wept when I left SeaWorld for France in 2001, because I was leaving
Kasatka and the other whales I loved more than anything else. Now,
a dozen years later, I was weeping because I felt I was abandoning her
daughter Takara, leaving her to be turned into a baby-making machine by SeaWorld, her calves taken away from her to populate marine
parks across the world.

When I took medical leave in May 2012, no one knew I was about
to end my career—though many of my colleagues were afraid I might.

The SeaWorld Human Resources Department was trying to prevent my taking protected time-off under the Family Leave and Medical Act, which would give me insurance coverage to treat my injuries while I took unpaid leave. It provided the guarantee that my job would still be available for me if I could return. If they didn't allow me to have that grace period, I wouldn't be able to even begin to recover—and I would not have the chance to decide whether I could feasibly get back to work. Eventually, after I told the vice president of the Human Resources Department that the company was violating federal law, SeaWorld relented and I went on leave.

It took me almost three weeks to realize that my career was over. Something I had read a year or so earlier helped push me forward. "Keto and Tilikum express the stress of orca captivity" was written by two former SeaWorld trainers, Dr. Jeff Ventre and Dr. John Jett—a physician and a research professor, respectively. Published on January 20, 2011 on the website of The Orca Project, it was very sharply critical of their former employer. When I first heard that the two were speaking out against SeaWorld, I was angry. Even though I was disenchanted with the corporation and was having almost daily battles with management over whales and safety, I still defended the company against outside detractors. Some of the staff at the Shamu Stadiums in the three parks knew about the paper but it circulated like subversive material. The most loyal employees refused to read it. I refused as well. But my friend Wendy Ramirez eventually convinced me to look at it.

I had expected to read some kind of biased treatise. Instead, the paper made plain everything I already knew—and convinced me that Jett and Ventre were as concerned about the whales as I was. I was also impressed by the fact that they could leave their jobs as trainers and contribute to our scientific understanding of the effects of captivity on orcas. Their paper played a role in the decisions I was going to make, helping to convert me from being angry at all critics to being their supporter because they were telling the truth.

Ventre and Jett have impressive academic credentials. They would publish a peer-reviewed article accepted by the *Journal of Marine Animals and Their Ecology* in 2013. Entitled "Orca (Orcinus) Captivity and Vulnerability to Mosquito-Transmitted Viruses," it examined the deaths of Kanduke and Taku. While it focused on the bizarre causes of death of the two SeaWorld orcas from mosquito bites, the paper documented the problems faced by the whales in great detail, from the whales' dental problems to the huge amounts of intense heat and radiation from the sun that the whales were exposed to in the SeaWorld parks, a situation that can have an "immunosuppressant" effect on the orcas. Jett and Ventre said they often observed sunburned dorsals—perhaps a factor in the collapsed fins afflicting SeaWorld's captive male orcas. That paper validated what I saw when I did my work.

The science helped with intellectualizing my decision, with getting my head wrapped around it. But when it came to the heart, the decision was cathartic, an emotional, soul-changing upheaval. After taking medical leave from SeaWorld, I needed three weeks to have the calmness to realize I was closing this chapter for good. The process of leaving had been tumultuous. I had to retain an attorney to fight the VP of Human Resources to exercise my federally protected rights to protected leave. But once I had recovered presence of mind, I could not escape the fact that I was losing the whales, losing Takara.

When it hit me, I was alone in my apartment. I was lying in bed and immediately grabbed my cell phone to call my best friend, Wendy Ramirez, the only person who would truly understand the depth of my loss. As her phone rang, the tears streamed down my face as I repeated, "Please pick up, Wendy. Please pick up." Her phone went to voicemail. All I could manage to say was, "I really need you right now. I lost her. I can't believe I've really lost her. She's gone." I hung up and collapsed in the middle of my bed, burying my face in my hands. I cried the same gut-wrenching cry from 11 years earlier.

I tested the waters about speaking out about SeaWorld's treatment of orcas. The Orca Network told Jeff Ventre and Tim Zimmermann of *Outside* magazine that an unnamed trainer wanted to speak to them. Eventually, I divulged my identity to Tim, who then put me in touch with Gabriela Cowperthwaite, who was directing a documentary about the orcas of SeaWorld. She and Tim told me they thought it would help the project tremendously for someone like me to be in it. I would be a source of information fresh from two decades as a trainer at the corporation. I was working for SeaWorld during the time Alexis and Dawn were killed. My experience was so recent I could testify to the ongoing protocols and procedures of SeaWorld's killer whale program. Carol Ray, one of the former trainers who appeared in *Blackfish* told me after the documentary's New York City premiere that "I wished so badly you were going to speak and say that it wasn't like that anymore at Sea-World. I wished more than anything you were going to say things had changed and their lives were better now. But you confirmed it's actually worse." She said she had hoped that the bad things she remembered from the 1980s and 1990s were things of the past and that I would say, "That doesn't happen anymore." There was such sadness in her eyes.

Still, it was hard to make the leap. I initially agreed to collaborate, but then got cold feet and backed out only days before we were going to shoot. I just wasn't ready and was fearful of reprisal from SeaWorld. While I was in SeaWorld, I had been told time after time that, if I left and spoke out, I would be hurting the whales; that they would then cut back on my contact with the orcas, which I believed enriched the lives of the whales, thus diminishing the quality of their existence in SeaWorld. It was a vicious, cyclical argument that proved tremendously successful as emotional blackmail. That psychological conditioning was embedded deep in me like a thorn, and, despite the logic of doing so, it was difficult for me to pluck it out.

Eventually, I made up my mind not to return to SeaWorld. The filmmakers approached me again. This time, I decided to go forward. A week after I resigned my position at SeaWorld, I was in Seattle sitting down to be interviewed for *Blackfish*.

I remember it being a gorgeous day. I hadn't slept well the night before my interview. So many things were running through my mind. I did not want to be exploited by SeaWorld's enemies the same way SeaWorld had exploited the whales. I knew it was important to choose the right medium and the right journalists to speak to. I wanted my views to be reflected accurately. I was taking a leap of faith. I was going to be out there, speaking my mind, to everyone. SeaWorld would be hearing it all too.

Gabriela and the camera and lighting crew made me feel relaxed and comfortable. I sat for four and a half hours of questions and answers. When I'm nervous I'll drink a ton of water. I think I drank six to eight bottles of water by the end of the session. After we finished, I knew there was no turning back. As Jeff Ventre had told me, "Are you ready? It's a one-way door."

Gabriela and Tim decided to keep my participation in *Blackfish* a secret until the film was screened for reviewers. Even the other former SeaWorld trainers in the documentary knew only that there was an experienced trainer fresh out of the company who was interviewed in the film. No one in the industry suspected it was me. No one knew if the mystery trainer was male or female—or even which park I was from.

I was the last interview Gabriela filmed before *Blackfish* went into post-production. They had deadlines to meet, most importantly for submission to the Sundance Film Festival, the annual and legendary marketplace for independent films founded by the actor Robert Redford in 1978. It sounded like the holy grail to me and so I put it out of my mind. I had no way of knowing how big or small *Blackfish* would end up being. Would the film go straight to DVD? Would it even make it that far? My hope was that it would air on cable on either Animal Planet or National Geographic. Or, if things went really well, perhaps on HBO. Of course, I had one great fear: that SeaWorld would sweep in with all its lawyers to quash the film before anyone could see it.

In late November, I was thrown into a crash course in the movie business. Tim called to tell me that a press release was about to go out announcing that *Blackfish* had made the list of Sundance's official selections. This was huge news but I tried not to get too excited. We still had no idea how the film would be received at Sundance. Would it generate buzz? Or would it flop? After qualifying for the festival, the goal was for your film to be seen by the right people, be bought and get a distribution deal. We crossed our fingers and hoped for the best.

At Sundance, *Blackfish* was originally scheduled for two screenings. But as word got out about the subject of the documentary, a third was added, then a fourth, a fifth and a sixth. An extra screening that wasn't part of the schedule was thrown in because of demand. We had buzz.

The Sundance premiere on Saturday, January 19, 2013, was sold out; people stood on line in ten-degree weather for nearly three hours, hoping for wait-list tickets to become available. The film's account of how Tilikum killed Dawn Brancheau—and the orca's horrific life in captivity before that—clearly moved audiences. The section about orca calves being taken from their mothers to stock marine parks was particularly heartrending. Quickly, there was a battle over who would get to distribute it. HBO wanted it; so did IFC Films and a couple of others that would surprise us.

A couple of days later, I woke up to a text from one of my best friends, Joseph Kapsch, who works in entertainment news. He told me *Blackfish* had just been picked up by two companies, Magnolia Pictures and CNN Films. The documentary was going to have a summer theatrical release through Magnolia and then hit cable on CNN prime time in the fall.

SeaWorld would be heard from, of course. Gabriela had offered the company a chance to have its representatives appear in the film, to tell its side of the story. SeaWorld chose not to cooperate. However, as the premiere approached, they began to hear rumors that I was in the documentary. Friends of mine who were still working as orca trainers told me that on the day before the Sundance opening, senior management at SeaWorld called around asking employees if they knew whether I was in *Blackfish.* No one did because I had the foresight not to tell anyone. By the morning of the premiere, SeaWorld was certain I was in *Blackfish* and was frantically trying to find out what the film was going to say. They were not happy when they found out.

They began to try to discredit the film—and every former trainer who spoke out against SeaWorld in the documentary. One way was to try to find fault with my years of experience. Furious that I had chosen to speak out, they insinuated internally that I was not rehired at SeaWorld San Diego after my stint in France because of what they mysteriously described as a "character flaw," that I was never loyal to the company. If so, what does it say about their corporate standards that I was rehired at SeaWorld San Antonio? And then promoted again and again after that? SeaWorld also said that I was enamored of the spotlight and must be reveling in the glow of popular attention and the glamor of the red carpet.

They couldn't belittle my accomplishments. I was their creation. I had accumulated 14 years of experience at two different SeaWorld facilities. The most substantial criticism SeaWorld could lodge against me was that I was often two to five minutes late for work—and that I was difficult. They are right about that last part. I argued with them about everything: putting those huge whales in eight-foot-deep pools for entertainment reasons; the forcible insemination of the great dominant females of the parks; the stripping away of calves from their mothers. Yes, I was difficult to work with because, through the years, I increasingly voiced my opinions about those practices out of loyalty to the whales. I'm happy if they think that was a character flaw.

But SeaWorld also made life difficult for the people I loved. When I made the decision to speak out for the first time, I knew I was going to lose a lot of friends—or people I thought were friends. I accepted and understood that former coworkers who still admired SeaWorld and colleagues still in the industry would have to keep their distance from me. I knew that folks who were truly close to me and who truly loved me would continue to take my side. I'm not saying relations weren't strained at times, but the people who were truly my friends managed to stay in my life and I remained in theirs.

My friends who were still at the company told me that they were being watched closely; some said they were even warned by senior management to "be careful." Out of caution, some of them "unfriended" me from their Facebook accounts. They told me that their bosses were going through the friends lists on that website to check for my presence. I remember Wendy calling me in tears, apologizing for removing my name from Facebook. I wasn't upset. I said, "You need to protect yourself. I want you to protect yourself."

That was a stunning change. During our 20-year friendship, Wendy and I spoke about everything—the whales, SeaWorld, gossip, our lives. Now we couldn't. It was all silence. As we realized that was ending, as we finished that phone call, she told me, "Just don't forget all the good times. Don't forget about all the double waterwork we used to do together with Kasatka and Orkid and Takara. Don't forget those days."

I can't expect friends who are still trainers at SeaWorld to just walk out on their jobs. They have families to support. All I can say is that I love them and that I hope they fight for the whales from within the organization and they stay safe.

A typical example of the way SeaWorld went after me involved the incident where I lacerated my face after performing with Corky. The injuries from that accident were shown in *Blackfish*. SeaWorld went into overdrive to try and discredit my account of what happened. While my version has never changed, the company has now provided the press with four completely different sets of details. First, SeaWorld said that absolutely no whale was involved and that I simply dove on my own into the shallow area of the pool in the slide-over. A former Florida trainer, who doesn't even know me and has never worked with me, said, "No whale was involved and he walked into the screen." I never at any time walked into a screen and even SeaWorld discredited his statements, admitting that was not the way I was injured. For its second version, SeaWorld conceded I was indeed performing with a whale in the water then contradicted itself, saying I wasn't and that somehow I slid myself across the stage. Then, they had Wendy record a video segment on their "Truth about *Blackfish*" page where she said that absolutely no whale was involved and that "he simply ran and dove into the concrete." Sea-World posted that video the day after my testimony before the California State Assembly. Now, SeaWorld's fourth account is that I was performing in the water with a whale but did the maneuver incorrectly leading to my injury. It is consistent with their culture of blaming the trainer for incidents in the pool.

I have medical records as well as the testimony of former Shamu Stadium supervisors, senior trainers and camera operators—not to the mention the 6,000 people in the stadium that day.

My relationship with Wendy has changed radically. Now, our phone conversations are rare and filled with silence. She is a senior manager and her role is to protect the company. Our friendship will never be the same.

One of the people I loved and respected most is a former SeaWorld trainer who I worked with during my apprentice days in San Antonio. She has asked not to be named in this book. But I learned a lot from her. She and her beautiful family were devout Christians who were taught that homosexuality is wrong. But she and I were such good friends that she was one of the few people at SeaWorld San Antonio who knew I was gay. She never treated me differently. It never changed how she and her husband felt about me. I was incredibly moved by that. This was the South in the 1990s. I was still recovering from what Mark McHugh said about almost not hiring me.

Eventually, I left for California, and she gave up her career to focus on her family. She remained a supporter of the company, however, believing that it continued to have the best interests of the animals as a corporate priority. At the very least, she knew that the trainers loved the whales. She was always a strong advocate for the orcas and the rest of SeaWorld's menagerie. She fought with management over issues ranging from the sea lions going blind because of chlorine and ozone levels in the water to whether orca calves were being properly nursed.

One night, not too long after *Blackfish* was released, she and I had a lengthy argument. She felt I was not giving enough credit to Sea-World for the good it was doing; she also said that people she described as "radical animal rights activists" were having too much of an influence over me. She kept returning to the fact that the trainers had been doing the right things for the animals over the years. I kept trying to get her to understand that this fight has never been about the trainers, that *Blackfish* never says the trainers were villains.

I asked her if she thought it was ethical for SeaWorld to profit from its Shamu spectaculars. "Yes," she said, "because God gave us dominion over all the animals."

I am not a theologian, but I worked myself back into our debate by asking her a question. "When you come to SeaWorld with your kids and take them to the top of Shamu Stadium after the show, where you can look out at those pools and see the size of the facilities for the whales, when you see most of them floating stationary at the surface of the water, in your heart do you truly think that is good enough for these animals, with everything we know about them and their needs?"

She said, "No."

At the end of May 2012, after I went on medical leave, SeaWorld received a decision on its appeal against the OSHA rulings imposed on the corporation in the aftermath of Dawn's death. OSHA declared that SeaWorld had placed higher priority on its financial interests than on the safety of its employees. Administrative law judge Ken Welsch upheld OSHA's citations and fines. The money is miniscule in light of the $2.5 billion SeaWorld is worth: $75,000 total. But the defeat stung because the judge backed OSHA's contention that SeaWorld was ultimately responsible for putting Dawn in harm's way. SeaWorld took the case to the US Court of Appeals. On April 14, 2014, that court also upheld OSHA's charges after the US Department of Labor's independent occupational safety and health commission refused to hear SeaWorld's appeal.

The judges in both courts were scathing toward SeaWorld. With his administrative law decision, Judge Welsch said that SeaWorld was bending over backwards not to describe Tilikum's behavior with Dawn as "aggressive." In a detailed decision, he declared, "If Tilikum's killing of Dawn Brancheau was not an aggressive act, perhaps classification of the killer whale's behavior is irrelevant. Whatever the motivation ascribed to a killer whale, any unpredictable behavior has the potential of causing death or serious injury to a trainer working in close contact with the whales." SeaWorld's legalistic attempt to mischaracterize the incident had come to naught.

Welsch went on to deride several other SeaWorld practices as inadequately protecting the safety of trainers. "Trainers are expected to decipher precursors and then choose the appropriate response with split-second timing, keeping in mind that they are performing in front of an audience." He clearly saw who the loser was in SeaWorld's corporate blame game. "If the animal engages in undesirable behavior, it will be attributed to mistakes the trainer made." The judge also highlighted SeaWorld's priority: to minimize the audience's perception that something has gone wrong by having the show continue. He cited a memo by Mike Scarpuzzi after the 1999 incident between Kasatka and Petey. Scarp was angry that the show had been canceled. "The show did not need to be cut short," he wrote. "This brought unnecessary attention to the incorrect behavior and placed the control of the show to the whale. We have reiterated our existing policy to utilize any and all resources before canceling a show."

The judge was derisive. "SeaWorld insists it did not recognize the hazard posed by working in close contact with killer whales. The court finds this implausible and no reasonable person would conclude that . . . Whether the trainers were fully immersed and swimming with the killer whales for a waterwork show performance, or standing poolside or on a slide-out for a dry work show performance, SeaWorld knew its trainers were at risk for being struck or drowned by a killer whale."

The Court of Appeals was briefer in its judgment than Welsch but no less definitive in its view of SeaWorld. Concluding that OSHA did not overstep its authority in its dealings with the company, Judge Judith Rogers wrote for the court, "Statements by SeaWorld managers do not indicate that SeaWorld's safety protocols and training made the killer whales safe; rather, they demonstrate SeaWorld's recognition that the killer whales interacting with trainers are dangerous." SeaWorld, she wrote, "acted irresponsibly" and "violated its duties as an employer."

The corporation then had to deal with the impact of *Blackfish*. The documentary received great reviews. The *New York Times* said its account of Tilikum and his plight in captivity in SeaWorld was "delicately lacerating." The website Rotten Tomatoes gave the film an amazing 98 percent approval rating. The *Washington Post* called the film's portrayal of the treatment of orcas in marine parks "damning." When *Blackfish* was presented on cable TV, it became CNN's most watched show for all of 2013—with its biggest share in history of the valuable audience demographic of 18- to 23-year-olds. The film was nominated for best documentary at BAFTA, the British equivalent of the Oscars. It was among several shortlisted for an Academy Award.

Blackfish has had broad social and economic consequences. Ordinary folks got into the act. A petition drive on change.org was instrumental in ending a Taco Bell promotion that provided customers with discounted tickets to SeaWorld. The fast food chain also said it was ending its relationship with the marine park. Another change.org drive appears to have convinced Southwest Airlines to end a 26-year cross-promotional program with SeaWorld. Several musicians called off their appearances at the company's parks as a result of seeing *Blackfish,* including Martina McBride, Barenaked Ladies, 38 Special, REO Speedwagon, Cheap Trick, Trisha Yearwood, Heart, Willie Nelson, Trace Adkins and The Beach Boys.

The public statements and tweets by celebrities have not only been heartening for all of us who worked on *Blackfish* but have truly helped propel the movement for change. Ann Wilson of Heart said, "I've seen photos of people getting splashed [by orcas] and it looks like fun but when you look underneath you see the dark side. What they do is slavery, plain and simple." Cher said that SeaWorld was a "heinous corporation" and that its executives were focused on the bottom line and not on the welfare of the animals. Willie Nelson said on CNN after he dropped out of appearing at SeaWorld, "I don't agree with the way that they treat their animals so it wasn't that hard a deal for me to cancel." The comedian Russell Brand called SeaWorld "a stain upon humanity posing as entertainment." And the music impresario Russell Simmons said, "We need to realize that these are beings that suffer the same as we suffer, they want freedom the way we want freedom."

Politicians know a popular issue when they see one—and, from state governments to Washington, DC—they have joined the grassroots call for change. In April 2014 in California, home of the crown jewel in SeaWorld's empire, Assemblyman Richard Bloom, a Democrat, proposed bill AB2140, "The Orca Welfare and Safety Act," a piece of legislation that would essentially end the way the corporation is currently run. If passed, it would become "unlawful to hold in captivity, or use, a wild-caught or captive-bred orca . . . for performance or entertainment purposes, . . . to capture in state waters, or import from another state, any orca intended to be used for performance or entertainment purposes, to breed or impregnate an orca in captivity, or to export, collect, or import from another state the semen, other gametes, or embryos of an orca held in captivity for the purpose of artificial insemination, except as provided."

In February 2014 in New York, which has no parks with orcas, State Senator Greg Ball, a Republican, proposed a complete ban on captive killer whales within the borders of the Empire State. It passed unanimously in the Senate. While symbolic, Ball's legislation is proof that the sentiment generated by *Blackfish* is nationwide, affecting Americans who may never even have been to a marine park. I was asked to support Senator Ball and it was my honor to speak to other New York senators in Albany about my experience.

Along with experts like Dr. Rose and Dr. Giles, I co-sponsored and testified in California in support of Assemblyman Bloom's bill. It was infuriating to hear SeaWorld continue to refuse to acknowledge that it separates calves from their mothers. As I wrote earlier in this book, there is no question that calves are taken from their mothers— and that females are impregnated again and again, from an unnaturally young age.

Many of us who worked on *Blackfish* were astonished when the news broke in June 2014 that two California representatives in the US Congress had proposed updating federal rules on the welfare of captive killer whales, particularly the size of the pools and other living conditions. Furthermore, 40 members of Congress put their names to the letter the Californians authored criticizing the United States Department of Agriculture (USDA) for not updating its rules for captive marine mammals in 20 years. None of us knew it was coming, and we were ecstatic. It passed unanimously.

SeaWorld, meanwhile, questioned the congressional proposal to set aside $1 million to study the issue. It said peer-reviewed scientific papers already existed on the subject. The company likes to pretend it is a scientific organization for the purposes of public relations. But it gets little respect from scientists. The eminent New Zealand orca scientist Dr. Ingrid Visser has repeatedly asked SeaWorld to stop misquoting one of her studies every time it tries to argue that dorsal fin collapse occurs commonly in nature. The company says that 23 percent of the whales she observed had collapsed dorsals. She said the figure refers to a category that includes collapsed dorsals but was mostly made up of disfigured or crooked fins. She saw only one collapsed dorsal in the wild. The proper statistic would have been 0.1 percent.

As *Blackfish* began having a broad public impact with its January 2013 premiere at Sundance, SeaWorld refused to acknowledge that the film was having any kind of effect at all. Perhaps that was because a little financial engineering was going on. SeaWorld was preparing for an initial public offering of stock just three months later. It was important that SeaWorld Entertainment Inc., as the new public company was to be called, look financially sound and able to stand down any criticism in order to have a successful IPO.

SeaWorld has been through various groups of owners. The founders in San Diego sold the company to the publisher Harcourt Brace Jovanovich (HBJ) in 1976. HBJ in turn sold the parks in 1988—by then including Orlando and San Antonio—to Busch Entertainment Corporation, a division of Anheuser-Busch. In 2009, Busch sold SeaWorld and Busch Gardens to the Blackstone group for $2.3 billion—and Blackstone, a prominent investment bank, was preparing to harvest some profits by taking SeaWorld public. The IPO was apparently successful, with the original $27 share price jumping to close to $40 in a month. Blackstone took about half a billion dollars in profits with sales of stock after the IPO, according to Ryan Dezember and Michael Wursthorn in the *Wall Street Journal*. The *Journal* said other beneficiaries of the IPO were likely to be the Florida State Board Administration, the Texas Teachers Retirement Fund and the California State Teachers Retirement System, which had invested in the original SeaWorld purchase. It is a curious financial ecology that profits from and feeds off SeaWorld and its orcas.

Despite SeaWorld's solid numbers, the public pressure that originated with *Blackfish* was tenacious and longer-lived than the new public company's financial health. By August 13, 2014, SeaWorld still refused to admit that the film had had a detrimental effect on its business. It did concede, however, that the Bloom proposal in California—which just happened to have been inspired by the documentary—had dented attendance. In a quarterly statement required of publicly traded firms by the Securities and Exchange Commission (SEC), SeaWorld said it expected revenue to decline 6 or 7 percent in 2014. The company had earlier predicted an increase. As a result of that revelation, SeaWorld stock plummeted more than 33 percent to less than $19 at the end of that day.

Two days later, SeaWorld announced that it was expanding the pools in its facilities and investing in improvements in the orcas' habitat. Critics quickly pointed out that SeaWorld had to take a financial hit for the company to realize that it had to remedy its public image by belatedly throwing some money at the whales. On August 19, 2014, it was revealed that SeaWorld would not appeal the OSHA ruling to the US Supreme Court. It would have to abide by the federal agency's prescriptions and make it safer for trainers to work with the whales. Meanwhile, the company's fortunes continued to plummet. In early December 2014, the stock hit a record low of $15.32.

The world appeared to be turning against SeaWorld. Was victory in sight?

12

A VISION FOR
THE FUTURE

The prospect of a SeaWorld in financial decline does not fill me with glee.
The company may be motivated by greed and it may have exploited
both orcas and trainers, but SeaWorld is, paradoxically, the best hope
for the 30 killer whales that it owns.

In its confrontation with orca advocates over proposed legislation
to ensure the well-being of its killer whales, SeaWorld does little to
hide the fact that it is, first and foremost, a business and more interested in conserving its assets and profits than in conserving species. During testimony for California's proposed orca law, a lobbyist
representing SeaWorld said that if Assemblyman Bloom's bill passed,
SeaWorld would simply move its whales out of California because it
could no longer make money on them in the state. Or else, the lobbyist threatened, if California forced SeaWorld to change its killer whale
policies, then California itself should foot the bill. "You ban them, you
buy them."

The corporation lined up witness after witness to testify to the economic losses the San Diego area would suffer if SeaWorld decided to decamp. The core of the company's arguments to keep things as they are was financial and economic.

SeaWorld is missing an opportunity here. If it had a true vision of the future, the company could argue that it is the only institution that can afford to take care of most, if not all, of the 30 whales it owns—because those whales cannot be released into the wild. They have become so dysfunctional due to years of captivity that they would likely not survive in nature. Their socializations are abnormal; they are also hybrids of orcas that would never have occurred in nature; and they are now increasingly inbred. The responsible way to free captive whales is to reinsert them into the family units they were originally taken from. But the whales in the system who were taken that way are a small number: Kasatka, Katina, Ulises, Corky, Tilikum. I do not know whether the records of their pods of descent have enough information to determine where they could be reintroduced—and whether their families will even take them back. We don't even know if Kasatka's mother survived her capture.

The remaining whales were born in captivity. SeaWorld has so tampered with the fertility cycles of its female killer whales—who are fertilized at abnormally young ages—that they may never be able to adjust to the society of free matriarchal whales. Furthermore, true freedom would be a difficult adjustment because the orcas of SeaWorld don't know how to hunt for their own food. They have also been conditioned psychologically to interact with humans in complex reward-for-behavior scenarios that could make integration into the wild world of the ocean frightening. Their health—their teeth especially—has been badly compromised. Without the constant pulpotomies that we performed to relieve their tooth abscesses, they would become even

236

more susceptible to infection or die of hunger and malnourishment. Only SeaWorld has the staff and the know-how to pay close attention to the ills of captivity.

The problem is that SeaWorld can't make that argument because it would contradict the current image it projects of itself as the benign protector of the orcas in its care. All of the reasons its orcas cannot be returned to nature stem from the fact that they have been psychologically and physically damaged by captivity.

So what can SeaWorld do? It can take responsibility and revolutionize its business model to appeal to the burgeoning generation of Americans and people around the world who are increasingly convinced that keeping orcas—or any animal—in circus-performer captivity is morally and ethically wrong. SeaWorld can accede to the prescription of California's orca bill and build out sea pens that the public can visit—for the price of admission—to learn how captivity transforms cetaceans. A sea pen is an open ocean enclosure anchored to the ocean floor that provides a vastly more natural environment for the orcas. It is the closest sanctuary that human beings can construct for orcas whose lives and behavior have been compromised by captivity. SeaWorld cannot fully make up for its sins but it can atone—and teach the rest of humankind about its mistakes in the process.

At the very least, there should be an attempt to gather up all the solitary killer whales in captivity—that is, from marine parks that own only a single orca—and put them in a more social environment. Kshamenk, the Argentine orca whose sperm was used to inseminate both Kasatka and Takara, is one such lonely whale, swimming in Mundo Marino, a marine park outside Buenos Aires. Lolita lives alone in the Miami Seaquarium; Kiska in Marineland in Ontario. The sizes of their tanks are constricting. The conditions under which these solitary whales live are sickening—and all for greed.

I once thought sea pens were not the way to go, but more and more I hear discussions that conclude that such structures are indeed feasible. Certainly the expertise to care for the whales exists. Most if not all of the employees now in charge of the orcas could continue to look after the whales in these enormous open water sanctuaries.

They would no longer be performer-whales. The current Shamu Stadium spectacles have no educational content; anything informative is miniscule in comparison to the glitter that increasingly hogs the limelight. There is no dignity to the shows.

I would stop the artificial insemination program. I want this to be the last generation of orcas in captivity. SeaWorld and other marine parks can help the rest of the planet learn this lesson—and make some profit in the process of improving the lives of their surviving captive whales. And as the years go on, the company can formulate new ways to make a business out of truly educating the public about marine life and the real lives of orcas, born free and living free.

Will SeaWorld do this? Even after the company announced the expansion of the orcas' habitat—what would appear to be a major concession to years of criticism—CEO Jim Atchison said, "We are not apologizing for what we do or how we do it."

Atchison claimed that the pool expansion plans predated *Blackfish*. I don't see how that is possible. For five years at SeaWorld of Texas, we tried to get the corporation to allow us to build one more small back pool so the whales didn't have to spend so much time in the 8 foot deep med pool. That would have given Texas nearly the same amount of water volume as the California and Florida parks. We were repeatedly denied.

The corporation is clearly putting a Wall Street–friendly façade over what has turned out to be bad judgment—the decision to fight popular opinion over the treatment of captive orcas. The fact that

SeaWorld is now a publicly traded company means that it has other pressures to contend with. It must show a profit every quarter otherwise its most important audience—the stockholders—will divest themselves of their shares in search of more satisfying investments. Looking at it through that prism, the decision to expand the pools is good public and investor relations and probably a strategic move to prevent a bigger drop in admissions to the parks. It was just as important for Atchison to maintain that its policies were never wrong. That strategy backfired as SeaWorld stock continued to fall. On December 11, 2014, Atchison announced he was stepping down.

I cannot be optimistic about change coming from the top at SeaWorld. I suspect that someone in upper management is already planning to expand SeaWorld's operations overseas—perhaps, including sales of calves to new marine parks in Russia, China and the Middle East. Indeed, in an SEC filing prior to its IPO, SeaWorld declared that it was looking for "potential joint venture opportunities that would allow us to expand internationally by combining our brands and zoological and operational expertise with third-party capital." I worry about the news of orcas once again being captured in the wild by the Russians—and a new market for killer whales and an expanded gene pool.

Already, SeaWorld is enmeshed in a controversy over the young female orca Morgan in Loro Parque. Morgan was ill and rescued by the Dutch, who nursed her back to health. By law, she was to be returned to the wild. But because the aquarium holding her claimed at the time that they had problems identifying her pod, she wound up in SeaWorld's Spanish affiliate. Now, animal rights activists are fighting to free her even as SeaWorld has listed her as one of the orcas the corporation owns. Dr. Ingrid Visser says, "It is unclear how her ownership was transferred to SeaWorld." She has spent the last four years fighting court battles for Morgan in association with the Free Morgan

Foundation. "Morgan was the first new blood to come into the captivity industry in nearly two decades," says Dr. Visser. "That made her possibly the most valuable orca held in a tank at that time." According to Dr. Visser, SeaWorld has since been trying to breed Morgan with Keto, the male orca who killed Alexis Martinez. Any offspring that Morgan produces will be owned by SeaWorld, says Dr. Visser, "clearly illustrating why they were so desperate to gain ownership; that it wasn't about rescuing her, it was all about her breeding value." In the meantime, Morgan's residence at Loro Parque has not been peaceful. Dr. Visser says she recorded more than 320 puncture and bite marks on the young whale after only seven months at the Spanish affiliate of SeaWorld.

I foresee SeaWorld expanding overseas, where it would no longer be beholden to pressure from US legislators and public opinion. The premise of the company—to make money off the façade of conservation—has not changed from the 1960s and 1970s. And, if Americans learn to see through the terminology—"conservation through education"; "raising awareness for the species"; "in the care of man"—then there will be fresh audiences overseas who may still buy into the mythology.

It is intriguing that SeaWorld is being taken to task by some of its stockholders. In a lawsuit, the Rosen Law Firm alleged that the company had failed to make clear in its SEC filing to register its IPO that it had "improperly cared for and mistreated" its orcas; featured and bred Tilikum; and "consequently created material uncertainties and risks existing at the time of the IPO that could adversely impact attendance at its family oriented parks." The lawsuit specifically claims that the company "made material false statements" when it denied the allegations made in *Blackfish*. (At the time of writing, SeaWorld declined to comment on the lawsuit.)

If SeaWorld had a visionary leader, he or she would realize that the stock downturn was proof of a more critical development in the marketplace: that the potential audience has become savvier about animal rights. SeaWorld can shore up longer-term profits—and public goodwill—if it gets with the new spirit of the times and allies itself with the changing public philosophy. We are all evolving on social issues.

Speaking out against SeaWorld, however, has presented me with a very personal conflict. Some of the SeaWorld officials designated to defend the corporation's training methods are people I admire and who once were friends and supporters of mine. Kelly Flaherty-Clark always treated me with nothing but kindness. I admire her even though we are now on different sides of the debate over orcas. Her loyalty to SeaWorld did not keep her from testifying at the OSHA hearings that Dawn Brancheau did not break any rules or training protocols during her fatal session with Tilikum. Her testimony directly contradicted that of SeaWorld's expert witness Jeff Andrews.

When the time came to decide to speak out against SeaWorld, the most difficult hurdle for me was realizing that I would be on the opposite side of Chuck Tompkins, head of Animal Training for SeaWorld. He has always been supportive of my career and I felt as if I would be betraying him. I know he loves the whales. If there was a problem with a whale, he was always ready to help. When the trainers in Texas and I were concerned after Sakari, Takara's calf, hurt her jaw, Chuck assured us with a plan of action in case the baby orca was still not eating or opening her jaws 48 hours after the incident. He was a great counselor when it came to talking about our relationships with the orcas, warning us never to underestimate them. And when I came out against SeaWorld, he did not join in the vicious attacks on me that came from other officials of the corporation.

If you believe that God gave humankind dominion over all animals, we are entrusted with a huge responsibility. We should not use our power to inflict harm and pain—and profit from it. The battle for the future of SeaWorld's orcas is part of that debate on the ethics of humankind's relationship with the other inhabitants of this planet. Television journalist, author and animal rights activist Jane Velez-Mitchell put it this way: "This is the emerging social justice of the 21st century."

My life and career have evolved through four stages as the job I wanted more than anything else became a kind of grieving for a shattered dream. In the beginning, I was completely naïve: everything about the whales was wonderful even though I couldn't tell normal from abnormal, or healthy from unhealthy. Proximity to the whales was thrilling and seemed to be all that mattered. Then, I reached the second stage, when I realized that all was not right with SeaWorld; but I was still too low on the totem pole to do anything about it. I was still enthralled with my dream job and in love with the whales; and I believed that the company felt the same way about the whales and me. Then the moment came when I realized all that was false—but still held out hope. I knew the company was not really there for the orcas or me, that it was all about money; but I had become a high-ranking trainer and believed I could battle the wrongs and influence change from within. But I couldn't. This book is about how I reached the fourth stage: leaving, leaving behind my complex relationships with the orcas, abandoning my identity. I had always seen myself as a killer whale trainer—until I could not. All trainers are at one stage or another. I am in the final stage of grief over my career.

What am I today now that I have left SeaWorld? When I began this part of my life's journey, I was wary about being labeled an activist because I didn't want to be seen as the kind of radical animal rights agitator that SeaWorld loathed. Those feelings were reinforced when I teamed up with the people making *Blackfish*. During the promotion of the film, there was a conscious effort by the crew to make sure it was not labeled an "activist" film. We had huge and necessary support from the animal rights community, but being categorized as "activist" would work into SeaWorld's strategy of discrediting its critics as unreasonable radicals from the fringe. SeaWorld has always argued that the constituents of those views hurt the animals they claim to be trying to help.

The "activist = radical" tag provokes such immediate, unthinking reactions among my former colleagues at SeaWorld that, after what I thought was a sedate interview on *Real Time with Bill Maher* in July 2013, a number of them accused me of crossing over and becoming "a radicalized extremist." You would have thought I was a 9/11 hijacker if you had heard the tone of our conversations.

How would I choose to describe myself then? I don't really see myself as the man with the megaphone, though I'm glad there are people who do that. I see myself as speaking on behalf of those who have no voice themselves, who cannot speak for themselves: the whales. The perfect word is "advocate." There is still a lot of work to be done to change laws and win hearts and minds.

Former trainers and colleagues turned animal rights advocates John Jett and Jeff Ventre, along with former SeaWorld trainers Carol Ray and Samantha Berg, have formed the website Voice of the Orcas, which is an invaluable resource for information and insight about what's happening in the marine park industry. I'd like to help as well, counseling active trainers harboring doubts about what to do with their careers and how to deal with doubts that may have arisen through the years about the work they are doing. I want to be their advocate too.

I've been interviewed so many times about the whales that my answers are almost automatic. But one question stopped me. It was the ninth in a list of 13 emailed to me for a story in the United Kingdom. "If you knew then what you know now, would you do it again?" It would take me three weeks to be able to answer with clarity.

I valued my years with those whales. I loved the orcas. If I didn't have the career I had, I would never have been able to help expose the industry for what it is. I would never have been able to have the hands-on, first-person proof of just how intelligent, just how remarkable the whales truly are and, at the same time, realize how incredibly inadequate our efforts have been to give them everything they need to be able to thrive and be healthy in captivity.

A simple "no" would mean I was abandoning my dreams—and abandoning those whales. The memories are priceless. But if saying "no" means that these whales could have been free, that they would never have had to live a life in captivity in SeaWorld, then the answer is "No, I wouldn't have done it."

One big tough question I get asked a lot is: What do you say now to the kids who idolize you and want to be you when they grow up? Should they still have the same dream? What does the boy who grew up to get his dream job as an orca trainer tell another kid with the same dream today?

When I was in Texas in the final period of my career, a mother and daughter used to come to see me. The young girl was just like me: she wanted to see the Shamu show all the time. They would stay after to ask a lot of questions, just like I had done when I was a kid. The girl wanted to be a killer whale trainer as fast as she could—and she and her mother were willing to do whatever they needed to make that happen. She was probably 11 when she first started asking questions. And because her commitment to her dream reminded me so much of

244

myself, I didn't hesitate to give them all the encouragement and advice that I could. I became their favorite trainer and they would come to the park to watch me do shows and take photographs of me at work. It was a genuine friendship.

Then I left SeaWorld and went over to the other side. When *Blackfish* premiered at Sundance, I knew that both mother and daughter would be confused. The girl was 15 at the time, old enough to be really planning how to get started in the industry with the right education, extracurricular volunteer work and training. So I called her mom and asked if I could talk to her daughter. She put me on the phone with her. I let her ask me questions first. They were immediate and came from someone who was already attached emotionally to the whales: "How could you leave Takara? Do you miss her? Would you return to SeaWorld?"

I told her the truth. I missed Takara a lot but I couldn't return. I said I was fortunate and had an incredible career with those whales. Then I told her, "I don't have the right to tell you or any other child that it's not right for you to have the same dream I had. The responsibility I have is to share my story and to tell you exactly all the good and the bad I witnessed during my career." My job now is to tell the truth—both the inspiring stories from what was a storybook career and the horrors that emerged from the corporate exploitation of the whales and trainers.

Will there no longer be a need for trainers if my advocacy for the whales reaches its goals? The answer to that question is, most likely, "No." Even if we stop SeaWorld's breeding program, there will still be killer whales in captivity for decades to come because of whales born in captivity. (There were several born in the last two years, including to Kalia, who was artificially inseminated at the age of eight, in July 2013, and gave birth to her calf on December 2, 2014.) They will live out the rest of their lives in the care of man—though hopefully in a habitat where their lives will be of a higher quality than they now have at SeaWorld. For those whales, I do believe there is a role for kids like my confused young fan to grow up to fill. These whales will need caretakers who will hopefully stand up and fight for them.

This book has been about water. But since leaving SeaWorld to confront the corporation, I have stepped into the fire. Speaking out and becoming part of the controversy was a leap of faith, a conversion experience that I feel is purifying me. I didn't want to grow old and live with regret that I did not speak out. As a trainer, I knew too much and my heart was too heavy with doubt from years living the ideology of SeaWorld. I had to tell the truth. It was what I owed the whales.

I regret that there is only so much I can do for the whales I have worked with, swum with, and loved. They may, with time and the efforts of advocates, get a better life than they have now. But they will never experience what humans had no right to take from them in the first place.

For me, it will always come back to one orca, Takara. She will never know what it is like to be free. Because of that, I know that a part of me will never be free either.

EPILOGUE

LIFE WITHOUT TAKARA

One of the paradoxes of my life is that, for all my love of animals, I never really had a pet as an adult. My erratic and often long hours at Sea-World made it almost impossible to have one. I couldn't keep a dog waiting 12 or 14 hours for me to get home. It would have been cruel.

There was a much more sentimental and emotional reason I did not want pets. I didn't want to lose them. I've written about my tears and breakdowns when I left Kasatka and the other whales as a result of taking the job in Marineland in France; and then the pain when I left Takara to become an orca advocate. Whenever the thought arose of bringing an animal into my own home, I became wary and anxious. The life spans of dogs and cats are short. I didn't want to make another living being a part of my life, to become family, only to lose him or her.

Beowulf changed all that for me.

It was about 2009 or 2010. I was dating a guy who was in the Navy. He was housed with four other military men. One of them, Tom, was the owner of a half-pitbull, half-Dalmatian mix named Beowulf after

247

the legendary Scandinavian hero. But this Beowulf wasn't male; she was a force of nature.

I first saw her when she, her owner and his friends were still stationed in Monterey, California. Tom loved her, but when she stopped being a puppy, she started to become aggressive, getting into fights with other dogs. She was trouble. One day, Tom took her out running and, despite a shock collar around her neck, Beowulf couldn't be stopped from attacking a man on a bicycle. She slammed into him, knocked him off the bike and latched on to his leg. The shock collar was activated to its highest—a 10—again and again but she would not let go until Tom got a hold of her. He loved her but worried about legal and medical liabilities. He didn't know how to stop the aggressions, which were escalating. He decided it was time to euthanize her.

I heard what he was planning to do. I knew little about Beowulf but I never liked the idea of putting down a dog. I convinced Tom to let me take her with me to Texas for three months; I'd try to work out her problems and get a handle on her aggression and then he could have her back. He agreed and shipped her to me on a plane.

Three months later, when Tom called, I didn't know what to say. I had fallen in love with her and was afraid he wanted her back. To my relief, Tom asked if I wanted to keep her. What can I say? I am drawn to dangerous animals. We were a perfect fit.

Aggression will always be part of Beowulf. I could train her not to be hostile to specific animals and people. But I had to condition her to tolerate each one separately. If she hasn't been trained by slow approximation to accept your presence, she won't. She will never be a friendly dog. I keep her away from most people. And so she only goes out with me. I can't be away from home longer than a few days because no one else can get close enough to feed her unless I've conditioned her to accept them. When I travel, she's by my side. We've lived in California,

Texas and now in New York City. Wherever I end up, she'll be with me. I'll never abandon her.

Beowulf is also obsessed with water. She will swim for hours and will sweep down fast rapids, diving to get a ball, a stick or whatever we're playing with. She is another dangerous animal that means everything to me.

Like the whales, aggression doesn't mean that an animal is bad. It just means they're complex. That is Beowulf's key to my heart—she's difficult but she let me in, allowed me to be close. Like Takara and her mother and the other orcas.

Beowulf

ACKNOWLEDGMENTS

I come from a family that covers a spectrum of two extremes when it comes to compassion for animals. On one end, I have a relative who has exhibited such cruelty to animals that he once killed his own dog because he said he wanted to know what it felt like. On the opposite end of that spectrum is my sister Missy Hargrove, who shares my love and compassion for all animals. She always has pets and is so tenderhearted that she will save snakes snared in fences even though she is scared to death of them. She picks up mosquito hawks caught in the rain, whose wings are so drenched they cannot fly—then blows on them until they are sufficiently dry enough to fly off. Missy, where would I be without you? Despite our interrupted childhoods away from each other, we have always been close and there for each other through the good and the bad. You are an inspiration for being so open and tenderhearted to all animals. I am so proud you're my sister. I love you the most!

Quentin Elias—
My greatest love. Our life together in Paris and the south of France was out of a storybook. We were in our late twenties, invincible, and had it all. Your tragic death at only 38 years of age in 2014 in New York City still haunts me. You told me to never leave you and I never did. I'll see you when I get home.

My Publisher, Palgrave Macmillan Trade—
The team of Elisabeth Dyssegaard, Karen Wolny, Lauren LoPinto, Lauren Janiec, Christine Catarino, Laura Apperson, and Michelle Fitzgerald: Thank

you for believing in me and my life story with these whales, and believing that people need to hear my story for change. All of you have been great to me, and I'm proud and fortunate to have you bring my story to life.

My literary agent, Farley Chase—
During our first meeting in your office in Manhattan, after I explained my experiences and vision to you for just ten minutes, you completely got it. Thank you for all your hard work and truly believing my story needed to be told.

My co-writer, Howard Chua-Eoan—
A friend for more than ten years, you were the first to press me to write this book; thank you for lending your talents to make this book possible. Howard is grateful to Josh Tyrangiel and Ellen Pollock of *Bloomberg Businessweek* for giving him time to work on this project. He also wants to thank Phil Bildner for counsel, Dan Mathews for support and Brett Garrett for coffee.

Tom Wihera and John Laffin—
Two of the toughest guys I know. You both have my admiration for your resilience and for what you both have accomplished in the military. You guys are true role models. Our friendship came quick, easy, and real. Your support in New York City for the opening weekend of *Blackfish* meant a great deal to me personally. Tom, congratulations on your beautiful wife, Christina, and for giving me my "greatest gift."

Lisa Gisczinski—
You had the courage to stand by me, your friend of more than 20 years. It says everything about you. I love you.

All my friends and former colleagues who are still with SeaWorld who still support me—
After all the friendships of former colleagues I lost, your support means the world to me. We know right from wrong and what is really happening here. I understand your need to protect yourself and stay silent, for fear of

retribution from management. Every person has their own journey. Please stay safe. I love you guys.

David Sepe—
We have more than a ten-year history; brought together in 2003 and then again in 2014 by the same person but this time in tragedy. No more lost years.

Ryan Buckley—
CNN is lucky to have you. Who wouldn't be lucky to have the eternal Mr. Sunshine and 4/4? Everyone loves Ryan. Thank you for supporting me and being a great friend.

Chad Allen Lazzari—
Friends for 20 years. I am so proud of your immense accomplishments and who you have always been as a person. So proud of our history. You are one of the most valuable people to me. All love to you, your mom, and your grandmother.

Joseph Kapsch—
I have never laughed so hard or had so much fun while living the party life in Los Angeles. How did we survive all the situations we got into? And we did it with the best humor. You are truly one of my best friends . . ."This light is making us crazy."

Mark Schapira—
One of my best friends, you have always supported me, and we've shared some of the craziest times in Los Angeles (and New York). Love you, Mark.

John Atchley—
You have shown generosity and consistent loyalty and support of me as a friend for more than 13 years. Thank you for everything.

Bruce Martin—
I was 18, a runaway, with no money and no possessions. I was fortunate that fate and intuition brought me to the right people at just the right time. The security and direction you provided with the purest of intentions came when I needed it the most. You will always be special to me.

OSHA & Lara Padgett—
Thank you for ensuring that employers are providing a safe and healthful workplace. We had serious safety issues for decades at Shamu Stadium and with no union to protect us or make sure we had rights as employees we were alone until your perseverance.

To all the doctors and specialists that have worked on me through the years as a result of all the killer whale injuries—
To the six different orthopedic surgeons, I'm sorry I wasn't ready to accept your advice to end my killer whale career, and thank you to the one who injected me with everything known to science to buy me three more years with the whales so I could have time to come to terms with closing that chapter. To my great sinus surgeon here in New York City, my pain management specialists, all my primary care doctors and my podiatrist who diagnosed my fractured foot and said I needed surgery (which I continue to put off)—thank you. And finally, thank you to the medical osteopaths who put my back and neck back together countless times and to the Manhattan Sports Medicine Group.

Eric Balfour and Erin Chiamulon—
Your presence with us as we spoke to the members of the California State Assembly on this issue, and your passion and knowledge, contributed greatly. You are wonderful people and I enjoyed my time with both of you.

All those, including the Kotler family, who travelled to Sacramento, CA, to support us during our testimony before the California State Assembly for "The Orca Welfare & Safety Act"—
I watched as they let the hundreds of you who couldn't get seats inside the chamber flood in from the hallways. You came from all parts of California,

other states, and even from other countries, just to have ten seconds at that mic to show your support. In that moment I was both humbled and inspired and knew I made the right decision to speak out. Thank you.

Assemblyman Richard Bloom (D-CA) and his staff—
Thank you for authoring the historic bill AB 2140, "The Orca Welfare and Safety Act."

NYS Senator Greg Ball (R-NY) and Assemblyman James Tedisco (R-NY)—
Thank you for authoring similar legislation in New York State named the "Blackfish Bill."

Howard Garrett, Dr. Naomi Rose, Dr. Deborah Giles, Dr. Lori Marino & Dr. Ingrid Visser—
Your combined knowledge, experience, and research has taught us all, including me, about the real lives of orcas living free in the wild. Thank you for your contribution to my book.

Gabriela Cowperthwaite—
I know you made *Blackfish* from the right place in your heart, and you pushed this longstanding debate into the forefront of mainstream consciousness. Thank you and your producer, Manny Oteyza, for caring about this issue and me and always treating me ethically and protecting my anonymity.

Tim Zimmermann and Elizabeth Batt—
For your tireless contribution to progress awareness on this issue while upholding the highest of journalistic ethics, thank you.

Ceta-Base—
Thank you for your contribution of invaluable factual data and statistics on captive orcas.

To my following family who have truly loved and supported me—
Ricky and Pauline Hargrove, Jeannie and Bruce Alexander, April and Trey King and their families; Jack and Darlene Tindel, and their children Jack and Tracy and their families; Lynn and Linda Brackin, their children and families; Jamie Brackin-Semon, her family, including her mother, Linda.

My grandparents Walter and Merle Brackin who have passed—
I remember how powerful it was to feel the strength of your unconditional love, knowing you would always protect your family. You are both loved and missed by all of us who were blessed to have you as family.

Darlene Tindel (Aunt Sissy) and Tracy Tindel-Green—
You have shown me such tremendous support during my killer whale career but most importantly now. You know how much I loved you growing up and wanted to be around you. I knew I was loved and I was safe. Thank you for giving me that. I love you.

April Hargrove-King—
You are more my sister than cousin, you stood by my side through all the years of total madness and you were never fazed by it and I love you so much for it. You were my perfect date for the New York City premiere of *Blackfish*. And what a perfect day together at Coney Island before the premiere.

I'd like to thank the following friends who have also always supported me—
Christina Freedman, Lana Gersman, Frank Santisario, Veronica Rosmaninho, Alex Caputo, Hezi Imbar, Tim Friese, Dave Lendon, Darryl Colen, Marcos Prolo, Kelly Culkin, Cheryl Semcer, Matthew Walker, Tim Brock, Tony Marion, Jure Klepic, Juan Carlos Gutierrez, Ron Lynch, Michelle Guillot, Randy Musgrove, Kim Clemons, Jennifer Parkhurst and her beautiful son Indy.

Alex and Greg Bruehler, who were both killed in October 2009 while riding a tandem bicycle when a man drove onto the shoulder of the road

hitting them at 70 mph with his truck; they left behind their seven-year-old daughter, Kylie—
Alex and I were trainers together at SeaWorld of California and her husband, Greg, worked in animal care. You are both loved and missed.

Former trainers Carol Ray, Sam Berg, Dr. John Jett, Dr. Jeff Ventre, and Dean Gomersall—
We worked at different SeaWorld parks at different times but we are forever bonded by our parallel experiences from the past and the present. You are wonderful people who have contributed so much awareness. We are most powerful as a united front. Very challenging for SeaWorld to overcome that we collectively cover every SeaWorld park from 1987 to 2012.

To my other sisters and brother—
Lenora Hargrove, Sheila Archuletta, and Ashley and Matt Hargrove, and their families—I love you.

My father Steve and his wife Elsie—
More than 20 years are completely gone but at the end of the day, it's about today. For reasons known to only you and me, thank you for what you have given me since 2010 and your support.

My mother Anne—
Thank you for giving me a loving and happy childhood when I was a young boy. I choose to remember all those years when a little boy could not have loved his mother more.

Beowulf—
My dog and my best friend who sees and loves me at my best and worst. Together in California, Texas, and New York City. With me when my life was still training killer whales and now that it's not. You endured all the hotels getting back to New York City during all the *Blackfish* film festivals and promotion. You were beside me as I wrote every word in this book. I may have saved your life but you saved mine. You are my "greatest gift."

BIBLIOGRAPHY

Chapter 2
Friedersdorf, Connor. "The Fantastical Vision for the Original SeaWorld." *Atlantic.*
    March 21, 2014.

Chapter 6
Garrett, Howard. Email correspondence with authors.
Giles, Deborah. Email correspondence with authors.
Marino, Lori. Email correspondence with authors.
Rose, Naomi. Email correspondence with authors.
Rose, Naomi. "Killer Controversy: Why Orcas Should No Longer Be Kept in Cap-
    tivity." Animal Welfare Institute, Washington, DC, 2014.

Chapter 8
Robeck, T.R., K. J. Steinman, S. Gearhart, T. R. Reidarson, J. F. McBain and S. L.
    Monfort. "Reproductive Physiology and Development of Artificial Insemina-
    tion Technology in Killer Whales (*Orcinus Orca*)." *The Society for the Study of
    Reproduction.* 2004.

Chapter 9
Marino, Lori. Email correspondence with authors.
Marino, Lori, Chet C. Sherwood, Bradley N. Delman, Cheuk Y. Tang, Thomas P.
    Naidich and Patrick R. Hof. "Neuroanatomy of the Killer Whale (*Orcinus orca*)
    from Magnetic Resonance Images." *The Anatomical Record Part A* 281 no. 2
    (2004): 1256–1263.

Chapter 10
Montero, M. A. "La orca 'Keto' sí atacó y causó la muerte de Alexis, el adiestrador del
    Loro Parque," October 4, 2010. www.abc.es/20101003/coumunidad-canarias/
    orca-keto-ataco-causo-20101003.html.

BIBLIOGRAPHY

Chapter 11

California Bill AB2140. The Orca Welfare and Safety Act.

Dezember, Ryan, and Michael Wursthorn. "The Blackstone-Blackfish Connection." Moneybeat. Blogs.wsj.com. *Wall Street Journal,* December 24, 2013.

Jett, John and Jeffrey Ventre, "Keto and Tilikum Express the Stress of Orca Captivity." The Orca Project. January 20, 2011.

Jett, John, and Jeffrey Ventre. "Orca (Orcinus) Captivity and Vulnerability to Mosquito-Transmitted Viruses." *Journal of Marine Mammals and Their Ecology* 5, no. 2 (2012): 9–16.

Judith Rogers statement. United States Court of Appeals for the District of Columbia Circuit. No. 12-1375. SeaWorld of Florida, LLC, Petitioner v. Thomas E. Perez, Secretary, United States Department of Labor, Respondent.

Ken Welsch statement. Secretary of Labor, Complainant, v. SeaWorld of Florida, LLC, Respondent. OSHRC Docket No. 10-1705. United States of America Occupational Safety and Health Review Commission.

Chapter 12

Rosen Law Firm. Class Action Cases: SeaWorld Entertainment. www.rosenlegal.com /cases-335.html.

INDEX